State, society, and the UN system: Changing perspectives on multilateralism

Edited by Keith Krause and W. Andy Knight

**United Nations
University Press**

TOKYO • NEW YORK • PARIS

United Nations University Press
The United Nations University, 53-70, Jingumae 5-chome,
Shibuya-ku, Tokyo 150, Japan
Tel: (03) 3499-2811   Fax: (03) 3406-7345
Telex: J25442   Cable: UNATUNIV TOKYO

Typeset by Asco Trade Typesetting Limited, Hong Kong
Printed by Permanent Typesetting and Printing Co., Ltd., Hong Kong
Cover design by Kerkhoven Associates

UNUP-885
ISBN 92-808-0885-0
03500 P

JZ
4984.5
.S73
1995

Contents

Acknowledgements

We would like to acknowledge the help we received from various individuals and institutions during the development of this project and the preparation of this book. Our most immediate debt is to Robert Cox, whose broader conceptual framework for the MUNS (Multilateralism and the United Nations System) programme was used to locate our project, and to the manuscript reviewers for UNU, whose extensive comments made for a vastly improved final product. Financial support for our conference on Changing State/Society Perspectives on the United Nations System (held in Toronto, 18–21 March 1992) from the United Nations University in Tokyo is gratefully acknowledged, as is the administrative support of the York Centre for International and Strategic Studies.

In addition to the conference participants whose chapters are in this volume, a number of other participants also gave helpful comments and advice. These include David Dewitt, Grant Littke, Pierre Lizée, Sorpong Peou, Pat Sewell, Sandra Whitworth, Michael Williams, and Shodja Zianian. Comments on a draft of our introductory chapter by many of the participants of the ACUNS (Academic Council on the United Nations System) workshop held at Dartmouth College in the summer of 1992 proved very useful. Thanks also to Jennifer Milliken for reading drafts of the introduction and conclusion.

The coordination and administration of the conference were made easier by staff of the Centre for International and Strategic Studies, in particular Heather Chestnutt, Steven Mataija, and Rosemary Thompson. Rose Edgecombe graciously typed several of the chapters for the final volume.

Finally, this research project drew on the experience of the editors in preparing a Canadian case-study for another country-study multilateralism project undertaken by ACUNS in collaboration with the Ford Foundation and the now defunct Canadian Institute for International Peace and Security (CIIPS). While it has built upon that project, our research also represents a point of departure from it.

Introduction

Evolution and change in the United Nations system

Keith Krause and W. Andy Knight

The academic study of the United Nations is enjoying renewed popularity lately, after several years languishing as a backwater within International Relations.[1] Different scholars are studying the scope (and varieties) of multilateralism after the Cold War, the possibilities for reform of the UN system, the domestic sources of state policies towards it, the potential for expansion of the peace and security functions of the United Nations, and so on.[2] Some reasons for this renewed interest are easy to discern. Action in several regional conflicts (peace-keeping, peace-building, observer missions, or good offices) in Somalia, Afghanistan, Namibia, and Cambodia has given renewed legitimacy to the peace and security function of the Security Council and the Secretary-General's Office. The use of Security Council resolutions as the instrument to enforce international law against Iraq's invasion of Kuwait also activated the peace and security mechanisms of the United Nations, as have setbacks in such enforcement in the Yugoslavian successor states. In addition, concern among some Western states about the political tenor of the activities of organizations such as UNESCO and the FAO (Food and Agriculture Organization) and concern with the "efficient" use of resources have on occasion threatened the continued existence of these institutions and led to serious efforts at internal reform. Finally, several overarching multilateral issues that had been eclipsed in recent years, such as economic development, the environment, or human rights, are ascending the agenda of international attention.

From a broader vantage point, several forces in global politics have altered the basic parameters of the post-1945 world order. The most significant include the end of the Cold War confrontation and the near-disappearance of the Soviet Union/Russia as a superpower, the virtual end of the decolonization process, the emergence of new states, changing patterns of global production and economic activity, and a new emphasis on representative institutions and human rights that challenges the "right" of states to non-interference in their internal affairs. These changes to world politics (and the global distribution of power) will have an impact on the pattern of international governance embodied in the institutions of the United Nations. Whether or not existing institutions will prove adaptable enough to accommodate new demands and challenges is an open question. What is clear, however, is that these institutions will not receive such demands and challenges as "empty vessels." The institutions of the United Nations embody the relationships of power and understandings of "world order" that governed post-1945 international politics, and this institutional expression of world order limits or constrains their future potential.

The central thrust of this book is to examine against this changing backdrop the relationship between particular state/society complexes and the "world order" represented by the institutions of the post-1945 United Nations system. The authors of these studies go beyond a narrow analysis of government-to-government relationships between states and central UN institutions to discuss also the evolving reciprocal links between societies and the multilateral institutions of the post-1945 world. In general the authors make two analytic moves. The first is to highlight the domestic factors and forces that shape a state's policies towards multilateralism. The second is to examine the impact of the multilateral diplomacy of the UN system on domestic political and economic structures and forces, and the broader ideas and structures that shape the context within which state policies are formulated. The goal of each study is to gain a better understanding of not only how states/societies participate in the changing global multilateral system, but how such participation has affected various forms of state and domestic state–society relations, and how the UN system has been influenced by the different pressures for change that have emerged out of its member states.

One forerunner to this book was the effort (sponsored by the Academic Council on the United Nations System) to examine policies towards reform of the UN system through several case-studies, primarily of major powers.[3] The cases in this volume were selected to fill in some gaps and mirror the coverage of this earlier study, and to focus attention on seldom-studied smaller states. Germany and India, for example, have been strong supporters of multilateralism and the UN system, although arguably they have not had a voice commensurate with their relative position of power within world politics. Both (as chapters below point out) have expressed some discontent with existing arrangements and distributions of power and influence within the system. Sweden and Romania have each (in different ways) regarded the UN system as a means for projecting on a wider stage particular domestic understandings of how political life should be organized, and have regarded themselves as "net contributors" to the UN system. Smaller states such as Chile, Jamaica, and Sierra Leone have been on the receiving end of the benefits and costs that have accrued from membership and participation in the multilateral system. The theoretical and practical implications of the perspectives articulated by these states, while not dominant, must be included in any comprehensive evaluation of the future directions for multilateralism in the UN system.

This study also departs from previous work and attempts to overcome some of the methodological and conceptual limitations of earlier approaches, limitations that stem from its statist and pluralist orientations. It also draws out from the cases a framework that can guide further studies on the UN system. Since this book is part of a larger project (sponsored by the United Nations University) exploring different facets of "Multilateralism and the United Nations System," it is embedded within, and draws upon, the approaches developed within that project.[4] The meaning and potential of "multilateralism" have come under recent scholarly scrutiny, and many different definitions of it have been offered.[5] Most simply, multilateralism can be regarded as "an institutional form that coordinates relations among three or more states on the basis of generalized principles of conduct."[6] But, as noted by Robert Cox: "to define a meaning of multilateralism ... we must begin with an assessment of the present and emerging future condition of the world system, with the power relationships that will give contextual meaning to the term."[7] To comprehend the forces that aid or hinder multilateral activity, one needs to understand the process of structural change within states/societies, in multilateral institutions themselves, and at the level of world order.

The "state/society perspective" and state policies towards the United Nations system

The particular contribution of this volume is to focus attention on the forces at work within and between states, through the lens of what can be called a "state/society perspective." Such an approach starts from the premise that traditional approaches to the study of international organization do not capture the many ways in which states approach their participation in multilateral relations or the many factors that influence state policy, and that their failure to do so has theoretical and practical consequences. Among the processes or forces that this approach highlights are such things as historical influences, the configuration of state power and civil society, or the role of individuals. More will be said about this below, but one general implication of this approach is that scholars must examine not only what occurs within international and domestic political "space" (while keeping the two spheres separate) but what occurs *across* the domestic–international divide. This boundary must be to some extent erased, in order to examine forces and factors that work across it. Multilateral participation, as expressed within the United Nations system, provides an excellent issue area in which to examine this interplay of domestic social and political forces with broader currents in world politics.

This can be contrasted with most theoretical explications of foreign policy and state behaviour, which have attempted to build general models from the experience of one or two (usually Western) states.[8] These models perhaps do not even explain foreign policy formation in their primary case, but they are almost always inadequate when applied to different contexts. What unites the contributions to this volume is that most authors have tried to use methods appropriate to their case and have, where appropriate and necessary, gone beyond existing approaches to the study of the formation of state policy towards the United Nations. The broader conceptual umbrella for this can be called a "state/society perspective," and it serves to highlight a broader set of political struggles beneath the state (within society) and between society and the state.

In general, a state/society perspective adopts a more comprehensive approach to analysing foreign policy-making concerning multilateral organizations and the UN system, and is more "sociological" in its conception of the state and its role in international and domestic politics. It draws attention to the interactive struggles between the society and the state apparatus and "consider[s] the 'state' not as a single entity with a single interest, but rather as a 'naturally' divided entity, made up of particular relationships" that can cut across state boundaries.[9] This approach differs from realist or "world system structuralist" approaches, in that the domestic political context is not considered irrelevant to theory-building or purely determined by systemic processes.[10]

It also differs from functionalist or liberal institutionalist approaches, which adopt a pluralist account of state–society relations in which the state is conceived of as an "honest broker" that aggregates the competing interests articulated by different groups in society (whose interests are exogenously determined).[11] Rather, it insists that "the state cannot be isolated from civil society: it is defined by the series of links that form both the state and the societal groups."[12] Groups within the state (such as the military in Chile) or within the society (such as labour unions in Jamaica) not only can exert greater influence on state policy than other groups; at various times they can actually shape the process by which interests are articulated and aggregated, to the benefit of some groups and detriment of others. Thus, while some foreign policy orientations towards multilateral institutions may reflect the diversity of interests expressed within a state/society complex, others may reflect the state apparatus having been captured by a particular group within society. Hence the degree to which state representatives can pursue policies within international organizations that run against the interests of various groups within society is an issue that has to be addressed in each particular case. Some authors have argued that a state's insertion into the United Nations system and its activities in the multilateral arena actually increase the autonomy of state rulers, making them less responsive to (and less representative of) their societies. One example of this is the way in which economic policy planners in states such as India attempt to advance their ideas via the World Bank or International Monetary Fund (IMF) when they have been thwarted within the Indian bureaucracy; another would be the ability of the ruling élite of a "predatory state" such as Sierra Leone to buttress its position and extract resources from society.

At the meta-theoretical level, this approach bears some resemblance to a "social constructivist" orientation, which argues that the dynamic processes operating at the level of the international system simultaneously and mutually constitute state actors and the systemic structures within which they act.[13] It also fits alongside what some authors call "neo-structuralist" approaches, which take as their subject matter "an overall transformative process wherein all states and societal forces are constantly being transformed through participation in the world system as a whole in terms of their fundamental characteristics and structure."[14] Factors analysed by realists, liberal institutionalists, or world system theorists do not disappear from this account, and indeed some contributions to this volume come close to operating within these perspectives. But this is used as a point of departure to push the overall analysis beyond government-to-government relationships between the state and central institutions of the UN system. The goal is not so much to create a "new" theory of state/society participation in the UN system, as to add to the array of approaches scholars can use to apprehend the subject matter.

The "state/society perspective" and the United Nations system

A different account of the processes of change unfolding at the level of the UN system itself is a crucial aspect of a state/society approach, and a necessary counterpoint to the specific dynamics presented in the case-studies. Thus the remainder of this introduction discusses changes in the UN system and in the overarching conceptions of "world order," and attempts to situate the individual chapters against a broad backdrop of evolution in the multilateral institutions of the UN system. One caveat must be registered, however: the loose equation of "multilateralism" with activities within the UN system is clearly an oversimplification.[15] A focus on the UN system (broadly conceived) excludes much multilateral activity, but it does at least delimit the scope of the following analyses, and brings somewhat greater theoretical attention to bear on the generally institutionally focused analysis of the United Nations. It does not imply, however, that all activities within the UN system are multilateral, or that the proper focus of attention ought solely to be the operations of UN organs.

Most accounts of the UN system treat it as a complex bureaucratic structure organized with a hierarchical division of labour. On the surface, this is obvious: the United Nations has principal organs, main committees, standing committees, subsidiary organs, specialized agencies, and semi-autonomous bodies (like the IMF, the International Bank for Reconstruction and Development [IBRD], the International Development Association [IDA], and the International Atomic Energy Agency [IAEA]) scattered around the globe, supported by the Secretariat, and reporting to the Secretary-General. As an intergovernmental structure, the UN system also recognizes and draws upon non-governmental organizations, and has been functionally designed to achieve certain objectives of the international community, codified in the Charter. These objectives include maintaining international peace and security, advocating protection of fundamental human rights, ensuring the sovereign equality of nation-states, and facilitating socio-economic progress and advancement. This large, complex, and fairly permanent social system has been characterized as a "superbureaucracy" or a "new Byzantium," and envisioned in mechanical terms as a complex machinery of international governance.[16]

But there is another way of looking at the United Nations system: as the concrete expression of the power relationships of post-1945 international society, and as the arena in which competing ideologies and values have clashed. Such a "sociological" orientation at the systemic level mirrors and complements the "state/society perspective" adopted for examining domestic political change, and is one way to escape the "dissatisfaction with the individualist foundations of neo-realist international relations theory, foundations which encourage an understanding of international cooperation and institutions as collective results of the self-interested strategic interaction of states."[17] It also resonates with certain approaches to the study of international organization, particularly with those scholars who have proposed that sociological concepts and methods for the study of domestic societies be applied to the study of "international society" or drawn parallels between the devices for maintaining order in the anarchical societies of so-called "primitive" peoples and those that supply a modicum of order in the modern states system, in the absence of an international government.[18] Key analytical concepts used in sociology (legitimacy, authority, influence, status, socialization, stratification, social control, norms, rules, belief systems) have also found their way into the international relations literature that deals with the mechanisms and means of international governance.

Hence the UN system encompasses the institutions noted above, but is also the expression of a particular "world order," understood as the "political, economic, social, ideological, and cultural structures that define the behaviour and power relationships among human groups."[19] These historically determined structures are "those persisting patterns of thought and actions that define the frameworks within which people and states act."[20] The United Nations system is the post-1945 incarnation of these structures of world order, and its possible evolutionary trajectories are constrained and channelled by them. This perspective allows one to move beyond a state-centric focus, in the same way that an account of the competing forces at work in domestic politics moves beyond institutionalist/statist political science.

Discussions of possible reforms to, or evolution of, the institutions of the UN system must be examined against the way in which the structures that underpin them have (or have not) changed. This does not, however, mean that the UN system is nothing more than a transparent forum through which is refracted the interplay of power relations between states. As Inis Claude noted:

> Political institutions evolve, not along lines rigidly set by their creators and definitively stated in constitutional documents, but in response to a dynamic process that combines the propulsive and directive impulses of trends running through the political context and of purposes injected by participants in their operations.[21]

The objectives of the founders, and the constitution of the organization, act as constraints on the United Nations, and its institutions continue to embody the power relations that dominated at their founding. Ultimately, however, these structures do not control altogether its evolution, and the UN system has developed over time a degree of relative autonomy, with different parts of it possessing an underlying *Weltanschauung* that affects the kinds of pressures it responds to and the kinds of policies that emerge from it.

Principles and ideas embodied in the UN system at its creation

In historical terms, the UN system can be compared to the League of Nations and Concert of Europe systems, both of which possessed some institutional expression and incorporated particular visions of world order. The Concert of Europe established a loose procedure of great power governance of European politics that permitted the interests of smaller powers (such as Poland) to be sacrificed in order to safeguard its central principle of the "balance of power." Its focus was almost exclusively on political/security issues. The League of

Nations system was a set of weak institutions whose paralysis was the product of changing power relationships in which the declining powers (Britain, France) were unable to create the consensus needed to empower multilateral institutions to address problems of international peace and security, while the ascendant powers (the United States, the Soviet Union) were unwilling or unable to play a greater role in multilateral arrangements for domestic, historical, and ideological reasons. However, a range of functional institutions (concerning communications, health, labour, and so on) broadened the agenda of multilateralism beyond its previous political/security focus, and new ideological norms (the concepts of self-determination, or "one state – one vote") were introduced into the discourse.

A historical account of the evolution of the UN system would be superfluous.[22] From the perspective of this project, however, it is important to note that the political, economic, social, ideological, and cultural structures of the post-1945 world were embedded in the UN system as constitutive principles and as underlying ideas. Constitutive principles in world politics (the "rules" that determine the nature of social relations without determining outcomes) include the sovereign state as the subject of international law, concepts of non-intervention, and the principle of self-help.[23] The underlying ideas included the legitimacy of great power governance on peace and security matters, the validity of resort to war as an ultimate arbiter, an essentially "liberal individualist" conception of human rights (including the right to property, the free flow of information, and other negative rights), and a capitalist global economy based on comparative advantage and an international division of labour. All of these underlying ideas have been challenged in various institutions of the UN system, and in some cases the institutional expression of these ideas has evolved through a process of adaptation (such as the innovation of peace-keeping), or the struggle has crippled the effectiveness of the institutions embodying them (the battle over UNESCO being a case in point). Seldom, however, have the constitutive principles of world politics themselves been challenged.

Concrete expressions of these political, economic, social, ideological, and cultural structures are not difficult to find. Within the core of the UN system, the structure and powers of the Security Council are rooted in the acceptance of the legitimacy of great power governance; this gave rise to the veto of the five permanent members, and to the relatively unrestricted scope of Security Council powers.[24] This was different from the veto that every state possessed in the League of

Nations system, but it matched well the post-1945 configuration of power. It was also clear that the main concern of the Security Council would be with threats to international peace and security, as one goal of the institution was to save succeeding generations from the scourge of war. But the increasing gap between the 1945 configuration of power and the realities of global politics in the 1990s gave rise to demands for institutional reform. These have ranged from proposals to alter the membership of the Security Council (by giving permanent member status to Germany and Japan, adding permanent members from Asia, Africa, and Latin America, or creating "semi-permanent" members), to changing the method of electing the Secretary-General, to altering the procedures for collective UN action (by bypassing the veto).[25]

In other cases the underlying ideas of post-1945 world order have been embodied within the formal and informal institutional practices. For example, UNESCO incorporated into its founding ethic the principle of the "free flow of information," based on the principle that news was neutral and objective, and a commodity that should be traded in a fashion analogous to the economic principle of comparative advantage. In its early years, UNESCO even had a Division of the Free Flow of Communication, and policies protecting infant national news agencies (such as in India and China) were frowned upon.[26] The counter-reaction to this, incarnated in the call for a New World Information Order, was based on a perception that the penetration of the South by Western media sources posed a profound challenge to national self-expression and cultural integrity.[27] A similar observation can be made with respect to the ideology underpinning the division between the International Covenant on Civil and Political Rights and the International Covenant on Economic, Social, and Cultural Rights.

Other scholars have made parallel arguments with respect to the economic ideology of "embedded liberalism" that governed the institutionalization and administrative norms of post-1945 international economic institutions such as the World Bank or International Monetary Fund, or to the "New Deal regulatory state" that informed American planning for post-war multilateral arrangements.[28] The Economic and Social Council (ECOSOC) was a subsidiary body in the global economic regime, and even the institutional innovations of the UN Development Programme (UNDP) and the UN Conference on Trade and Development (UNCTAD) failed to dent the dominance of the institutions controlled by the developed states. The

"New International Economic Order" (NIEO) of the 1970s challenged this "embedded liberalism," but with little success.[29] The more recent adoption by the IMF and the World Bank of the guiding principle of "structural adjustment" (explored in the chapters on Sierra Leone and Jamaica) represented the new orthodoxy of global economics, with its emphasis on market forces, subsidy removal, and openness to global trade and foreign investment.

Shifts in underlying ideas and beliefs are neglected in studies of government-to-government relations of the UN system, in part because it is difficult to trace causal links between these changes and outcomes. A focus on the changing politics of foreign aid policy, for example, can neglect the background debate (conducted in international institutions and elsewhere) over appropriate strategies for development (favouring industry over agriculture, or export-led versus infant industry arguments) and the impact of political cultural factors that shape a state's entire policy towards development assistance.[30] The authors of the case-studies in this book, when examining particular activities of their state in the UN system, attempt to bring out these collective images or embedded beliefs. Their analyses of which forms of multilateral participation are favoured (economic versus political/security, development versus trade, regional versus global, and so on) attempt to show how the choices states make reflect different beliefs held by ruling élites (or more broadly in society) that are seldom explicitly articulated in the formal domestic decision-making structure, but that may none the less be projected from the domestic political order outward to multilateral arrangements.

Change in global politics and the response of the UN system

It is difficult to distinguish ephemeral changes from durable underlying shifts in world politics. There can be little doubt, however, that several developments since 1945 have directly challenged the original vision of world order that was articulated in the institutions of the UN system.[31] The major movements in multilateralism include, *inter alia*, such issues as: the stagnation and recent resurgence of the peace and security role of the United Nations; the rise of the principle of self-determination, its expression in the decolonization process, and the expansion of the UN system; changing definitions and strategies of development (including the NIEO and the shift to structural adjustment); and the adoption of new issues such as the environment and sustainable development or human rights. Challenges to the underlying ideas that governed the immediate post-war order arose within each of these issue areas, and the changes of recent years may turn out not to pose greater difficulties for the UN system than some of the dramatic events associated with these shifts in multilateralism. Three of them – the political/security role of the United Nations during the Cold War, the UN response to the decolonization challenge (inclusiveness/universalism), and the debate over welfare and justice that revolved around economic development issues – will be discussed below.

Two caveats are worth noting, however. First, many of the changes that have occurred since 1945 have not challenged the constitutive principles of the "Westphalian state system," and such challenges have been relatively much weaker or slower to manifest themselves.[32] Challenges to the constitutive principles of the state system have been mounted by segments of the environmental movement, indigenous peoples, the women's movement, human rights advocates, and other forces in world politics that are ill accommodated within the current inter-state structure. Human rights advocates, for example, often question the cornerstone principle of non-intervention in the internal affairs of states, while indigenous peoples struggle against the principle that the sovereign state is the subject of international law.[33] Most often, however, these challenges have been expressed in the interstices of global politics, and have yet to storm its central institutional bastions.

Second, against the tapestry of rapid change one must also acknowledge the significant continuities in world politics. The point is *not* to argue that world politics are static and unchanging, but rather that the dynamic of change can be evolutionary and adaptive rather than transformational.[34] Viewed over the long run, the evolution of international society can be thought of as a dialectical process that produces contradictions at various levels of world politics; these contradictions are "the antagonisms that lead to [its] modification."[35] Examples of continuities in the constitutive principles or underlying ideas of world politics (all of which are undergoing evolution) would include:

- the perpetuation of the territorial nation-state;
- continued support for the principle of sovereignty;
- the reluctance of citizens and governments to transfer authority and allegiance from the state to a supranational body;
- persistent reliance of states on self-help measures to achieve national objectives;

- the use of violence to achieve such objectives;
- the continuing derivation of international legal norms and obligations from custom and formal consent;
- divisions between the rich and poor.

These distinctions have practical consequences for the way in which we think of the past and future of the UN system. On one level, many challenges and changes in global politics have been accommodated by incremental institutional adaptations that are oriented to the maintenance of the existing order. On a deeper level, however, the UN system has also been an arena for competition between alternative "transformational" visions of world politics that are directed to changing the existing order, and that have found some expression in different institutions and practices. A purely institutional focus on the UN system would concentrate only on the first type of adaptive response, while ignoring the potentially greater underlying shifts or contests under way. In any case, the same broad "sociological" approach that the authors of the case-studies apply to their states must also be used to examine the evolution of the UN system itself. The three examples that follow highlight some of the key changes in multilateral institutions and practice that form the backdrop against which the case-studies unfold.

The UN response to the Cold War challenge

The Cold War greatly restricted the potential scope of UN activity in peace and security matters. By 1947, the wartime expectation that the victorious powers would remain united to preserve a stable international security environment and collectively punish defectors had been proved false. Bipolar East–West tensions and rivalry, the concern with spheres of influence, and the balance of nuclear terror and arms racing quickly dominated global politico-military relations. These factors limited the United Nations' role in securing and maintaining international peace and security, at times completely marginalizing the organization in the conflict management area.[36] In addition, the ideological competition between the superpowers was played out in the UN arena as attempts to resolve international disputes kept being vetoed by one party or another.[37] It soon became obvious that when any of the permanent members became involved in a conflict, the Security Council would likely not be involved in its resolution. As a result, the United Nations resembled more a battlefield than a dispute resolution mechanism, and the primary role of the organization in maintaining international peace and security was severely limited.

But the pressures for action in the peace and security arena did not vanish, and the UN system responded in four ways. The first was an attempt to shift decision-making power for peace and security matters away from the Security Council to the General Assembly. As early as 1947 an Interim Committee was established to provide the Assembly with a mechanism for dealing with political disputes. In 1950 the Assembly adopted the "Uniting for Peace" resolution, which empowered the Assembly to address breaches of international security if the Council failed to do so.[38] Through this the General Assembly "formally laid claim to a substantial role in the area of security concerns that the Charter had assigned primarily to the Security Council."[39] The second response was the establishment of a number of institutions and practices to address the problem of nuclear weapons and the arms race. The United Nations established the Atomic Energy Commission (1946) and the International Atomic Energy Agency (1957) to encourage the peaceful use of nuclear energy while ensuring that nuclear materials and equipment were not diverted to military purposes. In 1968 the Nuclear Non-Proliferation Treaty was drafted under UN auspices and as of 1993 had been signed by 155 states. The United Nations has also been the umbrella for a number of disarmament and arms limitation treaties, most notably the 1992 Chemical Weapons Convention. The General Assembly has also established bodies to deal with specific disarmament concerns, such as nuclear weapons testing, disarmament and development, or the arms trade.

Both of these responses were minimalist adaptations to difficult circumstances that did not really ameliorate either superpower tensions or arms races. But the third and fourth responses were more imaginative, and deviated far from the post-1945 vision of the United Nations. The third response was the invention of peace-keeping.[40] This invention was a substitute for the inoperable collective security mechanisms of the Security Council, and it has proved to be one of the United Nations' most indispensable innovations. Lester Pearson, one of the originators of the concept of UN peace-keeping, described it as an intermediary technique between "merely passing resolutions and actually fighting," and Dag Hammarskjöld placed this invention under "Chapter $6\frac{1}{2}$" because it fell in the grey zone between the two means given to the United Nations for maintaining international peace and security – pacific settlement and collective enforcement.[41] Overall, the United Nations has created 16 observer missions and 10 peace-keeping operations, half of which have been established since 1987. This highlights the way in which an innovative response to the problems of maintaining international peace and security can, over time, become taken for granted as an indispensable international institution.[42] Peace-keeping has also come to be seen as a useful response to a range of disputes short of war (including ethnic, cross-border, tribal, and other civil conflicts) that were not fully anticipated by the framers of the Charter.

The fourth response was the adaptation of the role of the Secretary-General. This began with Dag Hammarskjöld, under the auspices of "preventive diplomacy" and his reinterpretation of the Secretary-General's discretionary powers under Article 99 of the Charter.[43] The preventive diplomacy concept was initially restricted to areas in which the superpowers were not directly involved, and over time it has taken many different forms, from commissions of inquiry and fact-finding missions to military observation and truce supervision.[44] Some UN peace-keeping operations, such as the United Nations Emergency Force or the UN Force in Cyprus, were exercises of preventive diplomacy in the sense that they were used to reduce the impact of Cold War competition in the respective regions. Preventive diplomacy therefore reinterpreted existing Charter provisions to suit the changed international conditions in which the UN system found itself. More recently, in 1987 Secretary-General Pérez de Cuéllar created an information-gathering and early-warning agency (the Office of Research and Collection of Information – ORCI) under the umbrella of preventive diplomacy.[45] Although ORCI itself has been discontinued under recent UN reforms, pressures to provide adequate early warning and information gathering to enable the United Nations to respond more quickly to nascent international crises still exist.[46] Finally, preventive diplomacy was given a high profile in the 1992 report of the Secretary-General, *An Agenda for Peace*.[47]

The end of the Cold War may or may not herald a structural change in world politics, but it does create new opportunities for "peace-making" and "peace-building," as suggested in the *Agenda for Peace*. This document emphasizes new dimensions of security and an expanded UN role in the realm of international peace and security. But it also reconfirms the sovereign state as the "fundamental entity of the international community" and does little to challenge the principle of non-intervention in internal affairs. Thus the future evolution of the United Nations' capabilities in this area depends to a great extent on which ideas of world order and the role of major powers in maintaining international peace and security become dominant. If a directorate of great powers takes control, the UN role will be secondary, as it was in the war to expel Iraq from Kuwait. If, however, the United Nations is called upon to take the lead where individual states fear to tread, and the principle of non-intervention becomes less sacrosanct, then its role will be more prominent and probably much more creative. The international response to the Iraqi invasion (and the measures taken to protect the Kurds), the wars in the former Yugoslav republics and Somalia, and the peace process in Cambodia do not yet provide clear indications of which ideas will dominate.

The UN response to the decolonization challenge

Several important challenges to the original vision embodied in the UN system have come from states not present at the founding of the organization. Although these states had no input into the original rules and norms that governed state interaction in the UN system, they could use the principles embodied in the Charter (such as universality, self-determination, sovereign equality, justice, and peaceful transition) to demand membership in the United Nations and subsequently to challenge some of the dominant principles and processes prevailing in the organization.[48] But before the Non-Aligned Movement and the Group of 77 developing countries (G77) coalesced to stake out an alternative vision of world order that ran counter to the one originally embodied in the United Nations, these states had to "join the club." The issues promoted by newly independent states (and the response of the UN system) are given great attention by several authors in this volume, in particular in the Indian and Sierra Leonese cases. It is worth reviewing here, however, the way in which the simple admission of these states to membership challenged the institutional principles and practices of the United Nations.

The response to the call of new states for admission to the United Nations was, until 1955, generally negative. The United States in particular viewed UN membership through Cold War lenses, and opted to exclude potential members of the opposing camp from the United Nations (the Soviets wanted both friends and foes admitted as a "package"). By 1955, the backlog of applicants had grown, and the deadlock was broken by a joint Canadian–Soviet initiative that saw

16 new states join the organization. The principle of exclusion (based on functional criteria) was replaced by *universality*, which essentially dictated that most states entered the organization soon after independence.[49] This saw the organization swell in membership throughout the 1960s, and more recently with the admission of the successor states to the Soviet Union. The idea of universality has become so automatically applied that the Secretary-General has suggested that perhaps it has begun to harm the organization, as the admission of micro-states and states without effective sovereignty degraded respect for the institution.

The second phase of the response to decolonization was the adaptation and expansion of UN institutions, in particular the Security Council and the Economic and Social Council (ECOSOC). In 1966, the Security Council was expanded from 11 to 15 members, and the "Afro-Asian bloc" succeeded in entrenching guaranteed representation in five of the elected seats. The ECOSOC was expanded from 18 to 27 seats, with Afro-Asian states guaranteed 12. The principle of balanced and "equitable" geographic representation became a leit-motif throughout the organization (from its first debate in the Security Council in the 1950s), and today it has extended to an implicit "rotational" selection of the Secretary-General. This development changed the underlying ideas of the United Nations, as it ran counter both to ideas of great power management and to the model pushed by middle powers (such as Canada) of "functional representation" on the various UN bodies.[50]

Finally, the new states enforced some changes in the principles and ideas that structured the organization. The Trusteeship Council, which was initially set up under Chapter XIII of the UN Charter with the interests of colonial powers in mind, became instead a body that expedited the independence process. The new states succeeded in expanding Chapter XI of the Charter and established the principle that "all non-self-governing territories should be subjected to international examination and criticism."[51] The 1960 General Assembly Declaration on the Granting of Independence to Colonial Countries and Peoples (Resolution 1514 (XV), 1960) called for a speedy end to colonialism and proclaimed emancipation for dependent people around the globe. This was followed in 1961 by the establishment of a Special Committee on Colonialism (now known as the Committee of 24) to examine its application and implementation. During the next two decades the Assembly adopted a series of "action plans" to expedite progress toward independence for many states, and passed a number of resolutions decrying apartheid, racism, and various forms of colonialism. As Brian Urquhart argued, without the United Nations, "the process [of decolonization] would have been far more protracted, far more violent, far more disorderly and would have created far greater tensions in the world than it, in fact, has done." The United Nations acted as "an instigator, a catalyst, a face-saver for the colonial powers and as a bridge between the old and the new countries."[52] Members acted to preserve the status quo as much as possible while at the same time trying to adapt to the massive pressures for change from outside the organization. One result of this, however, was a much deeper clash of ideas and visions within the organization throughout the 1970s and 1980s, reflected primarily in the economic sphere.

The UN response to changing conceptions of economic development and socio-economic rights

The influx of new states into the UN system brought a number of demands and pressures to the UN system that it was ill prepared to handle. The key demand of new states was the need to accelerate the process of economic development to close the gap between them and the industrialized states. Dealing with the historical disadvantage and legacy of colonialism, and the structural inequalities of the global liberal economic system, was a source of frustration for most new states. The rapid "stages of economic growth" promised by Western modernization theorists (such as Walt Rostow) did not materialize in underdeveloped countries. Even the regional economic development ideas of such economists as Raul Prebisch and the Economic Commission for Latin America in the mid-1950s only marginally improved Latin American states' share of world trade, and did little to improve the situation for African states.

To many in the third world, the nascent "dependency theories" seemed best to explain their plight as peripheral (and exploited) participants in the global economy. Drawing on the critique of liberal economic theories contained in dependency theories, Western industrial states were increasingly accused of siphoning off surplus from the peripheral states for their own economic growth.[53] The UN system was used to mount a challenge to the established liberal economic order, and by the 1960s the counter-hegemonic ideology of the New International Economic Order had emerged.[54] Most G77 states sought a forum in which to express their concerns over trade and development issues; they wanted, however, not only to create a new organization, but also to entrench different norms and ideologies of economic development in the institutions and practices of the UN system. Their challenge was expressed in the third world consensus at the first UNCTAD in 1964 and caused a marked divide between the North and the South. The success of the OPEC (Organization of Petroleum-Exporting Countries) cartel in the 1970s, combined with the breakdown of the Bretton Woods system, gave an impetus to this critique.

The development of the third world alliance is dealt with in greater detail in the Jamaican case-study. In general, the G77 sought ways to shift power away from the North to the South within those institutions of the UN system that could conceivably improve their lot.[55] At the same time, they utilized their majority in the General Assembly to condemn the North and influence world opinion and to pass declarations calling for "third-generation" economic and social rights, which invoked the new principle of restitution or compensation.[56] The UN system responded to these economic and social demands, first, with an expansion of the machinery of the United Nations in economic and social areas; second, with the "expansion" of international law to accommodate the changed situation; and, third, with attempts to coordinate its development assistance programmes better.[57] This involved the creation of the UNDP, followed by attempts to restructure it as a strong central coordinating organ and to strengthen the United Nations' capacity to offer technical assistance to developing countries.[58] However, there was little change in the institutions that exert the most control over the developing countries' economies (i.e. the General Agreement on Tariffs and Trade (GATT), the IMF, and the World Bank). Although developing countries have taken an increasingly active role in the various GATT rounds, they have not been successful in transforming that organization into a trade forum that would advance their interests.[59] The IMF has even expanded its influence in developing countries through a programme of conditionality and structural adjustment that has virtually transformed the economic structures (and political management mechanisms) of several third world states (as is discussed in the Thai case).

The tactics and rhetoric of the G77 had few concrete results. Western states viewed these moves as part of a Marxist, anti-Western, and particularly anti-American conspiracy devised by the Soviet Union. At first, they largely ignored UNCTAD, in favour of the Bretton

Woods institutions – the GATT, World Bank, and IMF – which the Group of 77 viewed as antagonistic to their interests. By the late 1970s there was some agitation (particularly among US delegations to the United Nations) for the introduction of weighted voting, particularly in budgetary matters. This was followed by more serious attempts to force reform in the UN system, including the withdrawal of the United States and Britain from UNESCO, similar pressures on the FAO and the International Labour Organization (ILO), the suspension of payments to specialized agencies, and the withholding of assessed contributions from the regular UN budget.[60] The result seems to be that third world states were forced to acquiesce on matters formerly seen as vital in order to preserve the main outlines of the UN system. The Western industrialized states are arguably more firmly in control of the organization today, and the G77 is fragmenting as some of these states move into the category of newly industrializing countries while others fall to the status of a fourth world.[61] In addition, the regionalization of third world issues has contributed to the dilution of the solidarity of the G77.[62] What began as an attempt radically to transform the UN system has been forced into a reformist agenda in which the parameters of what can be changed are determined primarily by the dominant states within the organization.

The future response of the UN system

Although it is impossible to detail the future response of the UN system to changes in world politics, from the United Nations' pattern of adaptation to deep changes in the post-1945 world it is possible to sketch some trajectories. The institutions of the UN system are under great pressure, not only because financial and political limits are being placed on their activities, but because the gap between the conditions and structures these institutions were designed to cope with and the emerging world order is increasing. There is a wide consensus that the institutions need to change to meet new challenges, even if this means stretching or radically reinterpreting the existing constitutive principles and underlying norms of international practice.

Several examples of how this has been manifest within the central institutions of the UN system can be offered. For instance, the haste with which former republics of the Soviet Union were recognized and admitted to the United Nations was not consistent with some traditional understandings of the rules of state recognition.[63] The Security Council resolutions concerning the Kurds in Iraq appeared to reinterpret Article 2(7) of the Charter concerning non-interference (although it should be noted that the humanitarian intervention in Iraq was *not* conducted under the auspices of the resolution). Likewise, Security Council resolutions concerning the extradition of Libyan nationals for the bombing of an American civilian airliner highlight the wide scope of authority of the Security Council (and the absence of any quasi-judicial checks on the constitutionality of its actions).[64] Finally, the recent Security Council leaders' summit and follow-up report by the Secretary-General advocate a sharp reinterpretation of the peace and security mechanisms of the United Nations that goes beyond the traditional requirements for consent of states in conflict, and expands the meaning of "threats to international peace and security."[65]

The authors of the present studies highlight some of the pressures being brought to bear on the UN system, ranging from German and Indian pressure for a greater say on the Security Council to a Romanian emphasis on enhanced peace and security mechanisms, to a Swedish and Jamaican emphasis (with different degrees of urgency) on development issues. In general terms, there are three possible responses of the institutions of the UN system to the pressures posed by changing world order configurations. The first response, the incremental adaptation of existing practices without questioning the constitutive principles or underlying ideas of world politics, will be the most common. Examples would include the admission of new members to the United Nations, changes in Security Council consultative practices among the permanent members, the emergence of a norm of "non-use of the veto" in the Security Council, and various administrative and bureaucratic reforms. The history of the organization and the current constellation of interests within it suggest three reasons why this will be the most common response. First, most major states (and certainly the most powerful UN members) advocate only incremental and managerial reforms.[66] Second, most challenges to the system can be *reinterpreted* as calls for incremental adaptation (as a form of co-optation), one example of this being the argument that various groups need to be "brought into" the system more effectively. The UN system itself exerts powerful pressures on participants:

the web of interactions created by participation in the hegemonic system can, through a gradual process of learning and adjustment, induce elites to buy into the normative underpinnings of that system. Through frequent participation in the institutions erected by the hegemon, elites in secondary states are exposed to and may eventually embrace the norms and value orientations that those institutions embody.[67]

Finally, it is likely the United Nations itself cannot bear much more radical change without its entire existence being challenged, given the difficulty in fashioning a compromise when all issues are on the table.[68]

The second response would address attempts to alter the underlying ideas that govern world politics, and in such cases the UN system will likely be the arena in which competing ideas or norms struggle for primacy or legitimacy.[69] As Cox argues, insertion into, and participation in, the UN system may give rise to "counter-hegemonic forces" that agitate for change in the underlying ideas of the post-1945 world order: "eventually, institutions ... can become a battleground of opposing tendencies, or stimulate the creation of rival institutions reflecting different tendencies."[70] Already one can see, around issues such as strategies for economic development, environmental policies, the claims of indigenous peoples, the feminist movement, and the demands for human rights and representative government, such a clash of perspectives within and between different international forums.[71] In general, however, these perspectives begin to clash within the UN system only *after* the previously silenced groups or perspectives have found their voices on the margins of international society and have pushed their issues up the agenda, precisely because the structure of the institutions is not at the outset conducive to advancing their claims.[72] The most evocative example of this is the way in which the alternative strategies of development emerged before coalescing into the demand for a New International Economic Order, which, despite some gains (such as in the UN Convention on the Law of the Sea), foundered on the resistance it encountered from industrialized states as expressed in other global economic institutions.

Finally, one could imagine the UN system becoming the *vehicle* for the expression or creation of a new, "post-Westphalian" vision of world politics. For example, the United Nations could be the forum in which the principle of non-intervention was radically amended to incorporate human rights considerations, or the great powers could surrender their veto and implement a more "democratic" system of UN representation. Such changes could not be accommodated without a severe reinterpretation of the constitutive principles of world politics; not surprisingly, all previous efforts at such changes have been stillborn. The ruling élites of member states have a vested interest in preventing reforms that would undermine rules of the game that they benefit from. Further, international institutional practice has been extremely reluctant to undermine the constitutive principles of world politics; one excellent example is the UN humanitarian intervention to protect Iraqi Kurds, which was *not* conducted under the authority of Security Council Resolution 688, in part because Iraq did not accept the resolution and the Security Council was reluctant to override this principle. The creation of standing or rapid deployment forces under the authority of the Secretary-General has similarly not found much favour with possible contributor states.[73] Moreover, the present institutional arrangements exist in a fragile counterbalance, and it is difficult to imagine that piecemeal reform would be acceptable (changes to Article 2(7), for example, would likely be linked to elimination of either the veto or the possibility of unilateral action). Lastly, the social engineering ethos that was part of the San Francisco experiment is dead; it is no longer possible to imagine that a club of (generally) Western state leaders with a shared world-view could produce a set of constitutional arrangements for global governance that were endowed with legitimacy. There is no consensus on what process could endow such future arrangements with any legitimacy, but this merely highlights the confusing situation within which we labour.

The state/society perspective and the case-studies

The authors of the studies that follow focus on the changing relationship between their state/society and the institutions of the UN system. The studies have been organized into three sections, the first dealing with two states (Germany and India) that are seeking (and can mount a plausible claim to) a larger voice within the system; the second dealing with two states (Sweden and Romania) that have seen the UN system as a means to project certain domestically derived visions onto a global stage; the third dealing with three states (Chile, Jamaica, and Sierra Leone) that are greatly affected by the shifting currents and ideologies of multilateral UN institutions. The factors analysed by traditional approaches do not disappear, but the scope of the analysis has been broadened beyond the government-to-government relationships between a state and the central institutions of the UN system. The chapters are organized around each state's insertion into (and changing participation in) the UN system. They examine the state/society complex's perspective relative to some of the major movements in multilateralism detailed above, including peace and security and the Cold War, the expansion of the United Nations, changing strategies and policies of development, and emerging multilateral issues (such as the environment, human rights, or the role of women). Against this backdrop, the authors then detail the most significant issues promoted or supported since 1945 and the way in which participation in multilateral activities may have changed, particularly over the past two decades. In the end, each author reflects on the importance of their state's policies and activities for the future of multilateralism, by assessing not only their state/society's impact on the evolution of specific institutions or policies of the UN system but also the implications of this for the evolution of the UN system itself, and for global governance in general.

The state/society perspective allows the authors to introduce a range of forces that are generally excluded from traditional analyses, but that could have an impact on a state's policy formation process towards the United Nations and multilateralism. This requires examining questions concerning the nature of the state and its position in the international system, the state–society configuration of power within each state, and the impact of the multilateral institutions on domestic structures and social forces. Five broad sets of factors that fit within the sociological framework of this study emerged from the various cases as potentially significant influences on different states' multilateral policies towards the UN system: historical influences; the relationship between state power and domestic political, social, or economic cleavages; the role of individuals; political cultural and ideological influences; and transnational or global forces. A more comprehensive discussion that synthesizes some of the insights from the case-studies will be presented in the Conclusion, but it is worth indicating briefly at this point how they emerged from the state/society perspective on multilateral participation that has been outlined here, and how they are excluded or occluded within more traditional conceptions. In general, some combination of these factors is essential to explaining why particular states have pushed certain forms of multilateralism within certain contexts, and what conditioned the way in which policy priorities were set.

Is there anything about a state/society's historical experience that can help explain the particular positions that a state takes towards multilateralism? Such influences are difficult to specify with precision, but they appear in some cases to leave a lasting imprint on a state's approach to multilateralism. The most suggestive case is the United States, which, as John Ruggie and Ann-Marie Burley have argued, attempted after the Second World War to "project the experience of the New Deal regulatory state into the international arena."[74] As the debates surrounding Ruggie's argument for "embedded liberalism" make clear, neither liberal nor realist accounts can explain how such essentially domestic historical experiences (which also reflect particular ideological commitments) can leave an imprint on a state's approach to multilateralism. In this volume, the German study makes clear that the legacy of Nazi Germany has exerted a profound influence on contemporary German policy regarding multilateralism since 1945, and in the Indian case the colonial experience has had an equivalent impact.

Also noteworthy is the potential role of idiosyncratic, often personalist, factors in explaining the policy orientations of certain states. Neither neo-realist nor neo-liberal accounts would easily accept that policies (over the medium or long term) can be explained by the character of a particular leader or the orientation of a specific ruling élite. Yet, rather than assuming the unimportance of such factors a priori, different case-studies posed it as a question: can the foreign policies of states be explained in some cases by the impact of a particular leader or the orientation of the ruling élite? It appears in some cases that foreign policy cannot be explained without at least some reference to the changing ideological leadership provided by people such as Michael Manley, Augusto Pinochet, or Nicolae Ceauçescu.

An equally striking occlusion in the traditional approach to understanding multilateralism is the relative importance of various *forms* of the state (the relations between the state, the economy, and society) in structuring or determining a country's pattern of multilateral activity. The "liberal pluralist" notion of aggregated interests expressing themselves as the "national interest" may fit "strong states" such as Germany, but it is not clear that such an approach is much help in explaining the foreign policy orientations of weak or fractured states/societies such as Sierra Leone. Similarly, economic forces resulting from particular patterns of land ownership, mode of production, degree of industrialization, or dependence on single-commodity exports could also, by expressing themselves through particular forms of state, have an impact on the policies that a state adopts towards and within multilateral institutions.

The more subterranean ideological and "political cultural" dimensions of the relationship between states/societies and the multilateral system are also obscured from view on other theoretical accounts, again on the a priori grounds that such factors are either unimportant or derivative. Yet various authors have suggestively identified an almost unconscious self-image that states (such as Sweden and India) operate with in the international arena, and highlighted the domestic functions of such images. Sweden's choice of Tanzania as the largest recipient of its foreign aid effort, for example, reflected an underlying commitment to "socialism" as an appropriate development strategy for Africa, and was consistent with its self-image as presenting a "third way" alternative to the dominant economic ideologies articulated by both superpowers.[75] India's commitment to the Non-Aligned Movement and its perceived leadership role in the international struggle against apartheid highlight the importance states often attach to defending consistently certain values and orientations.

Finally, a state/society perspective draws attention to the "internationalization of domestic politics" and the impact of multilateral institutional policies and ideologies on domestic struggles to define state interests (which are treated as exogenously determined in liberal and realist approaches to international relations). Forces within a state can gain strength with reference to ideas in circulation or institutions operating outside of the state itself. As Fred Halliday notes: "the existence of the state–society relation permits alternative means of conducting international relations, in as much as it encourages states and social forces to pursue international policies that will enhance their positions with respect to each other."[76] One prominent example would be the impact of structural adjustment policies and ideologies, which have reshaped political and economic institutions and social relations in many parts of the developing world. Such analyses challenge the notion that the relationship of influence between multilateral institutions and states runs only upward from states. Indeed, one strength of the cases that follow is that they highlight the impact the UN system can have on states and domestic political structures, an influence that is not readily apparent in studies that focus on great powers and the United Nations.

Conclusion

The changing pattern of global politics at the end of the twentieth century is apparent to all observers. What the consequences of these changes will be for multilateral cooperation within the UN system is, however, much less obvious. Previous changes in the configuration of power in world politics were legitimized and made concrete through the institutional systems established after major wars (the Westphalian system, the Concert of Europe, the League of Nations), and the way in which these systems embodied new constitutive principles or underlying ideas was clear. Barring a catastrophic major war, one must focus on the underlying forces and processes shaping the future world order in order to understand their future trajectory and impact on the institutions of the United Nations system. These forces and processes are most evident today in political struggles within states and in the attempts by states to affect the institutions of global governance.

The case-studies that follow go some way to enhancing our understanding of the forces for change in world politics. They tackle the issues raised from diverse approaches, and contain within them an implicitly (and sometimes explicitly) strong critique of previous approaches. These chapters also raise difficult and complex theoretical and conceptual considerations, but, together, they begin to provide a framework within which current changes in world politics, multilateralism, and the UN system can be comprehended. Ultimately, this will increase our knowledge of the future potential of the UN system as an instrument of multilateralism and a mechanism of global governance.

Notes and references

1. This introduction has benefited from the insights and contributions of many scholars, most notably the authors of the case-studies in this book, and the participants in the 1992 Academic Council on the United Nations System/American Society of International Law summer workshop on International Law and Organizations at Dartmouth.
2. Some examples of this would be Margaret Karns and Karen Mingst, "Domestic Sources of International Cooperation: A Conceptual Framework," paper presented to the International Studies Association annual meeting, 20–23 March 1991; Robert Johansen, "U.N. Peacekeeping and Military Force," *Third World Review* 12 (April 1990), no. 2: 53–70; James Blodgett, "The Future of UN Peacekeeping," *Washington Quarterly* 14 (Winter 1991), no. 1: 207–220; Bruce Russett and James S. Sutterlin, "The U.N. in a New World Order," *Foreign Affairs* 70 (Spring 1991), no. 2: 69–83; Leon Gordenker, "International Organization in the New World Order," *Fletcher Forum* 15 (Summer 1991), no. 2: 71–86; and the special issue of *International Social Science Journal* devoted to international organizations (45, November 1993). For sources on multilateralism, see note 5 below.
3. Eight states were represented in the final volume: Algeria, Canada, France, Japan, the Netherlands, Nigeria, the United Kingdom, and the United States (Chadwick F. Alger, Gene M. Lyons, and John E. Trent, eds., *The United Nations System: The Policies of Member States*, Tokyo: UNU Press, forthcoming).
4. For a theoretical overview see Robert W. Cox, "Multilateralism and World Order," *Review of International Studies* 18 (April 1992), no. 2: 161–180. The UNU project is under his in-

tellectual stewardship, and for background on his approach see Robert Cox, "On Thinking about Future World Order," *World Politics* 28 (January 1976), no. 2: 175–196; "Social Forces, States and World Orders: Beyond International Relations Theory," *Millennium* 10 (Summer 1981), no. 2: 126–155; *Power, Production and World Order* (New York: Columbia University Press, 1987); "Production, the State, and Change in World Order," in Ernst-Otto Czempiel and James Rosenau, eds., *Global Changes and Theoretical Challenges: Approaches to World Politics for the 1990s* (Lexington: Lexington Books, 1989), 37–50.

5. See John Gerard Ruggie, ed., *Multilateralism Matters: The Theory and Praxis of an Institutional Forum* (New York: Columbia University Press, 1993); Robert Keohane, "Multilateralism: An Agenda for Research," *International Journal* 45 (Autumn 1990), no. 4: 731–764.

6. John Gerard Ruggie, "Multilateralism: The Anatomy of an Institution," in Ruggie, *Multilateralism Matters*, 11.

7. Cox, "Multilateralism and World Order," 163.

8. This problem was first explored by Baghat Korany, "Foreign-policy Models and Their Empirical Relevance to Third-World Actors: A Critique and an Alternative," *International Social Science Journal* 26 (1974), no. 1: 70–94. See also Christopher Hill, "Theories of Foreign Policy Making for the Developing Countries," in Christopher Clapham, ed., *Foreign Policy Making in Developing States* (Aldershot: Gower Publishing, 1987), 1–16. For an example of the traditional approach, see Roy Macridis, ed., *Foreign Policy in World Politics*, 7th ed. (Englewood Cliffs, N.J.: Prentice-Hall, 1989).

9. Douglas Chalmers, "Corporatism and Comparative Politics," in Howard Wiarda, ed., *New Directions in Comparative Politics*, rev. ed. (Boulder, Colo.: Westview Press, 1991), 69–70.

10. It is impossible here to give a complete account of the various approaches to multilateralism. For a more comprehensive analysis of realist, liberal institutionalist, and world systems approaches to multilateralism, see Cox, "Multilateralism and World Order," 166–176.

11. As Robert Putnam describes this process:

at the national level, domestic groups pursue their interests by pressuring the government to adopt favourable policies, and politicians seek power by constructing coalitions among those groups. At the international level, national governments seek to maximize their own ability to satisfy domestic pressures, while minimizing the adverse consequences of foreign developments.

Robert Putnam, "Diplomacy and Domestic Politics: The Logic of Two-level Games," *International Organization* 42 (Summer 1988), no. 3: 434. On neo-liberal institutionalism, see Robert O. Keohane, "Neoliberal Institutionalism: A Perspective on World Politics," in Robert O. Keohane, *International Institutions and State Power: Essays in International Relations Theory* (Boulder, Colo.: Westview Press, 1989), 1–20.

12. Chalmers, "Corporatism," 70.

13. Alexander Wendt, "Anarchy Is What States Make of It: The Social Construction of Power Politics," *International Organization* 46 (Spring 1992), no. 2: 391–425. As Wendt notes (p. 392), this differs from neo-realist and neo-liberal accounts, which share a "rationalist" conception in which "questions about identity- and interest-formation are therefore not important." See also Nicholas Onuf, *Worlds of Our Making* (Columbia: University of South Carolina Press, 1989).

14. Barry Gills and Ronen Palan, "Introduction: The Neostructuralist Agenda in International Relations," in Ronen Palan and Barry Gills, eds., *Transcending the State–Global Divide* (Boulder, Colo.: Lynne Rienner, 1994), 4. As they put it, "state policies therefore cannot be explained in terms of a volitional being: the state does not pursue a 'national interest' ... Central to the neostructuralist agenda is the concern with the interrelation between policies and the wider socioeconomic and ideological domestic and international setting" (ibid., 6.)

15. As Ruggie notes, the adjective "multilateral" can apply to "three institutional domains of

interstate relations: international orders, international regimes, and international organizations" (Ruggie, "Multilateralism," 12).

16. David Pitt, *The Nature of United Nations Bureaucracies* (London: Croom Helm, 1986).
17. James Caporaso, "Towards a Sociology of International Institutions: Comments on the Articles by Smouts, de Senarclens and Jönsson," *International Social Science Journal* 45 (November 1993), no. 4: 479. Caporaso is highlighting a common thread of discontent with existing approaches that is evident in the articles of these three authors in the same issue of the journal.
18. As Evan Luard defines it, "international society" is

    a relatively permanent association of nations and other groups, linked together by ties of intercourse, trade, and diplomatic relations, not necessarily – any more than other societies – always peaceful, still less tightly organized and integrated, but possessing some common customs and traditions, common expectations concerning the relationships and behaviour to be expected among its members, even, in many cases, common institutions for discussing common problems.

    Evan Luard, *Types of International Society* (New York: The Free Press, 1976), viii. See also Hedley Bull, *The Anarchical Society* (London: Macmillan, 1977); Friedrich Kratochwil, *Rules, Norms and Decisions: On the Conditions of Practical and Legal Reasoning in International Relations and Domestic Affairs* (Cambridge: Cambridge University Press, 1989); Roger Masters, "World Politics as a Primitive Political System," *World Politics* 16 (July 1964), no. 4; Onuf, *Worlds of Our Making*.
19. Robert Cox, "Programme on Multilateralism and the United Nations System," unpublished paper, United Nations University (April 1991), 2.
20. Cox, "Multilateralism and World Order," 168–169.
21. Inis Claude, *Swords into Plowshares*, 4th ed. (New York: Random House, 1984), 6.
22. Good sources on this include Amos Yoder, *The Evolution of the United Nations System* (New York: Crane Russak, 1989); Claude, *Swords into Plowshares*, passim; Paul Diehl, ed., *The Politics of International Organizations* (Chicago: Dorsey Press, 1989); Clive Archer, *International Organizations* (Boston: Allen & Unwin, 1983).
23. Borrowing from Terry Nardin, constitutive principles (such as the rules governing the way pieces move in chess) *determine* that the game is chess and not checkers. They cannot be changed without the game changing to something other than chess, although the rules do not determine the outcome of specific games. See Terry Nardin, "International Ethics and International Law," *Review of International Studies* 18 (1992): 19–30. See also Kratochwil, *Rules*. From a legal perspective see Thomas Franck's discussion of primary rules ("the rights and duties typically enumerated in treaties or specified by the pedigree of customary usage") and secondary rules (whose role is "identifying the sources of rules and establishing normative standards that define how rules are to be made, interpreted and applied") in *The Power of Legitimacy among Nations* (New York: Oxford University Press, 1990), 183–184.
24. As Ruggie argues, American officials sought to make the idealist aspiration of collective security compatible with the practice of balance of power politics (Ruggie, "Multilateralism," 26). The issue of unrestricted scope came to the fore in the debate over Security Council actions in the Libyan extradition case. See the International Court of Justice decision in "Questions of Interpretation and Application for the 1971 Montreal Convention Arising from the Aerial Incident at Lockerbie" (Libyan Arab Jamahiriya vs. United States of America), 14 April 1992, and UN Security Council resolutions 731 and 748. We are indebted to Betsy Baker and Benedict Kingsbury for bringing this point to our attention.
25. For a brief overview, see Tad Daley, "Can the U.N. Stretch to Fit Its Future," *Bulletin of the Atomic Scientists* (April 1992): 38–42. For a comprehensive survey of Security Council proposals, see Hanna Newcombe, "Reform of the United Nations Security Council," *Peace Research Reviews* 8 (May 1979), no. 3. On the Secretary-General issue, see Joakim Parker,

"Electing the U.N. Secretary-General after the Cold War," *Hastings Law Journal* 44 (November 1992), no. 1: 161–184.

26. See Jeremy Turnstall, *The Media Are American* (New York: Columbia University Press, 1977), 208; Herbert Schiller, *Mass Communications and American Empire* (New York: Augustus M. Kelly, 1969), 34–39.

27. See UNESCO, *Many Voices, One World* (Paris: UNESCO, 1980).

28. See John G. Ruggie, "International Regimes, Transactions and Change: Embedded Liberalism in the Post-War Economic Order," *International Organization* 35 (January 1983), no. 2: 261–285; Ann-Marie Burley, "Regulating the World: Multilateralism, International Law, and the Projection of the New Deal Regulatory State," in Ruggie, *Multilateralism Matters*, 125–156; Jahangir Amuzegar, "The IMF under Fire," in Diehl, *Politics of International Organizations*, 242–258.

29. See Stephen Krasner, *Structural Conflict: The Third World against Global Liberalism* (Berkeley: University of California Press, 1985); Craig Murphy, "What the Third World Wants: An Interpretation of the Development and Meaning of the New Economic Order Ideology," *International Studies Quarterly* 27 (March 1983), no. 1: 55–76.

30. As does, for example, the otherwise interesting study by Ole Elgström, "Internal Bargaining and Foreign Aid Negotiations," paper presented to the International Studies Association annual meeting, Vancouver, 20–23 March 1991.

31. For an overview of the vast literature on change and adaptation of the UN system, see W. Andy Knight, "Change and Reform in the United Nations System," unpublished doctoral dissertation, York University, 1993; Ronald Meltzer, "Restructuring the United Nations System: Institutional Reform Efforts in the Context of North–South Relations," *International Organization* 32 (Autumn 1978), no. 4: 993–1018.

32. The clearest presentation of this type of change is Mark Zacher's analysis, "The Decaying Pillars of the Westphalian Temple: Implications for International Order and Governance," in James Rosenau and Ernst-Otto Czempiel, eds., *Governance without Government: Order and Change in World Politics* (Cambridge: Cambridge University Press, 1992), 58–101. Zacher's six "decaying" pillars of the Westphalian system (pp. 62–63) are:
    (1) periodic resort to war.
    (2) low levels of trans-boundary consequences of state activities.
    (3) low levels of economic interdependence.
    (4) low information flows that promote cultural distinctiveness.
    (5) a predominance of authoritarian or non-democratic governments.
    (6) a high degree of cultural, political and economic heterogeneity that makes policy coordination difficult.
    These are not exactly the same as constitutive principles, but the point is similar.

33. See, on humanitarian intervention, Thomas G. Weiss and Larry Minear, "Do International Ethics Matter? Humanitarian Politics in the Sudan," *Ethics and International Affairs* 5 (1991): 197–214; on the indigenous peoples issue, S. James Anaya, "Indigenous Rights Norms in Contemporary International Law," *Arizona Journal of International and Comparative Law* 8 (1992), no. 2: 1–39.

34. This argument for continuity needs to be distinguished from the static neo-realist analysis exemplified by John Mearsheimer's argument in "Back to the Future: Instability in Europe after the Cold War," *International Security* 15 (Summer 1990), no. 1: 5–56. More insightful attempts to deal with change in global politics include Barry Buzan and R. Barry Jones, *Change and the Study of International Relations* (New York: St. Martin's Press, 1981); Robert Gilpin, *War and Change in World Politics* (Cambridge: Cambridge University Press, 1981); Oran Young, *Resource Regimes: Natural Resources and Social Institutions* (Berkeley: University of California Press, 1982).

35. Ralf Dahrendorf, *Class and Class Conflict in Industrial Society* (California: Stanford University Press, 1959), 125–126.

36. Oran Young, "The United Nations and the International System," in Leon Gordenker, ed.,

The United Nations in International Politics (Princeton, N.J.: Princeton University Press, 1971), 17.

37. In 205 substantive issues raised in the Security Council between 1946 and 1987, the USSR cast 121 vetoes, the United States 58, the United Kingdom 27, China 22, and France 16. In addition to this there were several incidents when the so-called "hidden veto" was utilized. See W. Andy Knight and Mari Yamashita, "The United Nations' Contribution to International Peace and Security," in David Dewitt, David Haglund, and John Kirton, eds., *Building a New Global Order* (Toronto: Oxford University Press, 1993), 284–312.

38. GA Resolution 377 (V), 3 November 1950. See Adam Roberts and Benedict Kingsbury, *United Nations, Divided World: The UN's Roles in International Relations* (Oxford: Clarendon Press, 1988), 34; Geoffrey Goodwin, *Britain and the United Nations* (New York: Manhattan Publishing Co., 1957), 245–255.

39. Claude, *Swords into Plowshares*, 268. One could interpret recent moves by the permanent five members to enhance their cooperation and coordination as an attempt to reclaim some of this terrain for the Security Council. Interview with UN official, June 1991.

40. This ad hoc conflict management technique can be described as the employment, under UN auspices, of military, para-military, or non-military personnel or forces in an area of conflict, in order to separate and disengage disputing parties long enough to allow negotiations to take place between them.

41. Lester Pearson, "Force for the UN," *Foreign Affairs* 35 (April 1957): 401; Ramesh Thakur, "International Peacekeeping, UN Authority, and US Power," *Alternatives* 12 (1987): 461. For an elaboration of the role that UN observer missions and peace-keeping operations have played in the maintenance of international peace and security, see the second edition of *The Blue Helmets: A Review of United Nations Peace-keeping* (New York: United Nations Department of Public Information, 1990).

42. *An Agenda for Peace*, report of the Secretary-General pursuant to the statement adopted by the summit meeting of the Security Council on 31 January 1992. General Assembly Document A/47/277, 17 June 1992, 14.

43. See Dag Hammarskjöld, *Introduction to the Annual Report of the Secretary-General on the Work of the Organization,* 16 June 1960, UNGA 15th Session, supplement no.1 A (A/4390/Add.1); Claude, *Swords into Plowshares*, 312–334.

44. Examples of its use are the Middle East crises of 1956 and 1958, the Laos crisis of 1959, and the Congo crisis of 1960. A detailed list of UN missions is offered in Walter Dorn, "Keeping Watch for Peace: Fact-finding by the UN Secretary-General," unpublished paper, Parliamentarians for Global Action (October 1992).

45. Thomas Boudreau, *Sheathing the Sword: The UN Secretary-General and the Prevention of International Conflict* (New York: Greenwood Press, 1991), 116.

46. United Nations, General Assembly, *Review of the Efficiency of the Administrative and Financial Functioning of the United Nations: Restructuring of the Secretariat of the Organization, Note by the Secretary-General*, 21 February 1992, UNGA 46th Session, Agenda item 105 (A/46/882), 2.

47. See note 42.

48. The Charter obligated member states holding responsibility for dependent territories to facilitate the progress of these territories towards self-government and eventual independence.

49. Claude, *Swords into Plowshares*, 89–92; John Holmes, *The Shaping of Peace: Canada and the Search for World Order*, vol. II (Toronto: University of Toronto Press, 1982), 336–348.

50. See A. J. Miller, "The Functional Principle in Canada's External Relations," *International Journal* 35 (Spring 1980), no. 2: 309–328.

51. Claude, *Swords into Plowshares*, 364.

52. Brian Urquhart, "The Management of Change: The Role of the UN," in *Canada and the United Nations in a Changing World*, report of a UNA-Canada conference, Winnipeg, 12–14 May 1977, 44.

53. See Immanuel Wallerstein, *The Modern World System* (New York: Academic Press, 1974) and André Gunder Frank, *Capitalism and Underdevelopment in Latin America: Historical Studies of Chile and Brazil* (New York: Monthly Review, 1969); Enrique Cardoso and Enzo Faletto, *Dependency and Development in Latin America* (Berkeley: University of California Press, 1978); J. Samuel Valenzuela and Arturo Valenzuela, "Modernization and Dependency," *Comparative Politics* 10 (July 1978), no. 4: 535–557.

54. Edmund P. Wellenstein, "The North–South Dialogue: Another Confrontation or a Basis for a New International Economic Order?" in Jan A. Van Lith, ed., *Change and the New International Economic Order* (London: Martinus Nijhoff Publishing, 1979), 150–164.

55. Craig Murphy, "What the Third World Wants: An Interpretation of the Development and Meaning of the New International Economic Order Ideology," in Diehl, *Politics of International Organizations*, 226–241.

56. On the links between the NIEO and third-generation rights, see Van Lith, *Change and the New International Economic Order*. In 1975 the Charter of Economic Rights and Duties of States was adopted by the General Assembly. The three generations of rights are generally broken down as follows:
   • first-generation rights stressed civil and political rights and the right to property;
   • second-generation rights treated economic, social, and cultural rights as a priority and a prerequisite for the enjoyment of civil and political rights;
   • third-generation rights added the right to self-determination and the importance of the struggle for development.
   See Jack Donnelly, "Human Rights in the New World Order," *World Policy Journal* 9 (Spring 1992), no. 2: 249–277.

57. Institutional expansion included the UNDP, the Department of Social and Economic Affairs, and UNCTAD itself. Examples of legal changes include: laws to regulate the activities of transnational corporations; the UN Convention on the Law of the Sea (UNCLOS); and the International Covenant on Economic, Social, and Cultural Rights (adopted 16 December 1966).

58. See United Nations, *A Study of the Capacity of the United Nations Development System*, vols. 1 and 2 (Geneva: United Nations, 1969). There have also been a number of "development decades" to highlight the need for development in the third world.

59. See Gil Winham, "Gatt and the International Trade Regime," *International Journal* 45 (Autumn 1990), no. 4: 796–822.

60. The level of unpaid assessments to the organization's budget had risen to US$970 million by early 1993. In addition, unpaid assessments to the peace-keeping forces account (which is separate from the regular budget) stood at US$1,500 million (*New York Times*, 16 May 1993).

61. See Chung-In Moon, "The Future of the Newly Industrializing Countries: An Uncertain Promise," in Dennis Pirages and Christine Sylvester, eds., *Transformations in the Global Political Economy* (New York: St. Martin's Press, 1990), 153–194; Tim Shaw, "The Future of the Fourth World: Choices and Constraints on the Very Poor in the 1980s," in Pirages and Sylvester, *Transformations*, 195–229.

62. See Donald Puchala and Roger Coate, *The Challenge of Relevance: The United Nations in a Changing World Environment* (New York: The Academic Council on the United Nations System, 1989), 54.

63. See Michael Akehurst, *A Modern Introduction to International Law*, 5th ed. (London: Allen & Unwin, 1984), 57–68.

64. See note 24.

65. *An Agenda for Peace*, passim. See Keith Krause, "Redefining Security? The Discourses and Practices of Multilateral Security Activity," paper presented to the annual meeting of the British International Studies Association, Warwick, 14–16 December 1993.

66. See Keith Krause, W. Andy Knight, and David Dewitt, "Canada and Reform of the United Nations," in Alger, et al., *The United Nations.*

67. John Ikenberry and Charles Kupchan, "Socialization and Hegemonic Power," *International Organization* 44 (Summer 1990), no. 3: 291–292. See also the article on socialization of permanent representatives to the UN.

68. Advocates of a "third-generation organization" or a "successor vision" (such as the UNA-USA report) would disagree on this point. See Peter Fromuth, ed., *A Successor Vision: The United Nations of Tomorrow* (New York: United Nations Association of the United States of America, 1988).

69. An idea first argued in Ernst Haas, "Dynamic Environment and Static System: Revolutionary Regimes in the United Nations," in R. Gregg and M. Barkun, eds., *The United Nations System and Its Functions: Selected Readings* (Princeton, N.J.: Van Nostrand, 1968), 162–196.

70. Cox, "Social Forces," 136–137.

71. *Inter alia* see Peter Willetts, ed., *Pressure Groups in the Global System* (London: Frances Pinter, 1982); Chiang Pei-Heng, *Non-Governmental Organizations at the United Nations: Identity, Role and Function* (New York: Praeger, 1981).

72. For a provocative analysis of how the institutions themselves exclude or silence certain perspectives (from the standpoint of international law), see Hilary Charlesworth, Christine Chinkin, and Shelley Wright, "Feminist Approaches to International Law," *American Journal of International Law* 85 (1991): 613–645, especially 621–634.

73. The Secretary-General's report treads a fine line on this issue, but still advocates vesting authority in the Council and activating Chapter VII arrangements (*Agenda for Peace*, paras. 42 and 43).

74. Ruggie, "Multilateralism," 30, citing Burley.

75. Elgström, "Internal Bargaining," passim.

76. Fred Halliday, "State and Society in International Relations: A Second Agenda," *Millennium* 16 (1987), no. 2: 223.

Part I
Seeking a larger voice: German and Indian perspectives

1

The multilateral obligation: German perspectives on the UN system

Wilfried von Bredow

The re-emergence of Germany as one of the economically most potent and politically most important nation-states in the international
system is a near-miraculous success story. In recent years, many observers of Germany's growth have expressed doubts over the democratic reliability of the German nation, asking themselves whether
Germany would continue its policy of prudent and peaceful multilateralism, or fall again to the temptation of regional expansionism
and hegemonic rule. This is probably a typical non-question, because
the changes of the international environment have once and for all
eliminated the possibility of a Wilhelminian or National Socialist content in German policy. This does not mean, however, that German
foreign policy is not faced with choices.

With the end of the East–West conflict and the unification of the
two German states on 3 October 1990, the political establishment
and the public in Germany had to live through the difficult and sometimes painful process of re-evaluating their political priorities. This
process has not yet come to an end. It is interesting to note that one
of the major strands of the contemporary political debate centres
around what I like to call the "multilateral obligation" in Germany's
foreign policy doctrine.[1] For the Federal Republic of Germany and,
for very different reasons, the German Democratic Republic, a multilateral approach to foreign policy was a necessity after the Allied
Powers dictated the erasure of what their political élites perceived as

the unhealthy militaristic and imperialistic elements of traditional German nationalism. The Germans themselves accepted this "lesson of history" without much regret. A politically and morally sound pursuit of the national interest has to be embedded in a multilateral perspective; this became a fundamental principle of post-National Socialist Germany. What was conceived to be a device for Germany's domestication in the 1940s soon developed into a vehicle for Germany's rise to economic, political, and – to a considerably lesser degree – military power in the following decades. Multilateralism proved to be a more effective approach to addressing Germany's problems in the international environment than any unilateral nationalist strategy could ever have been. In other words, after 1949, Germany's national interests were to be pursued in a multilateral perspective. In the case of the Federal Republic, this is very evident in Adenauer's *Westpolitik*, in Brandt's *Ostpolitik*, and in the *Vereinigungspolitik* of Kohl and Genscher. Will this principle of German foreign policy survive the unification process without becoming debilitated?

I shall address this question by examining the development of Germany's relations with the UN system, as well as the current German debates about its new status, role(s), and responsibilities in the international system. These debates reflect some problems of collective identity, which stem, however, not from a kind of neo-nationalist outlook on the world, but, on the contrary, from a deep resentment and suspicion of nationalism. It is worth emphasizing this point: Germany's unification is perceived by most Germans not as a reward for their national policies but as a result of the breakdown of "real socialism" in Eastern Europe. The first section of this chapter will give a historical account of Germany's growth into the UN system. The following section will elaborate on the new position of Germany in the current international system, particularly with respect to the United Nations. The final section will describe and analyse the post-unification debate about Germany's new status in international politics and the consequences for its role in the UN system.

Growing into the UN system

The development of the relationship between Germany and the UN system can be divided into three periods: from 1949 to 1973, when neither of the two German states was an official member of the United Nations; from 1973 to 1990, when the Federal Republic of

Germany (FRG; West Germany) and the German Democratic Republic (GDR; East Germany) acted as formally acknowledged members of the world organization; and the period since German unification in 1990, when the five *Länder* (states or provinces) of the GDR joined the Federal Republic of Germany. In the same year, two members of the relatively small academic community of UN observers in West Germany published a book with the rather optimistic title *The Rediscovery of the United Nations.*[2] Who had rediscovered what, and why at that time?

Participation as non-members

The Charter of the United Nations created "a center for harmonizing the actions of nations" in order to maintain international peace and security, to develop friendly relations among nations, and to achieve international cooperation (Article 1). These goals were proclaimed at the end of a terrible war, during a collective mood of "never again," and a time when the concept of "One World" appeared to be realistic. There were, however, exceptions, at least for an interval. In 1945, it was somewhat inconceivable that the enemies of the Allied Powers during the Second World War could become members of the United Nations on the basis of equal rights and duties. This substantial and moral differentiation is engraved in the Charter of the United Nations: Article 53 (in Chapter VIII, "Regional arrangements") states:

1) The Security Council shall, where appropriate, utilize such regional arrangements or agencies for enforcement action under its authority. But no enforcement action shall be taken under regional arrangements or by regional agencies without the authorization of the Security Council, with the exception of measures against any enemy state, as defined in paragraph 2 of this Article, provided for pursuant to Article 107 or in regional arrangements directed against renewal of aggressive policy on the part of any such State, until such time as the Organization may, on request of the governments concerned, be charged with the responsibility for preventing further aggression by such a State.

2) The term "enemy State" as used in paragraph 1 of this Article applies to any State which during the Second World War has been an enemy of any signatory of the present Charter. Article 107 of the Charter (in Chapter XVII, "Transitional security arrangements") states: Nothing in the present Charter shall invalidate or preclude action, in relation to any State which during the Second World War has been an enemy of any signatory to the present Charter, taken or authorized as a result of that war by the Governments having responsibility for such action.

Although the enemy states clauses did not play an important role in the German debate after 1949, they certainly placed a stigma on Germany. The aggressiveness and murderous racism of National Socialist Germany led not only to Germany's defeat in 1945 but also to a moral isolation that could be overcome only by a credible turn towards the values of democracy and respect for human rights. Under the shadow of this defeat and international isolation, the majority of Germans accepted the stigma of their recent history and engaged the task of constructing a new society.

The perspective of a common world and cooperative global development under the joint leadership of the five permanent members of the Security Council was soon overshadowed by the onset of the Cold War. The East–West conflict, which had played only a secondary role in the decades after the Russian revolution, now developed into a firmly bipolar and harshly antagonistic structure of international relations. Germany became a victim of this development because its provisional division into a Western and a Soviet zone of occupation marked the beginning of a dual political development of separate states characterized by mutually hostile political ideologies, incompatible economic systems, and mutual contempt for each other's ruling élite. The city of Berlin became a symbol of the division of Germany and of Europe, generating a peculiarly cruel and inhuman kind of border relationship between the two Germanies. On the other hand, the Germanies also benefited remarkably from the Cold War and the East–West confrontation, for their status changed from losers to allies. The benefits were, however, unequally distributed: the Germans of the Western zones of occupation (since 1949 the Federal Republic of Germany) gained a parliamentary democracy and were integrated into a prosperous global market economy, while the Germans in the Soviet zone of occupation (since 1949 the German Democratic Republic) had to manage their lives under a totalitarian political system and an inefficient, centralized, state-planned "socialist" economy.

The core objectives of West Germany's foreign policy doctrine in its first period of existence, the chancellorship of Konrad Adenauer (1949–1963), were to establish the Federal Republic as a reliable ally in the Western world, to regain the status of a sovereign and internationally respected actor in regional and world politics, to overcome the traditional constellation of power, conflict, and war among European nations, and eventually to re-establish Germany as a united, democratic, and peaceful society. In the years of the Cold

War, this doctrine was necessarily embedded in a profoundly anti-communist context, which made intra-German relations difficult. Aside from the problematic aspect of German reunification, this doctrine could also be made to operate in West Germany's relations with other countries (such as France or Israel).

Perhaps more importantly, this approach established a precedent for the foreign policy behaviour of West Germany in the pursuit of its national interests (or what was perceived as its national interest by the political establishment): *multilateralism*. During the years of its existence, West Germany experienced considerable success in using multilateralism as a tool for promoting national interests. Over the same period, the international system evolved considerably, becoming increasingly characterized by multilateral approaches to various issues. The unique circumstances of Germany after the Second World War, a situation that prohibited a strictly nationalist foreign policy for the post-National Socialist Germany, put the Germans into the avant-garde of the pursuit of multilateralism. It was probably not the result of a deep insight into the developing complexity of the international system during the second half of the twentieth century but a consequence of sheer necessity that West Germany adopted a most promising method of pursuing its national interests. It is also true that these multilateral practices had a considerable influence in shaping the perceptions of West Germany's national interest and foreign policy objectives.[3] The multilateral approach has become part of German political culture and functions, among other things, as an effective antidote against the temptations of neo-nationalism and (too much) protectionism, especially in times of *Eurosklerosis* and general discontent with the development of international affairs.[4] Counter-currents like the apolitical xenophobia manifest among the younger generation gained momentum after Germany's unification, but these remain fringe phenomena.

One of the consequences of West Germany's commitment to multilateralism was its attempt to play a useful and constructive role in the UN system by becoming active in its special organizations, even during a time when the Federal Republic was barred from UN membership. The Federal Republic has participated in the Food and Agriculture Organization since 1950, the International Labour Organization since 1951, the World Health Organization since 1951, and UNESCO since 1951; by 1955, the Federal Republic had become a member of practically all of the special agencies, organizations, and conferences of the UN system. From 1956 on, it had become routine for the Federal Republic to take part in the founding of new specialized agencies or organizations (for example, the International Finance Corporation, the International Atomic Energy Agency, the Intergovernmental Maritime Consultative Organization, or the United Nations Industrial Development Organization).[5]

One of the early studies distinguished between three attitudes the Federal Republic might have adopted towards the UN system. Germany could either remain passive, attempt to promote the goals of the United Nations from its position as a non-member, or pursue its national interests and view the United Nations as an instrument for this goal. The author, in a kind of melancholy idealism, deplored the fact that the government of the Federal Republic chose the third of these options.[6] That it indeed chose the third option can be illustrated with reference to the "German Question." In 1951/52, during the coldest period of the Cold War, the General Assembly dealt with the proposal to hold free elections in both East and West Germany. The issue of free elections was at that time not a real one, but it figured as part of the propaganda war between East and West, since there was no real chance that the Soviet authorities would allow free elections in one of their satellites.[7] As the General Assembly was then more or less a forum for the common expression of Western policy towards the Eastern bloc, nobody seriously expected any resolution of the "German Question" that led to German reunification. The debate eventually petered out without any progress having been made, and, over the following years, the Soviet Union or its allies would occasionally use various forums in the UN system to denounce West Germany as a militaristic, imperialist, and neo-fascist society (implicitly pointing to the "enemy states" clauses), after which one of the Western delegations would take the floor to defend the Federal Republic.

The "active non-membership participation" of West Germany in the UN system between 1950 and 1973 was driven mainly by the political motive of impeding international recognition of East Germany.[8] This "negative" motivation made it necessary for the Federal Republic to demonstrate its multilateral constructiveness, even in UN specialized agencies that were not of direct interest to the West German government. Constructiveness in this respect often meant financial contributions. Because the "German Question," as an important element of the East–West conflict, was a handicap for policy, West Germany's multilateral efforts in the UN system during the 1950s and 1960s are probably best regarded as "potential multilateralism."

The attitude of the economically and otherwise much stronger of the two Germanies had, of course, a decisive influence on the UN policy of East Germany, which tried without success to gain equal status in the United Nations as a participating non-member.[9]

From 1949 to 1973, the Federal Republic, while not a member of the United Nations, played two different roles in the UN system. First, it tried to demonstrate a newly acquired sense for international cooperation and multilateralism as a low-profile, responsible actor in international politics. Secondly, it consistently sought to have the German Democratic Republic prevented from playing any role at all in the UN system. These attitudes were framed by the Cold War period of the East–West conflict. As the Cold War became anachronistic (primarily the consequence of achieving a nuclear balance of terror in the early 1960s) and the UN system began evolving into a forum for expressing the concerns of the emerging third world, these two role preoccupations of the Federal Republic became increasingly less suitable for meeting the new challenges of a still bipolar, but much more complex international system.

Double indemnity? Two Germanies in the United Nations Organization (UNO)

After the 1962 Cuban missile crisis, the East–West conflict began to change in appearance, if not in nature. The following years saw the slow development of *détente* in East–West relations, first between the two leading powers, the United States and the USSR (mostly in the realm of nuclear arms control), then between Eastern and Western Europe, and finally between the two German states. In other parts of the world (primarily Asia and Africa), the confrontation continued to be very tense and to include the use of military force. This was not so in the heart of Europe, where the international community pushed the two Germanies toward *détente*. With the Four Power Agreement on Berlin, the complicated timetable for the Conference on Security and Cooperation in Europe (CSCE), and the Basic Treaty between the two German states, the necessary conditions for their acceptance as full members of the United Nations were fulfilled. On 18 September 1973 the Federal Republic and the GDR became the 134th and the 135th members of the United Nations.

The two Germanies continued to play rather different roles in the UN system. The Federal Republic participated in more or less all activities of the United Nations or its specialized agencies, becoming one of the main financial pillars of the organization. The GDR, on the other hand, preferred to participate selectively in the UN system, and its financial contributions were minimal in comparison with those of the Federal Republic. Comparative studies of the two Germanies in the United Nations have, not surprisingly, revealed very different patterns of voting behaviour. East Germany, as a "socialist country," voted in near-total conformity with the USSR. West Germany usually voted in conformity with the United States and the member states of the European Communities (EC). There were, however, a considerable number of cases of disagreement between the United States and the EC member states. In such situations, West Germany tended either to abstain or to side with the European states.[10] Quite astoundingly, the "German Question," and the problems generated by the division of Germany, did not emerge as an issue in debates within the UN framework. One important reason for this was that, from the early 1970s onwards, this issue was debated in other forums, such as the CSCE.[11] At the UN level, there was practically no special bilateral cooperation or even mutual consultation between the two Germanies.

The 1970s and 1980s saw the United Nations drifting towards a peculiar kind of anti-Westernism. Western states – because of their historical reputation as colonial powers and, more recently, their image as rich industrialized powers unwilling to help the poor countries of the underdeveloped world – became the target of a growing number of resolutions by the General Assembly and other bodies.[12] These resolutions were coloured by the developing world's strong anti-colonialist, anti-imperialist (and anti-Zionist), and anti-capitalist attitudes, as well as by a military and economic perspective that identified the United States and its allies as the enemies of a peaceful development of humankind. These were largely rhetorical and symbolic, rather than substantive, policy efforts. However, for all its marginal political relevance, it gave the GDR the opportunity to establish itself in the mainstream of UN debate, whereas West Germany often found itself branded as one of the villains in world politics. The gap between the rhetoric and reality sometimes became absurdly wide, and on the level of the United Nations' day-to-day activities a double standard had to develop. The GDR did not really profit internationally from its voting behaviour in the General Assembly, and the Federal Republic did not really become ostracized, since, when practical problems arose requiring the financial involvement of UN members, the GDR usually refused or was unable to become involved, while the Federal Republic participated actively in all kinds of multilateral UN activities and actions.

In West Germany's official version (or self-perception), the Federal Republic contributed to the UN system in four main fields, namely:
- by promoting a secure peace on the basis of non-violence and the resolution of conflicts by non-military means;
- by participating in disarmament and arms control processes and the creation of confidence-building measures;
- by promoting the right to collective self-determination and human rights;
- by supporting the just sharing of economic burdens in order to help developing countries fight hunger and economic backwardness.

West German diplomats often underscore the institutional success of the Federal Republic's multilateral activities, referring in particular to its membership of the Security Council in 1977/1978, and its presidency of the thirty-fifth General Assembly in 1980. West Germany's Minister for Foreign Affairs from 1973 to 1992, Hans-Dietrich Genscher, had the reputation of being a shrewd politician and of using the United Nations as a forum for emphasizing the good intentions of West Germany's efforts in the international arena. He was famous for his skills in personal diplomacy and for the enormous number of "private breakfasts" he held every morning in New York while the General Assembly was in session. To a certain degree, the potential of West Germany's multilateral participation in the UN system was realized. Official admittance to the United Nations in 1973 was regarded as a reward for the successful construction of an economically prosperous and democratic society. On the other hand, the political establishment of the Federal Republic perceived the role of the United Nations in international politics as secondary. Paradoxically, the main preoccupations of the United Nations, from peace and disarmament to human rights and the economic development of the former colonies, made it necessary to demonstrate one's "good intentions," even though these were often in contradiction with the realities of international politics. This was the advantage (and the disadvantage) of an institutionalized double standard. The UN system did provide some scope for *Realpolitik*, but the structural confrontation of the East–West conflict, and the various conflicts between the richer countries of the Northern hemisphere and the poorer countries of the South, tended to push all actors in the United Nations towards symbolic policy commitments. In the case of the Federal Republic, this symbolic policy served four main functions:

- to show the world the picture of a peaceful and helpful Germany, in contrast to the image of Germany in the past;
- to prove West Germany a reliable ally within the Western alliances;
- to demonstrate to the developing countries a certain readiness to ease problems that had grown out of other Western countries' political intransigence;
- to demonstrate to concerned groups within West German society that the government was busy attempting to overcome the global threats caused by weapons, underdevelopment, and ecological catastrophes.

Although the "real issues" of international politics may have been dealt with in other arenas, the UN system gained importance as a symbol of the rapid globalization of inter/transnational relations. Multilateralism in the UN framework remained largely (if not completely) rhetorical, but this rhetoric became increasingly important in West German domestic political circles. At the end of the 1980s, even before the disappearance of the East–West conflict, the impact of globalization was felt even among convinced "realists." Evidently, the UN system was on the brink of taking over other, this time less rhetorical and more "executive," functions in international politics. This trend was alluded to by the editors of the book *The Rediscovery of the United Nations* in 1990.[13]

German unification and the end of the East–West conflict

The period of *détente* in the East–West conflict seemed to have come to an end by the late 1970s. There were no further arms control agreements between the United States and the USSR; the Soviet Union had invaded Afghanistan; there were growing internal difficulties in Poland and elsewhere in the Soviet system; NATO made its decision to deploy Intermediate Nuclear Forces (Pershing II and cruise missiles) on West European territory; and US President Ronald Reagan announced his intention to invest billions of dollars in the Strategic Defense Initiative. This abbreviated list of international developments indicated the re-emergence of Cold War perceptions and attitudes between East and West.[14]

In fact, the end of *détente* signalled not the return of the Cold War but the beginning of the decade-long last phase of the East–West conflict. The second half of the 1980s was marked by a surprisingly quick *rapprochement* between the United States and the USSR, motivated not so much by any new-found political wisdom but largely by sheer necessity on the part of the USSR. At first, the new climate of East–West relations seemed to be evolving into a more efficient "antagonistic cooperation" between blocs, in response to efforts to develop relations more in accord with the CSCE Helsinki Final Act (1975). This also seemed to motivate the two Germanies with respect to "inner-German" relations. In 1987, the General Secretary of the East German Communist Party, Erich Honecker, paid an official visit to Bonn and was received with all the usual honours. West Germany's Foreign Minister, Hans-Dietrich Genscher, remarked in his speech before the forty-fourth General Assembly of the United Nations on 27 September 1989:

The Federal Republic of Germany as a state in the heart of Europe is using all its political weight for more cooperation, mutual understanding and disarmament in a better Europe. This includes cooperation with the GDR. Both German states know their responsibility for peace in Europe. This responsibility is stronger than what separates us. Both German states have delivered in their community of responsibility [*Verantwortungsgemeinschaft*] some important contributions to détente and disarmament in Europe.... Both German states, in their respective ways, have to contribute to overcoming the division of Europe.[15]

Only seven weeks later, the Berlin wall came down. The leadership of the USSR did not want to intervene in the process of dissolution, first of the "Soviet empire," then of the Soviet Union itself. The leaders of this state, from Lenin on, had always proclaimed their model of socialism as the effective alternative to capitalism, the market economy, and Western bourgeois values. Now it disappeared like the Cheshire cat, not a grinning one but a grim one.

The division of Germany in 1945 was motivated mainly by political concepts that emerged from (or were intrinsic to) the operation of the nation-state system. The development of the East–West conflict into the Cold War painted an ideological veneer on this essentially political phenomenon, and the two Germanies became models of the Eastern and the Western ways of organizing a society. Both socio-political systems were mutually exclusive and made universal claims, making it clear to Germans that they were involved in a "winner take all" competition and that they could not contemplate (re)unification until one of the two systems had collapsed. By the same token, traditional hesitations and doubts about a unified Germany were devalued, and it was commonly accepted by political observers of central Europe that German unification would be a consequence of Europe's unification after the end of the East–West conflict. With the sudden and surprisingly peaceful end of the East–West conflict, those traditional doubts and hesitations became resurgent, particularly in France and the United Kingdom. No one, however, could legitimately deny Germans their right to self-determination, and those (like Mr Nicholas Ridley in England and a handful of German intellectuals) who argued against unification soon found themselves isolated.

Turbulent changes in the international system

Since 3 October 1990 the Federal Republic of Germany has been the only German member of the United Nations, and the GDR has ceased to exist. The rapid process of unification and the enormous financial, economic, social, and other problems that have followed have been absorbing most of Germany's political energy. Current historical developments, however, have a global impact, given the unprecedented number of interdependencies of all kinds. While Germans celebrated the fall of the Berlin wall (not yet foreseeing the giant price of unification), a very dangerous military conflict was developing in the Middle East that would soon confront the unified Germany with contradictory expectations and dilemmas. The end of the East–West conflict was not at all the beginning of a new era of international peace, or even of regional peace in Europe itself.

The German political establishment and the public had to respond to the turbulent changes in the international environment by redefining Germany's international political role. At the same time, an immediate effort was needed to re-create the German collective (national) identity. German unification was the result of international changes, not of national policies. It came about in a multidimensional process of international conferences and agreements, not by national determination. The majority of Germans, at least in West Germany, did not regard unification as the fulfilment of their political dreams. Unification, in sum, was primarily a multilateral event, and not so much a national one. Its consequences, however, created the conditions for a bout of collective narcissism and self-reflection that, while understandable, emerged at an inopportune time.

The changes in the international system, the new shape of Europe, Germany's role in regional and global affairs, and the new international insecurity exemplified by the techno-media war against Iraqi aggression were all topics of debate in Germany, and would serve as the initiation of a new German collective self-understanding. In one way or another all of these issues were connected with the recent and future development of the United Nations and the broader UN system.

A heritage from East Germany?

In 1990, many people in West Germany asked themselves whether or not the disappearing GDR had produced some institutions or policies that were worth transferring into the new Germany. This question was asked in various political contexts, from social policy to the management of top athletes; usually, the answer was a disappointed "no." This was also the case for East Germany's UN policy. Studies by East German authors on the results of the GDR's 17 years in the United Nations were unable to point to more than some superficial successes by their delegations in New York. Some rhetorically similar policies, such as a shared interest in disarmament, were characterized by some analysts as "common interests" pursued by both states in their UN policies.[16] This was not a very convincing argument: the GDR was a socialist/communist state, and its élite defined their political concepts and goals in Marxist–Leninist terms. This perceptual framework has been broken and the former élite of the country dispersed. Powerful institutions that act in the name of Marxism–Leninism no longer exist in the international environment (Cuba and China being peculiar exceptions, and probably only for a limited period). As far as the United Nations is concerned, the heritage of the East German past is nil.[17]

Reform of the UN system

Even before the end of the East–West conflict, the need to reform the UN system was widely discussed among experts.[18] It is not difficult to make an extended list of the problems that were perceived to need correction, from the over-bureaucratization of the Secretary-General's Office to the Byzantine complexity of the UN bureaucracy (and behaviour of bureaucrats), to the relative helplessness of the organization to intervene in dangerous political conflicts in the name of peace. One of the reasons for the immobility of the UN system was the impact of the East–West conflict on its performance. Thus, the end of the East–West conflict represents a point of departure for initiating far-reaching reforms of the United Nations and perhaps also of some of the specialized agencies in the UN system.

Reforming the United Nations is a general concern, but it also has a special German dimension. The end of the East–West conflict and the unification of Germany created a potentially more powerful nation-state. Whatever indicators one uses (with the exception of nuclear weapons), Germany today is the most influential state in Europe, and its political priorities command the attention of other European states. This may have been true before 1990, but it became more evident in the wake of Germany's unification. The dynamics and direction of the deepening and widening of the European Union (as shaped by the Maastricht accords of December 1991) and the attempt to create common West European policies towards the breakup of Yugoslavia are just two examples illustrating the growing weight of German opinion in the European context.[19]

These changes occurred too late to have an impact on Germany's reaction to the Gulf War. I shall return to the German Gulf War debate below; here, I shall concentrate on some of the general contributions to the UN reform debate from German sources. The relatively small community of political scientists and international legal scholars in German universities has been following the international debate with great interest. Political and/or academic contributions from these sources, moderately optimistic in tenor, tend to underline the difficulties of any far-reaching reform efforts.[20]

The difficulties of reforming the UN system can be illustrated by examining the problem of institutional anachronisms, the most salient of which is the composition of the Security Council. Evidently, the Security Council is the most important institution of UNO. If it functions adequately, there is a good chance that the goals of the UN Charter can be realized. In particular, the difficulties in securing, maintaining, and restoring peace in volatile zones of the globe can be practically tackled only by the Security Council. The Security Council was largely paralysed as an effective decision-making body during the decades of the East–West conflict, although it seemed to emerge from this crippled status during the Gulf crisis and the Gulf War. The anachronistic element of this institution, however, is the privileged position of the five permanent members of the Security Council. This construction reflects the immediate post-1945 constellation of power, which has lost relevance over the years and is now gone for good. A leading German international legal expert summarizes the debate on reforming the Security Council very cautiously:

Most proposals for a new structure of the Security Council, when closely examined, turn out to be useless ... France and Great Britain ... will probably not want to lose their privileged position, and all well-intentioned proposals to substitute their seats by a seat for the EC are just awkward speculations. One could only seriously think of a moderate augmentation of the permanent members with the intention to offer a better representation for third world countries. It is only conceivable that – as a second step of such a reform – Japan and Germany may nourish some hopes of gaining permanent membership of the Security Council.[21]

Until 1992, the German government tried to avoid a public debate on the question of Security Council reform. Foreign Minister Klaus Kinkel has, however, recently declared Germany's interest in a permanent seat on the Security Council, and Chancellor Helmut Kohl has rejected the idea of German membership of the Security Council without a veto.[22] The official attitude of the government appears to be intended to motivate other governments to call for Germany to be admitted as a permanent member of a reformed Security Council; this represents another example of Germany's "multilateral approach."

Social Democratic considerations

Another attempt to kindle German discussion on UN reform was made by the Social Democratic Party (SPD) in the German parliament. The main opposition party published a reform proposal that was debated in the German Bundestag on 23 January 1992.[23] The Social Democratic Party document is a detailed document covering a broad spectrum of proposed reforms. The most important among them are:
- strengthening the institutional position of the Secretary-General, including restructuring the reporting system with the appointment of four Vice Secretary-Generals;
- organizing UN financing more effectively;
- reviewing and changing the structure of the entire UN system so the interests of the developing countries can be better represented, and ecological problems more efficiently addressed;
- making the mechanisms of peaceful conflict resolution more efficient;

- expanding the mandate of the Security Council, abolishing the veto power of its permanent members, altering its composition to reflect global population distributions, and taking decisions in it on the basis of majority vote;[24]
- enlarging the competence of the United Nations to protect human rights;
- expanding the competence and ability of the United Nations to give immediate assistance in cases of disaster and catastrophe;
- broadening drastically the range of activities of the United Nations in the fields of development and environmental protection;
- deleting the "enemy states" clauses in the UN Charter;
- enlarging the range of options and activities of the United Nations to secure peace.

The approach of the opposition party to the problems and limits of reforming the UN system is characterized by optimism and idealism. This is a quasi-natural attitude of an opposition party on the moderate left, and should not be taken too seriously. On the other hand, there is indeed a general tendency towards political idealism in Germany's political (rather than academic) debate over UN reform; this was also reflected in the Bundestag debate on the Social Democratic Party proposal.

Regional or global organization of collective security?

In his address to the forty-sixth session of the UN General Assembly on 25 September 1991, Foreign Minister Hans-Dietrich Genscher presented 12 points outlining the core of the German government's foreign policy doctrine. Among them were the following goals:

- to develop the European Communities into a political Union and eventually into a United States of Europe;
- to allow all European democracies to have the option of joining the EC;
- to promote the CSCE Charter of Paris as the basis for an all-European integration process;
- to develop the CSCE into an efficient organization for dealing with political and military crises in Europe and the management of collective European security;
- to develop Euro-Atlantic cooperation from Vancouver to Vladivostok;
- to establish the United Nations as the central forum for multilateral action in the new world order.[25]

Again, this catalogue seems somewhat idealistic, even a little boast-ful; there is sometimes a hint of "nouveau riche" behaviour in Ger-many's foreign policy behaviour since 1990, which is perhaps under-standable given Germany's post-1945 stigma. Questions of style and rhetoric aside, observers may ask whether Germany's preference for empowering both the CSCE and the United Nations as the co-guar-dians of collective security might not also lead to conflict and compe-tition between them. The CSCE was not conceived to deal exclu-sively with European regional matters, since the United States and Canada have always been important participants in the CSCE pro-cess. Further, the breakup of the USSR has brought new Asian states into the CSCE, and Japan is considering applying for observer status.

The relationship between the CSCE and the UNO is unclear, however, even if one takes into account that the CSCE, during the Helsinki summit in July 1992, declared itself to be a regional ar-rangement under Chapter VIII of the UN Charter. This declaration provides some legitimacy for CSCE political intervention and peace-keeping actions in Europe and (perhaps) surrounding regions. Theo-retically, this functional division of labour between global and regio-nal institutions appears to be sound. There are, however, some outstanding questions, most of them deriving from the fact that the more than 50 member states of the CSCE will always have great dif-ficulty in arriving at common definitions of complex political situa-tions or, for that matter, in agreeing to a common policy for respond-ing to regional conflicts. Nevertheless, Germany is pushing hard to develop the CSCE into a working institution. Experts in the Ministry of Foreign Affairs apparently see no problem in the multiplication of the levels of multilateralism within the European region and with re-spect to other world regions. This perspective sometimes develops into a neat paradox of German diplomacy: Germany uses all its *national* means to convince other nations of the advantages of multi-lateralism.

New status – New expectations

Germany's self-perception in international relations is changing, but this is a slow process. The perception of Germany by other actors in the international system has, however, changed much more quickly. This perceptual gap helps explain why it is difficult on occasion to follow the logic of internal German policy debates in the new era. Two examples highlight this confusion.

The Gulf War 1990/91 and the hopes/fears of a new world order

During the first phase of the Gulf War (from the Iraqi invasion of Kuwait in August 1990 to the various attempts by the Security Council to restore peace), the attention of Germany's political establishment was absorbed by the unification process. In this light, the German reaction should not be criticized too harshly, although the surprise expressed by the German public over the international community's military response to Iraqi aggression revealed a surprisingly high degree of provincialism in its perceptions of international relations. This surprise can be described by examining two shifts in collective opinion:

- from enthusiasm for multilateral security programmes and the "new role" for the United Nations after the end of the East–West conflict, to deep consternation and even disappointment over the course of international events in 1991/92;
- from high and rising hopes for an international harmony devoid of ideological conflict, to a rather aggressive anti-Americanism, based on the perception that the United States was the only remaining superpower, and a nation with clear hegemonic ambitions.

The first of these shifts is clearly related to the international events of the preceding few years. The events of late 1989 and early 1990 seemed, in the eyes of many Germans, to be the dawn of a new era characterized by a universal movement towards disarmament, growing peace and security, and a significantly strengthened role in international relations for multilateral processes and international institutions such as the United Nations, which could provide the conceptual and political structures to move towards the future. In light of these expectations, the Gulf War was a traumatic shock. The second of these movements reflects more the traditional antipathy between the German political left and right (with Hans-Dietrich Genscher executing a strange mixture of right and left policies). The debate centred on the slogan "new world order," a term that was, indeed, introduced by US President Bush in a rather restricted, normative sense.

The United Nations was, to a certain degree, implicated in the strong criticism of American foreign policy by the peace movement and the political left. The Gulf War was seen as an American war, and the United Nations as merely an instrument of American interests.[26] Certainly, this is a rather simplistic interpretation (fuelled, however, by more than a handful of equally simplistic explanations and self-perceptions on the part of the American government and conservative politicians), but it has struck a resonant chord among some intellectuals and in universities.

Constitutional debates about the Bundeswehr

When the armed forces of the Federal Republic were founded in 1955, the memories of the Third Reich and of the atrocities committed by SS and Wehrmacht soldiers were still vivid enough that the Western powers insisted that the armed forces be under strong democratic political control. This condition was accepted by the leading politicians in the Federal Republic, and political (civilian) control has been written into the Federal Republic's constitution, the *Grundgesetz*. The constitution does not allow for the prosecution of an aggressive war, or for preparations for such a war. The armed forces are firmly integrated into NATO, and many politicians (and, indeed, public opinion) have interpreted the various articles of the Grundgesetz relating to the armed forces in a manner that makes it illegal for the Bundeswehr to take part in any military action outside of the territory protected by NATO. The majority of international and German constitutional legal experts do not agree with this interpretation, but this does not alter the consensus. Because of this "political fact," the Bundeswehr did not take part in the Gulf War, nor has it participated in any other UN peace-keeping operations.[27] Since unification, this attitude has come under criticism from outside as well as inside Germany.

Within the framework of a general constitutional debate, a special discussion has evolved over the question of whether some articles of the Grundgesetz should be revised to allow the Bundeswehr to take part in UN military operations. Until 1990, the official interpretation of the Grundgesetz excluded the legal possibility of a military intervention by West Germany beyond the territories of the Federal Republic or of NATO members. The government now wants to change this interpretation to include military missions in the framework of collective security actions by the United Nations or the CSCE within the catalogue of possible missions for the German armed forces. For this purpose, it has advocated a clarification of the constitution. The opposition has been either strictly opposed to any "out of area" missions of the Bundeswehr, or wants to include only UN peace-keeping operations in the catalogue (and explicitly into the Grundgesetz). Behind this question lies another, more difficult, one: whether Germany should take on the responsibility of participating in multilateral military actions.

The easy question

The German Gulf War debate revealed a deep-seated collective mistrust of the military as an instrument for conflict management. The Bundeswehr is today less popular than ever. Since 1990, the widespread illusion of the imminent dawn of an era of international peace and harmony after decades of East–West nuclear confrontation has been reluctantly abandoned. Yet even with civil war raging nearby in the former Yugoslavia, with its potential to create various difficult policy problems (for example, a refugee problem), Germany today is a more pacifist society than at any other time in recent history. This means that even participation in peace-keeping operations is for many Germans too "militaristic," although the great majority of political parties in the Bundestag favour German participation in such operations. The government tested public opinion by sending 140 soldiers from the medical corps to Cambodia as the German contingent to the UN Transitional Authority for Cambodia (UNTAC). This decision, taken mid-May 1992, was carefully prepared, and did not elicit any opposition from the Social Democratic Party. For the first time, even without an amendment to the Grundgesetz, German soldiers (albeit only medical personnel) participated in a UN peace-keeping operation. The German public did not react, although it may if there are casualties among any German contingents.

The majority of Germans have probably already accepted German participation in peace-keeping operations. This is perhaps because soldiers with blue helmets are understood to be not fighters but members of a kind of police force that may intervene in a conflict only with the consent of all the parties involved. Peace-keeping operations, in other words, are easy to consent to.

The difficult question

The more difficult question concerns German involvement in military operations such as the UN intervention against Iraq. According to Chapter VII of the UN Charter ("Action with respect to threats to the peace, breaches of the peace, and acts of aggression"), military intervention by the United Nations is, in certain circumstances, legal and legitimate. It may well be that in the future this kind of intervention will occur more frequently than it did during the years of East–West conflict. The German government favours amending the constitution to allow the Bundeswehr to participate in these types of UN actions. The SPD firmly rejects this option, although with some dissent from its right-wing elements. One of its foreign policy spokespersons, Norbert Gansel, is quoted as saying: "The government's attempt to open the possibility of world-wide fighting missions for the Bundeswehr by means of UN regulations will not succeed, even if it is wrapped in multilateral constructions."[28] The government, disagreeing with the majority of legal scholars on this issue, has declared that military operations, even within the framework of the United Nations, require a constitutional amendment. Without the support of the SPD, however, such an amendment is unlikely to be passed by the Bundestag, and neither the government nor the SPD seems willing to compromise its position on the issue.

Because of the unpopularity of involving German soldiers in military actions outside NATO territory, there will be no easy solution to this issue, and it may be that only changes in the international environment will alter the situation. In light of recent history, however, the possibility of such changes should not be ruled out. The political strategy of the government is slowly to "educate" the public in matters of international responsibility by having the armed forces participate in humanitarian actions of the United Nations. The Bundeswehr mission in Somalia in the summer of 1993 was one such case, but it became the subject of a political dispute between the government and opposition parties because the line between strictly humanitarian (non-military) and military actions could not be clearly drawn. Whether or not the "out of area" missions of the Bundeswehr will become an important issue in the 1994 election campaign will depend on developments in Somalia and elsewhere.

Germany's multilateral obligation

Unified Germany finds itself in a peculiar international situation. In the aftermath of the catastrophe of the Second World War, the German foreign policy perspective that had culminated in the quest for regional and (in the evil dreams of the National Socialists) world domination was eradicated. It was replaced by a new foreign policy tradition built on a commitment to multilateralism, cooperation, alliances, and economic integration. West Germany came to perceive itself as a trading state, a perspective that, along with its foreign policy manifestation, has come to enjoy broad public support.[29] These international and transnational perspectives have been further promoted by the dense network of interdependencies that have developed in the international system since 1945. Nation-states have not lost their relevance as actors in the international system but have been forced to share the stage with an increasing number and variety of actors. Multilateralism has become increasingly important, but it is a multiplicity of multilateralisms that have developed, rather than a neatly layered hierarchical system.

Germany soon became an efficient player in various multilateral frameworks. Certainly, the most important one has been the regional multilateralism of the European Communities. During the period of East–West confrontation, the transatlantic multilateralism of NATO and (later and to a lesser degree) the CSCE process was also very important. Engaging in global multilateral efforts, particularly within the UN system, has always had a strong moral appeal within Germany, although its political importance was in reality secondary to those of the European Communities, NATO, and the CSCE.

Today, and in the years to come, global multilateralism will become increasingly important. Germany seems to be well placed to understand and play a role in shaping this trend, as the government, along with a variety of non-state actors (ranging from corporations to socio-political movements), have come to rely on multilateral approaches in the pursuit of their agendas. On the other hand, the growing perception of Germany as an increasingly powerful nation-state functions as a temptation to define national interests unilaterally. This, in fact, seems to be the hidden expectation of some states (for example, France). Although it is unlikely, this may, in unhappy circumstances, lead to a spiral of self-fulfilling prophecies.

More probably, the development of Germany's international role will be characterized by continuing integration into the European Union, German participation in a fragile but evolving relationship between Eastern and Western Europe (which is in some respects reminiscent of a classic North–South relationship), a mixture of competition and cooperation in the Group of Seven leading industrial nations, and rapidly growing concern for global ecological problems and catastrophic situations in the poor South. These issues highlight the increasing relevance of the UN system, although the organization remains incapable of systematic and efficient action. What might be called Germany's "multilateral obligation" should be understood not so much as a normative prescription but as the essence of its collective international experiences since 1945. Behind Germany's current struggle to define its new role in international politics lies a comparatively solid belief, which has become ingrained in German political culture, that multilateralism is the best possible approach to foreign relations because it has already become an inescapable condition of international life.

Notes and references

1. The term "foreign policy doctrine" means the ensemble of values, norms, goals, and strategies of a state's foreign policy. Usually a doctrine changes only slightly over time unless it is severely challenged by radical developments within society or in the international system.
2. G. Doeker and H. Volger, eds., *Die Wiederentdeckung der Vereinten Nationen*, Kooperative Weltpolitik und Friedensvölkerrecht (Opladen: Westdeutscher Verlag, 1990).
3. The foreign policy of the German Democratic Republic was in this period closely linked with the foreign policy of the Soviet Union and was therefore also, albeit in a muted way, characterized by a multilateral approach.
4. This theme is elaborated upon in Wilfried von Bredow and Thomas Jäger, *Neue deutsche Außenpolitik. Nationale Interessen in internationalen Beziehungen* (Opladen: Leske and Budrich, 1993).
5. Renate Finke-Osiander, "Die UN-Politik der Bundesrepublik Deutschland," *Außenpolitik* 36 (1985), no. 3: 213.
6. Ernst-Otto Czempiel, *Macht und Kompromiß. Die Beziehungen der BRD zu den Vereinten Nationen 1956–1970* (Düsseldorf: Bertelsmann Universitätsverlag, 1971), 34.
7. It should be noted, however, that some German historians maintain a different view. Once the archives of the Soviet Union are opened to the public, this debate may be put to rest.
8. Volker Rittberger, "Die beiden deutschen Staaten in den Vereinten Nationen. Rückblick und Bilanz," in Deutsche Gesellschaft für die Vereinten Nationen, ed., *zur Diskussion gestellt* 33 (December 1990), 9.
9. Wilhelm Bruns, *Die UNO-Politik der DDR* (Stuttgart: Verlag Bonn Aktuell, 1978), 22.
10. Wilhelm Bruns, *Die Uneinigen in den Vereinten Nationen. Bundesrepublik Deutschland und DDR in der UNO* (Cologne: Verlag Wissenschaft und Politik, 1980), 147.
11. Wilfried von Bredow, *Der KSZE-Prozeß* (Darmstadt: Wissenschaftliche Buchgesellschaft, 1992).
12. The term "underdeveloped countries" is, of course, taboo because of its normative implications. A more neutral term for the countries in question was "third world," but this again reflects some preponderance of the first and second worlds. Today, most people use the geographic (geopolitical?) term "the South" and define the implicated problems as the "North–South conflict."
13. Doeker and Volger, *Wiederentdeckung.*
14. I deplore the general custom of using the terms "East–West conflict" and "Cold War" without any differentiation. In my understanding, the East–West conflict is (was until 1990) a deep structural conflict of the international system with its roots in the nineteenth century and emerging in contemporary history with the Russian revolution in 1917. The Cold War, on the other hand, is a specific period of the East–West conflict, from 1946/47 to 1962.
15. Hans-Dietrich Genscher, "Rede vor der 44. UN-Generalversammlung," *Vereinte Nationen* 38 (1990), no. 1: 24.
16. Wolfgang Kötter and Dieter Weigert, "Nach dem Ende der Teilung. Plädoyer für die Be-

rücksichtigung der DDR-Erfahrung in der gesamtdeutschen UN-Politik," *Vereinte Nationen* 38 (1990), no. 4: 131–134.

17. Wilhelm Bruns, "Die Geeinten in den Vereinten Nationen," Kurzpapier der Abt. Außen-politik- und DDR-Forschung der Friedrich-Ebert-Stiftung, 43 (August 1990), 5.

18. Rüdiger Wolfrum, ed., *Die Reform der Vereinten Nationen. Möglichkeiten und Grenzen* (Berlin: Duncker & Humblot, 1989).

19. The growing importance of Germany means the decreasing importance of other actors, and it is only natural that some of these other actors are less than enthusiastic about this development.

20. Some noteworthy recent publications from the academic community are, *inter alia*, Bruno Simma, ed., *Charta der Vereinten Nationen. Kommentar* (Munich: C. H. Beck, 1991); Rüdiger Wolfrum, ed., *Handbuch der Vereinten Nationen* (Munich: C. H. Beck, 1991).

21. Christian Tomuschat, "Die Zukunft der Vereinten Nationen," *Europa-Archiv* 47 (1992), no. 2: 43; author's translation.

22. *Frankfurter Allgemeine Zeitung*, "Kohl lehnt Sitz im Sicherheitsraat ohne Vetorecht ab," 10 July 1993.

23. The SPD proposal can be found in: Deutscher Bundestag, *Drucksache* 12/1719, 4 December 1991.

24 It is worth noting that the SPD did not address the question of whether or not Germany should strive for permanent membership of the Security Council. The SPD prefers an inter-nationalist image, contrary to its Bavarian sister-party in the Council, which has a more nationalist tradition of foreign policy.

25. Hans-Dietrich Genscher, Address to the 46th General Assembly of the UNO, *Vereinte Nationen* 39 (1991), no. 5: 168–171.

26. See, for example, Albert Statz, "Nachkriegszeit: Vereinte Nationen zwischen ziviler und militärischer Weltordnung," *Vereinte Nationen* 39 (1991), no. 4: 129–134.

27. In fact, the Bundeswehr participated marginally in this war by deploying some troops near the Turkish–Iraqi border. This was possible because Turkey is a member of NATO.

28 *Frankfurter Allgemeine Zeitung*, 24 June 1992.

29. Richard Rosecrance, *The Rise of the Trading State, Commerce and Conquest in the Modern World* (New York: Basic Books, 1986).

2

India in the United Nations and the United Nations in India

Hari Mohan Mathur

The United Nations was created on 24 October 1945, with 51 nations signing its Charter in San Francisco. India was one of the 51 original signatories of the 1945 UN Charter, and is also an original member of the World Bank, IMF, GATT, ILO, FAO, WHO, and UNESCO. India's deep commitment to multilateralism is further evidenced by the fact that Indian initiatives led to the founding of UNCTAD and the IDA:[1]

In the case of the International Bank, the original proposal was to call it the International Bank for Reconstruction. It was at India's insistence that the words "and development" were added to its title.[2]

The constructive role played by India in contributing to the founding of many other new organizations of the UN family is well recognized.

The United Nations was formed to create a new world order; to save succeeding generations from the scourge of war; to maintain international peace and security; to develop friendly and cooperative relations among nations; to address international problems of an economic, social, cultural, or humanitarian character; and to promote fundamental human rights and freedoms. The particular role of the United Nations in international peace and security closely paralleled India's foreign affairs philosophy and policy objectives, such that India was naturally attracted to the ideals upon which the United Nations was founded.

Because India was not independent when the United Nations was founded, its UN membership (and earlier membership in the League of Nations, of which India was also a founding member) in effect meant additional representation for British interests. Things changed, however, with the installation of an interim government in October 1946 as a preparatory step to independence in August 1947.

Since independence, India has participated actively in the work of the UN system, contributing significantly to the strengthening of the multilateral process. Although a developing country and in great need of aid from UN agencies, India has also contributed directly and indirectly to the multilateral process, via voluntary contributions to the UN system (by far the largest from the developing world, US$15.7 million in 1984), but also via its own aid programme for third world countries.[3] Every year India also plays host to tens of thousands of overseas students in its educational and research institutions, many of whom are supported by funding from the UN system. Additionally, India provides the United Nations with a large number of technical assistance personnel.

India's commitment to the United Nations and the vision of a new world that it represents is rooted in Indian traditions. A phrase from ancient scriptures, "Vasudhaiya Kutumbkam" (meaning "the world is one family"), expresses vividly the basic belief of Indian civilization in the oneness of humanity. Indeed, the Indian commitment to the United Nations has been rightly held as total. As a senior UN official in India recently remarked: "it has been a historical commitment, but above all, an emotional commitment which has resulted in it playing a leading role in all the deliberations and activities of the organization."[4] In assessing India's role in the United Nations, one researcher concluded that India is "one of the nations that has enabled the General Assembly to render judgement on controversial issues."[5] In recognition of its contributions to the work of the organization, India was recently elected to membership of the Security Council for a sixth term (1991–1992).

Major concerns of India's UN policy

Emerging as an independent nation in 1947, India saw itself as a new and significant international force. By virtue of its size, population, geographical position, history, and tradition, it felt entitled to a role in shaping the international order to suit its images and needs.[6] Spelling out the basic components of India's global concern, an early policy document stated:

In the sphere of foreign affairs, India will follow an independent policy, keeping away from power blocks of groups aligned one against the other. India will uphold the principle of freedom for dependent peoples and will oppose racial discrimination wherever it may occur. She will work with other peace-loving nations for international cooperation and good-will without exploitation of one nation by another. Towards the United Nations, India's attitude is that of whole-hearted cooperation and unreserved adherence in both letter and spirit to the charter governing it. To that end, India will participate fully in its various activities and endeavour to play that role in its Councils to which her geographical position, population and contribution towards peaceful progress entitle her.[7]

Over the years India has pursued several major issues in the United Nations. In the early years, the major concerns of India's UN policy were decolonization, anti-racism, non-alignment, and the settlement of international disputes by peaceful means.[8] Other matters pertaining to development, aid, trade, and environment have since emerged as additional areas of Indian policy involvement. Six of the most important issues pursued by India in the United Nations are discussed below.

Anti-colonialism

India's first major undertaking was to lead the fight against colonialism in whatever form, attempting to arouse the conscience of humanity against it. "As people of this country gained their independence only recently[,] they know what it is to be without freedom."[9] India argued that colonialism contradicted the concept of equality among nations, and, in a sense, Indian independence itself strengthened the movement for decolonization. India's anti-colonialism stance also has roots in Indian history and tradition: the history of India records how emperor Ashoka, having defeated the king of Kalinga in a war, later renounced the world, so great was his remorse at the thought of one people having to live in subjugation to the other. Another important factor shaping India's attitude towards colonialism was Nehru's world-view (discussed below).

The decolonization issue was first raised by India in the United Nations in 1946. India has since fought many battles on the issue, and the imprint of its intervention can be clearly seen in many cases. For example, India opposed suppression of the Algerian liberation movement by the French, instead suggesting a negotiated settlement. The General Assembly resolutions on the Algerian question contained the gist of these suggestions. In the United Nations, as Chester Bowles observed, "India has stood as a militant and uncompromising foe of colonialism and a champion of the rights of subject people to independence."[10] Indian political parties have also been unanimous and vocal in their opposition to colonialism, and the communists, with their opposition to "imperialist hegemony," have been particularly critical.

Racial equality

India has long been a frontline state in the fight against racism, beginning with Gandhiji's "satyagraha" in South Africa early this century. Opposition to apartheid as practised in South Africa and elsewhere stems from the Indian belief that discrimination on the basis of race is not only a violation of the United Nations Charter but also an affront to human dignity, and that racism constitutes a grave threat to world peace. Public opinion in India, cutting across all political lines, tends to support the struggle against racism. Consequently, India was in the forefront of the struggle against apartheid:

India was the first country in the world to raise the issue of racial discrimination in South Africa before the world body, the United Nations Organisation, in 1946. Since then India has been the first country to take innumerable initiatives to support Africa's liberation. It was also the first country to break off diplomatic relations with South Africa and introduce a general ban on trade and other contacts like sea and air travel with South Africa. India has consistently maintained the cultural and sports boycott of South Africa, according to United Nations directions.[11]

It has been India's belief that only the pressure of international opinion and action by international organizations could produce change in South African policies and practices. Accordingly, India exhorted the United Nations to exercise its influence and power to the benefit of the victims of racism, and the issues of race conflict and apartheid have been on the organization's permanent agenda.

While racism in South Africa came to be widely condemned, other forms of racism have lately emerged in other parts of the world but have failed to evoke a similar response. Developments in Fiji in 1987 bore distinct racial overtones. In his statement at the forty-third session of the United Nations General Assembly on 4 October 1988, the Minister for External Affairs gave expression to India's apprehensions as follows:

The international community should be opposed to racial discrimination no matter where it is practised. My delegation had referred last year to the unfortunate developments in Fiji that had distinct racial overtones. We had hoped that the groundswell of international public opinion would help restore the spirit of trust, harmony and concord which had prevailed in Fiji since its independence. As a member of the United Nations and as a member of its Committee on Decolonisation, India had been in the forefront to fight for Fiji's independence. It is a matter of great regret to us that the situation in Fiji has considerably deteriorated during the past one year. There are clear indications that an attempt is being made to institutionalise racial discrimination in Fiji.[12]

India has continued to press for more international action in support of the struggle for racial equality.

Disarmament and peaceful dispute settlement

India has spearheaded several disarmament initiatives, and from the beginning the Indian position has been that general and complete disarmament is the *sine qua non* for the prevention of wars and the preservation of peace. In opposing the arms race, Indian initiatives have not been restricted to simple proclamations of general principles; rather, proposals have dealt with concrete steps. As Djordjic put it, India has "sought and found various formulas for temporary and realistic solutions which are a step towards an agreement on general disarmament."[13]

India's first major initiative was its mid-1950s' proposal to ban nuclear testing, and it has long called for major powers to destroy their nuclear arsenals and for all states to restrict their use of atomic energy to peaceful purposes. The January 1985 summit held in India to launch the Six Nation, Five Continent Appeal for Nuclear Disarmament reflected this abhorrence of nuclear weapons. Indeed, the initiative by the six nations – Argentina, Greece, India, Mexico, Sweden, and Tanzania – helped refocus world attention on the imperative for nuclear disarmament. Another noteworthy initiative was the Action

Plan for Ushering in a Nuclear Weapon-Free and Non-Violent World, announced by the Prime Minister at the Third Special Session of the General Assembly devoted to disarmament in June 1988. This package of measures would have structurally linked the whole range of issues that are on the world disarmament agenda. The heart of the Action Plan is the elimination, in three stages, of all nuclear weapons by the year 2010. This represents a continuation of India's position and initiatives on nuclear disarmament.

India has also consistently maintained that international disputes must be resolved by peaceful means. India played a significant mediation role during the Korean War. When negotiations to end the conflict became bogged down over the issue of prisoners of war, India, with the support of other newly independent nations, was able to work out a compromise formula. The resulting resolution was adopted during the 1952 session of the UN General Assembly and ultimately became the basis for the settlement of the Korean conflict. Other Indian mediation initiatives have also borne fruit, and India's contribution to UN peace-keeping activities has been significant.[14] India has, for example, also contributed to UN peace-keeping forces in Korea, the Congo, Cyprus, Cambodia, and Somalia.

Third world solidarity

The admission of newly independent states to the United Nations during the 1950s and 1960s gave the organization an appearance very different from what it was at the time of its birth. India assumed a leading role in bringing third world nations together as a distinct (and majority) group in the United Nations: "when India speaks in the United Nations, it tends to speak as a representative of Asia or of the Afro-Asian world of under-developed and 'long-sinned' against millions."[15] Sharing a common background of colonial exploitation and confronting similar challenges of nation-building, they responded to the invitation to speak with their own voice on the world stage. As a distinct entity in the United Nations, membership in the third world group, which stood at 12 in 1946, grew to 56 by 1963 (out of 110 members).

By this time, the world had been split into two mutually hostile blocs. In encouraging solidarity among third world nations, India did not intend to form a third bloc. Rather, the Indian effort intended simply to keep the third world away from the superpower rivalry and the Cold War, in order to better concentrate their energies on the overriding task of development. India also felt that the United Nations could become an instrument through which the interests of the underprivileged masses of the third world could be advanced.

Development aid and economic issues

India has long maintained that the prevalence of poverty in the greater part of the world is a potential threat to world peace, and, moreover, that poverty in the midst of plenty is highly iniquitous. There is, therefore, a need for a greater flow of development resources from rich to poor countries.

India's difficult economic circumstances and its determination to progress within the framework of an open democratic society have consistently dramatized the need for development in the Third World. During the 1950s and early 1960s growing understanding of India's situation undoubtedly made more resources available for dealing with world poverty than might otherwise have been the case.[16]

The present situation in this regard is, in India's view, rather dismal. Aid flows are inadequate, terms of trade have deteriorated, and the debt burden of the third world is becoming unbearably heavy. The North–South dialogue remains virtually paralysed, and the issue of poverty is becoming simply a matter of rhetoric. The Indian official view is that "while there have been encouraging developments recently in the political sphere, the outlook in the area of international economic cooperation remains bleak."[17]

In general, India has been critical of the international aid establishment, particularly its style of functioning. One recurring criticism is that the global economic system is dominated by the rich countries and operated without regard to the needs, wishes, or counsel of the third world, even in matters that directly affect it. India has pleaded for an increase in assistance from international institutions and a greater role for third world countries within them. On economic issues, India has supported resolutions of the G77 group of developing countries calling for an International Decade of Development, a New International Economic Order (NIEO), and a Charter of Economic Rights and Duties. One of the early advocates of a wider role for developing countries on issues involving aid, trade, investment, and reform of international monetary institutions, India has made significant contributions to reform in this issue area. For example, "India has been instrumental in the founding of the International Development Association (IDA) and the United Nations Conference on Trade and Development (UNCTAD)."[18]

The environment

Environmental issues have surged to the forefront in recent years. In the Indian view, they are closely related to the problems of development, and therefore India attaches great importance to the issue of sustainable development, having drawn attention to the crucial link between economic development and environmental protection as early as 1972 at the First World Conference on Environment and Development, held in Stockholm. India has long been an ardent advocate of the development of crucial environment-friendly technologies, and, even more importantly, of the transfer of such technologies to third world countries so their wider use might help control the degradation of the environment.

The Indian perspective emphasizes the global dimension to these issues (global warming, for example), arguing that, to a large extent, the present environmental predicament is a direct result of the kind of development that has been practised in the developed parts of the world. India maintains that it is therefore important that they share a major responsibility in plans and action to reverse environmental degradation. At the recent Rio Earth Summit, India was an active participant, arguing that only a comprehensive multilateral approach can solve this problem.

Factors that shape India's policy orientation

Domestic factors loom large as determinants of India's policy orientation towards the UN system. As early as 1947, the Indian Prime Minister stated in the Constituent Assembly that:

Whatever policy we may lay down, the art of conducting the foreign affairs of a country lies in finding out what is most advantageous to the country. We may talk about international goodwill and mean what we say. We may talk about peace and freedom and earnestly mean what we say. But, in the ultimate analysis, a government functions for the good of the country it governs and no government dare do anything which in the short or long run is manifestly to the disadvantage of the country.[19]

It is always possible to discern the influence of domestic affairs in foreign policy. One study succinctly describes in general terms how domestic concerns got translated into foreign policy concerns in the Indian case:

Nehru and his colleagues found it easy to transform the non-violence of Gandhi into a foreign policy on "nonalignment" and "peaceful co-existence". Similarly, India's commitment to domestic democracy was easily projected at the international level into the position that the correct relationship among sovereign bodies is one country, one vote (not a vote weighted by economic or military power or by population numbers). Other important Indian objectives with economic content – egalitarianism, socialism, growth and modernization – are viewed as goals to be met among, as well as within nations. Finally, at the procedural level, the importance which the Indian Government attaches to its active management of domestic society is paralleled internationally by strong support in principle, and usually in practice, of supranational organizations such as the United Nations and the World Bank.[20]

Given that India is the world's largest democracy, and that its citizens enjoy guarantees of fundamental freedoms comparable with those of the developed Western democracies, Indian decision-making and policy positions must take diverse factors into account. In specific terms, one can isolate five important domestic influences on Indian policy towards the UN system: the political process, public opinion and pressure groups, personality factors, the bureaucracy, and ideological considerations.

The political process

The Indian parliamentary system means that general responsibility for major decisions concerning the United Nations rests with the cabinet, headed by the Prime Minister, although decisions and their implementation must be rendered acceptable by parliament. Decisions thus reflect the ideology and the policies of the ruling party, but as one analyst noted:

although foreign policy decisions are made in a parliamentary system of government by the party in power, the foreign policy outlook of the opposition parties inevitably affects such decision making not only because of the role the latter usually play in parliament, but also because of their influence over the political system as a whole.[21]

This influence is manifest during the annual discussion of the Minister for External Affairs' foreign policy statement, in debates during "question hour" or the budget session, in the Estimates Committee and the Consultative Committee on Foreign Affairs (whose membership reflects the relative strength of the parties in parliament), or through the inclusion of opposition Members of Parliament in visiting official Indian delegations to the United Nations.

Yet, while political parties make use of the many avenues available for airing their views on the best means to further the national interest in international forums, on the whole foreign affairs appear to be less important to them than domestic issues. This lack of interest in foreign policy was noted by sponsors of the First *Hindustan Times* Annual Debate on "India's Foreign Policy in the Changing World" held in 1992 in New Delhi. It noted that there was in particular "not enough thinking on foreign policy issues among political parties which were expected to provide political guidance to the bureaucracy in conducting the country's foreign policy."[22] This focus on domestic issues was also found in election campaigns: one study found that the space devoted to issues of foreign policy in the election manifestos of various parties has consistently been rather small (about 10 per cent).[23] On major policy issues, such as the role of the United Nations, the Commonwealth, the Non-Aligned Movement (NAM), and other multilateral institutions, there also seems to be a broad consensus among various political parties.[24]

As a consequence, changes in government have not produced fundamental shifts in approaches to foreign policy. In 1977, when the Congress Party was defeated after three decades in power, no major changes in foreign policy were made by the Janata government. "A shift from Mrs. Gandhi's Government to the Janata regime and back affected only the nuances of Indian foreign policy," although the Janata government was more self-conscious in the pursuit of genuine non-alignment and the maintenance of an even-handed relationship with the superpowers.[25] Similarly, there were few noteworthy changes when the coalition led by Janata Dal came to power briefly in 1989.

One exception to this has been the new policy of opening up the Indian economy to foreign investors, which has led to differences among political parties. The communists, in particular, are critical of government policy, which they consider to be a sell-out to the World Bank and the IMF, although this opposition has made no difference to the government's commitment to move forward with its economic reform programme.

Public opinion and pressure groups

The press in India, in articulating public opinion, devotes considerable attention to foreign policy issues. Traditionally it has been generally supportive of government policy. However, public opinion, when expressed in other more direct ways (such as demonstrations and marches), can exert considerable influence on the government's approach to specific foreign policy issues. Indeed, the pressure of public opinion has forced the government to change its course on several occasions. One dramatic instance (by Nehru's own admission) was India's unwillingness to sponsor the resolution to admit China to the United Nations at the fifteenth session of the General Assembly in deference to strong public sentiment against China, after having staunchly supported it during previous sessions.[26]

Traditionally, pressure groups have not been a significant influence on Indian policy-making: "groups such as the trade unions, student movements, professional societies, commercial, financial and industrial organizations and caste lobbies have a most limited scope of direct influence."[27] Lately, however, particularly since the changes in economic policies, organized groups have become vocal, even confrontational. Trade unions, especially those dominated by communists, have denounced these policies as an intervention by the World Bank and the IMF in India's domestic affairs. Privatization, the exit policy, and other reforms are seen as a threat to the high level of job security they have long been accustomed to as public sector employees. Their protests have made clear that the obstacles to reform will not be overcome either easily or quickly.[28]

The personality factor

Nehru's tenure as Prime Minister (1947–1964), during which time he also acted as his own foreign minister, also marked the years of India's high profile in the United Nations. Nehru enjoyed complete freedom of action in the foreign policy sphere, making all foreign policy decisions by himself, with cabinet and parliament for the most part being content to follow his lead.[29] The overwhelming dominance of Nehru's personality in the initial elaboration of India's external policies prompted one researcher to conclude that "foreign policy is always more autocratically determined than domestic policy."[30] The problems of world peace, anti-colonialism, and anti-racism formed the core of Nehru's policy preoccupations. Often enunciated in lofty moralistic terms, his policy reflected a mixture of idealism and considerations of the national interest. The central theme was non-alignment, a policy that emphasized independent action on the basis of the merits and circumstances of each particular case. Nehru's charisma and leadership role in the nationalist movement contributed to India's emergence as an independent nation, and his broad international outlook soon earned him a status that enabled him to shape the Indian orientation towards multilateralism.

Nehru's impact can also be found in India's anti-colonial and non-aligned policies. On the colonial issue, he saw in Indian independence the beginnings of a historic process by which the world would be freed of colonial domination, and regarded India's freedom struggle as part of a global movement on the part of all colonial nations to assert their right to self-determination.[31] Indeed, he simply extended the moral and political lessons from the success of India's struggle to the wider international arena. With respect to non-alignment, he clearly visualized that joining either bloc would surrender independence of action in addition to escalating tension. He was therefore interested in promoting an "area of peace" distinct from the realm of bloc politics, which was an "area of war." He realized that although India was a weak nation it could provide leadership in a divided world. He hoped that, by promoting the area of peace, he could serve as a "go-between" for the two camps, and so reduce tension between them.[32]

The foreign policy foundations laid by Nehru have remained intact, although subsequent domestic and international developments have resulted in shifts in nuance and style. India's domestic, economic, and security problems remained the central concerns of Nehru's immediate successor, Lal Bahadur Shastri. Indira Gandhi also maintained continuity with the past, although the visionary globalism of Nehru gave way to a more down-to-earth and explicit concern for India's national interest. Under Morarji Desai, the Janata government emphasized the moral necessity of global disarmament.[33] Rajiv Gandhi's policy emphasized the close parallel of India's vital interests to the global issues of peace, development, and the environment.[34] Under the leadership of the current Prime Minister, P. V.

Narasimha Rao, a more substantial break with the past has occurred in the domain of economic policy, as the Indian economy has ended its isolation and been opened up to market forces. In short, India's leaders have varied policy emphases in response to changing domestic and global conditions, but within a particular inherited framework.

The role of the bureaucracy

Although the personality factor is important, "Indian influence at the UN, however, does not depend entirely on the presence or absence of particular personalities."[35] Providing an element of continuity, the civil service makes important contributions to policy-making on issues pertaining to the United Nations. "In the Indian conditions, policy is largely formulated by the senior civil servants and the political leadership functions as monitors of this policy formulation."[36] Although the Indian Civil Service (with its legacy of highly competent impartial professionalism) is limited to "advising" the government, the advice offered naturally differs from adviser to adviser. A study of India's response to the Gulf crisis, for example, noted that "there were signs of divisions within the foreign policy establishment with prominent analysts and commentators questioning the wisdom of applying old standards and paradigms to the first major crisis of the post-Cold War era."[37]

The conduct of foreign policy is primarily the responsibility of the Ministry of External Affairs (MEA), within which there is a special UN division to deal with matters specifically related to the United Nations. In addition to the permanent mission at UN headquarters in New York, India is represented at all major UN agencies such as the FAO or UNESCO. But, in addition to the MEA, several other ministries are also responsible for policy-making related to UN matters (especially with respect to the specialized agencies). For example, the Ministry of Finance is responsible for dealing with the World Bank, the IMF, the UNDP, and other agencies concerned with international economic activities, while the Ministry of Education is responsible for dealing with UNESCO, and the Ministry of Health deals with WHO matters.

One major problem this creates within the bureaucracy is the lack of a coordinated approach. One Indian civil servant with long experience in planning has noted:

During the years that I was directly associated with planning, one had dealings with those who represented the World Bank and met a number of people connected with UNESCO, FAO, WHO and so on. But one found that each of these organizations was a preserve of some particular ministry here. There was no attempt on the part of the Government in India as a whole to look at the UN system as a whole.[38]

Another distinguished civil servant remarked that the representatives of the Indian government often adopted different attitudes in the GATT, UNCTAD, the World Bank, and other forums. As he put it:

the national representatives are answerable to different ministries at the National headquarters. Adequate care is not observed in coordinating their briefs. An integrated approach on the part of the national representatives would enhance their credibility and weight in international fora.[39]

Coordination is particularly difficult because various ministries suspect that the MEA will, in the course of its coordination efforts, usurp their authority and encroach on their jurisdiction. They are reluctant to part with the power and prestige that direct dealings with UN agencies give them, and are in any case confident of their ability to deal competently with matters that lie within their purview. Certainly it is true that ministries are in a better position to deal with particular activities of the United Nations because of their specialized knowledge. Nobody, however, disputes the principle that the manifold strands of UN policy would be better managed through a coordinated approach that would in turn generate better policy decisions.

Ideological and cultural/historical elements

The Indian position on the various issues it has raised in the United Nations has a particular ideological slant, coloured by the many developments that took place in the pre-independence period. As L. A. Viet pointed out, "More than most governments, India has couched its foreign policy in moral and ideological terms."[40] As other scholars have noted:

In India an intellectual and cultural Renaissance of the second half of the 19th century and the national movement of the first half of the 20th century threw up certain political ideals like anti-imperialism, anti-racialism, Asianism, cooperative internationalism, non-violence, and democracy. The intellectual leaders of the national movement were also strongly critical of the political-economic systems represented by capitalism, communism and Fascism.[41]

Inspired by these ideals, Indian leaders have seen themselves as supporters of non-violence, enemies of colonialism and apartheid, and the champions of disarmament movements everywhere.

For example, the Indian understanding of peace (an ideal India has always cherished) is derived from the ancient teachings of Buddha and Ashoka and from Gandhiji's more recent teachings. From a policy perspective, India's self-interest also requires peace, since the process of development cannot be sustained in conditions of war and strife. Although in India (as elsewhere) there has been, and unfortunately continues to be, a great deal of violence, there is still a strong belief in Indian thinking and philosophy in the desirability and necessity of replacing hatred with tolerance, violence with non-violence, and war with peace. It is this strong belief in peace, peaceful coexistence, and non-violence that India has attempted to project on the global scene. The major concern has thus been to widen the area of peace and promote the settlement of international disputes by peaceful negotiations. The five principles of peaceful coexistence (known as "Panchsheel") that India has propounded as the basis for relations among nations also have their roots in the Indian concern for peace and abhorrence of war.

This self-image has not, however, always proven to be in India's best interests. To outsiders, in particular, Indian actions have often appeared to contradict its own high principles. For example, "the forcible liberation of Goa in 1961 is perfectly justified as the final step in eliminating colonial rule in India, but it further eroded the moral credibility of India and Nehru as apostles of non-violence."[42] Similarly, the use of violence in the cases of Kashmir, the India–Pakistan relationship, and the sikhs has done some damage to India's legacy of non-violence and peaceful coexistence.

The Indian perspective and multilateral policies

As the above discussion has suggested, many factors have played a significant role in shaping the Indian orientation towards the United Nations. The two examples discussed below illustrate well the complex interaction between domestic political, historical, and social factors and the particular policy positions that India has adopted.

Security concerns, disarmament, and the Non-Proliferation Treaty

As noted above, disarmament is an issue to which India has accorded a high priority in the United Nations, based on its traditional opposition to the use of force as a means of settling international disputes. Instead, the emphasis has been on the use of moral force. As R. Tagore proclaimed:

we in India shall have to show the world what is the truth which not only makes disarmament possible but turns into strength. That moral force is a higher power than brute force will be proved by the people who are unarmed.[43]

Global disarmament efforts are also supported by the public, who understand that resources currently wasted on arms spending can be better invested in meeting the daily survival needs of the millions of poor.

However, India has not closed its "nuclear option," having consistently resisted international pressures to sign the 1968 Nuclear Non-Proliferation Treaty (NPT). Serious apprehensions were expressed by political parties of all shades on the NPT even during its drafting. India's opposition to the NPT was not based on an ambition to become a nuclear power, but because it considered the NPT to be unfair, discriminatory, and insensitive to India's security concerns. India's contention was that an international treaty for preventing the proliferation of nuclear weapons could be a powerful instrument of peace only if it was conceived within an overall and universal context of disarmament, and not as a simple exercise in imposing "unarmament" on unarmed countries.[44] India wanted a treaty that adhered to the principles of equality and mutual benefits, aiming at the prevention of both vertical and horizontal proliferation. Summing up the Indian position in parliament on 31 May 1967, the Minister for External Affairs criticized the proposed treaty as discriminatory:

The NPT was to be a step towards disarmament; we find in this treaty that it is not a step towards disarmament. The treaty merely aims at preventing a horizontal proliferation without preventing the vertical proliferation. In other words, it prevents the have-nots from acquiring nuclear power without any obligation being cast upon the haves either to freeze them, stockpile or to reduce them.[45]

The Indian position on the question did not change with the change in government in 1977. At that time, an Indian diplomat emphatically noted that the greatest weakness of the non-proliferation effort was its almost total preoccupation with countries that did not possess nuclear weapons and did not want them. He termed it a policy of trying to "disarm the unarmed."[46]

Along with this, India genuinely believes that atomic energy should be restricted to peaceful uses. Although India exploded a nuclear device in 1974 and thus acquired a nuclear weapons capability, it has made no effort to construct a nuclear arsenal, even in the face of nuclear threats to its security. On the other hand, India badly needs energy to carry out its development programme and, in the absence of other adequate energy sources, such as oil, atomic power appears to be a dependable option for meeting the growing demand for energy. Official policy has all along emphatically maintained that India's nuclear programme exists only to support its development needs.

There is, however, a small "pro-bomb" lobby that from time to time raises the demand that India make the bomb in order to strengthen its security position.[47] Its advocates argue that, if the nuclear weapons option is not exercised, it is an option that is of no use. And, with a nuclear mystique of prestige, power, and technological achievement, they do succeed in mobilizing support in favour of the bomb: even those who oppose the bomb are not yet prepared to forswear the nuclear option.

Thus the NPT debate is a recurring issue with many complex overtones in India. At the 1992 UN Security Council summit called to consider ways of strengthening the United Nations, the Prime Minister reiterated India's position, emphasizing that any attempt to control nuclear weapons must not stop at non-proliferation but strive to develop a global consensus and include on its agenda the elimination of all nuclear weapons.[48] At a 1992 meeting of the parliamentary consultative committee (attached to the Ministry of External Affairs), members urged the government to safeguard the country's status as a "nuclear weapon technology state."[49] Representing different political parties, the committee gave expression to national sentiment when it demanded that, as long as other countries continue to possess nuclear weapons, India should retain its nuclear option.

These security concerns seem not to have diminished in the postwar era. As one political commentator has highlighted, the disintegration of the Soviet Union has enhanced the dangers and the likelihood of the spread of nuclear weapons.[50] Not only might orphaned ex-Soviet nuclear weapons be under inadequate control, but unemployed, even destitute, nuclear scientists of the former USSR are willing to sell their services. Both could fall into very undesirable hands. Secondly, the proposal for a nuclear weapon free zone in South Asia, open to strong objections even at the best of times, has now become meaningless, as a consequence of the woefully belated confirmation that Pakistan does possess all the essential components for construct- ing a nuclear bomb, and is able to assemble one at a moment's notice. It is rank hypocrisy to talk of regional non-proliferation when the re- gion possesses nuclear weapons already. As a result, each time the issue is raised, the general feeling in India against signing the NPT is strengthened.

Issues of aid and development

Rapid economic development has always been a matter of the highest priority for India. In this context, aid has been valued as an important tool for accelerating the pace of development. The government, pressed for financial resources to finance its development pro- grammes, has welcomed aid on a selective basis, particularly when it comes from multilateral sources. India has been a major recipient of development aid from the UN system in general, and from the World Bank in particular. Against the resources required for development at the desired pace, however, the availability of aid has remained in- sufficient. Further, the overall flow of aid, particularly from multilat- eral sources, has declined in recent years. As one UN official in India observed:

we now have a situation where UN agencies, which have been widely praised for their efforts in the past, are now languishing for lack of funds. The case in point is UNHCR [UN High Commissioner for Refugees], twice awarded the Nobel Peace prize and today literally on the verge of bank- ruptcy. UNFPA [UN Population Fund] has also inexplicably been denied funds already pledged to it; IFAD [International Fund for Agricultural De- velopment], universally acclaimed for its orientation to small farmers, is at risk due to a funding quarrel between its major donor groups over what is, by today's standards, relatively a very minor sum; and we all know that the tremendous potential of IDA [International Development Association], proved beyond any possible shade of doubt by its successes, particularly in India, is being frustrated by lack of funds.[51]

The decline of aid is occurring at a time when needs have vastly in- creased. India's lament is that the international community is not giv- ing priority attention to the issue of alleviating global poverty. In

United Nations forums, therefore, India has been asking for an increased flow of resources for development purposes, most particularly for the poverty alleviation programme.

In addition, the whole philosophy of aid has also come under strident attack from several quarters. In recipient countries, coupled to the long-standing criticism that aid thwarts the process of self-reliant development, aid has been criticized because it benefits already affluent groups, not those most in need. Another criticism is that aid agencies operating in the field (including multilateral ones) tend to pry into details unconnected with their work and carry this information back to where it can later be used against India's national interests. These critics see nothing but sinister designs in the operations of the donor agencies.

One study of the World Bank's aid programme to India echoed some of these criticisms.[52] Discussing the effects of the Green Revolution on village society, the study found that financial resources made available by the World Bank to Indian agricultural credit institutions were accessible solely to wealthy and influential farmers.[53] Although agricultural productivity increased substantially, the new package also increased the power of the rich farmers, who were able to monopolize the opportunities that came with the increased flow of money through the credit institutions. "The real impact of the Bank's support to agricultural development in India has been felt in accentuating class inequalities and solidifying the power of the rich peasant."[54] Further, by concentrating development efforts in areas with assured irrigation facilities, the Green Revolution has also led to regional inequalities, with the level of development in dry regions remaining practically unchanged.

The study also found that the Bank has a philosophical bias that it propagates by establishing close links with politicians, bureaucrats, and members of the Planning Commission. A large number of policy makers and bureaucrats have also been employed by the Bank for short or long periods. The Bank has thus succeeded in creating a lobby for itself in influential quarters, an influence that has even percolated down to local state levels through agricultural investments. "It is no mean achievement on the part of the Bank that the state governments compete with one another for Bank projects."[55] Overall, this study argues that the World Bank is concerned with promoting not the interests of the third world, but those of the capitalist Western countries:

The industrialised countries have created a complex network of institutions to influence the philosophy and priorities of development of the Third World and the World Bank and the International Monetary Fund perform the task of structural integration of developing countries with the world capitalist system. The World Bank and the IMF, the twins of Bretton Woods Conference, are involved in a global effort to promote the interests of the industrialized countries.[56]

The study concludes that, "while the Bank proclaims its neutrality in politics, in its actual functioning it is deeply involved in politics of foreign aid."[57]

Thus the whole approach of aid agencies to development issues in countries such as India is now an open concern. The focus of the present international economic order seems to be on preserving the pre-eminence of developed countries, and international cooperation on issues of concern to developing countries, such as financial flows, trade, debt, and commodity prices, seems to have taken a back seat.

One issue that is currently generating much heated public debate is the "Dunkel draft" for an updated GATT agreement. One editorial comment on the draft code has condemned it as blatantly unfair:

the resulting take-it-or-leave-it draft code ... is loaded in favour of nations with economic might. It does little to accommodate the majority of the nations which, largely because of centuries old colonial stranglehold over their economies, are late starters in industrialisation. Indeed, the draft makes sure that the nations comprising the Third World remain dependent for technology – along with foreign exchange required to get machines and knowledge – on a handful of developed market economies. Though the Dunkel document ostensibly sifts and binds the positions of 108 nations, it really underpins the position of a few dominant ones.[58]

Expressing deep disappointment, the editorial concludes: "expecting fairness from an arrangement designed to strengthen unequal relations will be as futile as squaring a circle."[59]

At a symposium organized by the National Working Group of Patent Laws in Bombay in January 1992, speakers representing a cross-section of eminent economists, jurists, politicians, consumer organizations, industrialists, trade unionists, and farmers dwelt on the dangers posed by the Uruguay round of GATT negotiations.[60] The symposium resolved that the Prime Minister should convene an all-party meeting to discuss the implications of the Dunkel draft text and develop a national consensus on this issue of fundamental national importance.

Reacting strongly to the Dunkel draft, three former senior officials have also issued a statement in New Delhi saying that the draft militated against India's interests and that its acceptance would interfere with India's ability to make macroeconomic decisions and frustrate the pursuit of its development priorities.[61] The statement emphasized that the proposed agreement on Trade Related Aspects of Intellectual Property Rights goes against major elements of the Indian Patent Act 1970 and would require major changes in the Act, which should not be acceptable to the parliament. On trade-related investment measures the text would oblige India to treat foreign investors on a par with nationals; this would, according to the statement, impede India's self-reliant development programmes and accentuate its balance-of-payments problem. Further, the statement added that the revised GATT would oblige India to provide expanding and unrestricted space in its economy for the services, products, and capital of foreign multinational companies, and to remove limits on the inflow of equity capital and other imports for the foreign service industry. This would undermine the country's agricultural development programme by allowing, for example, foreign patent protection of seeds, plants, and biogenetic substances. Finally, by far the most pernicious aspect of the Dunkel document, according to the statement, was the establishment of a Multinational Trade Organization, which would, in collaboration with the IMF and the World Bank, be able to review India's trade policies and impose retaliatory measures and sanctions.

Having sensed the widespread public hostility towards the Dunkel draft, the government established an expert group to study its full implications. Various interest groups were promised full consultation before the final Indian position on the Dunkel text was formulated.

The impact of the UN system on India

These differing perceptions of the national interest have influenced the overall Indian perspective on the UN system, and the final orientation that emerges has been the sum of these diverse viewpoints. The last example also illustrates the way in which all aspects of Indian life are touched by the work of one or another multilateral agency. The United Nations has vastly expanded its activities parallel to virtually every activity of the government, with at least one UN agency being involved in the areas of education, health and nutrition, water and sanitation, irrigation, environment, agriculture, industry, drugs, and others. Several agencies can be involved in the same area, with inevitable duplication of effort, although each carves out a slightly different focus. With their array of development programmes and projects, therefore, UN agencies have a considerable presence in India. As studies of the effectiveness of aid have shown, the Indian record contains many lessons for other developing countries.[62]

Several ongoing programmes and projects in the field have emerged from the policy-oriented research, or global experience, of UN agencies.[63] The Training and Visit System of Agriculture Extension developed by the World Bank and the Oral Rehydration Therapy popularized by UNICEF are two such programmes. India, along with other countries, has benefited from these programmes and the ideas on which they are based. Themes selected for major global UN conferences also have an effect on government thinking, even to the extent of influencing the organization of government agencies. For example, in one Asian country new departments that came into being or were reorganized following various major UN conferences include: Department of Environment (after the Conference on Environment and Development in Stockholm); Department of Science and Technology (after the Conference on Science and Technology for Development in Vienna); and the Department of Non-conventional Sources of Energy (after the Conference on New and Renewable Sources of Energy at Nairobi).[64]

Working with the UN system has also increased the innovative capacity of state bureaucracies. One Indian expert, who had been closely associated with the World Bank, recounts that:

The picture one gets from Indian technocrats involved in preparing and implementing World Bank projects from the Indian side is also favourable. They consider the World Bank a welcome external source of pressure in favour of technical and administrative excellence. They say that it is possible to smuggle into World Bank projects good ideas which they have failed to get past the conservative Indian top levels.[65]

He also regards the intellectual contributions of the World Bank to be significant. Working collaboratively with Indians, the Bank has helped India to fashion its developmental strategies in many sectors:

The World Bank has placed a well-deserved emphasis on adequate project preparation, and India has acquired valuable expertise in this field which it is able to transfer to other LDCs. The stress of the World Bank on the long-term view, on the rational and professional handling of issues has strengthened the hands of those in administration, who value these concepts, reducing the impact of ad-hocism, narrowness, shoddiness and excessive politicization of decision-making. Its contribution has been most valuable.[66]

The proliferation of UN agencies, particularly those that became involved in development projects, soon meant that even in remote interior villages people now know about the United Nations, the World Bank, the IMF, and other UN agencies. Most of the activities of UN agencies operating at the ground level, such as the UNICEF and WHO-aided vaccination programme, bring concrete benefits. Much the same applies to the activities of UNESCO, the ILO, the FAO, and other agencies. Finally, as a consequence of UN interest and support, a number of non-governmental organizations (NGOs) concerned with such issues as environment, participatory approaches, and women's development have emerged. However, the impact of development can also be very disruptive. World Bank-aided projects such as dam construction have resulted in the displacement and resettlement of thousands of people. The Narmada Dam project, which has achieved worldwide notoriety, is a case in point, with some environmentalists calling it India's greatest environmental disaster.[67] The victims of development, then, perceive the development agencies of the United Nations in a totally different light. Nevertheless, despite this ambivalent reaction, on the whole the image that the United Nations has created is a favourable one.[68]

On the level of economic policy, multilateral organizations have also had a great impact on the Indian economy, in part as a consequence of the Gulf War. Thousands of Indian workers in the affected Gulf countries were repatriated, although no jobs were waiting for them in India. More seriously, their remittances, which constituted an important source of foreign exchange earnings, virtually stopped, engulfing the country in a balance-of-payments crisis. As a stopgap measure, the government was forced to take a loan from the IMF. Attached to this loan, however, were conditions requiring India to follow a wide-ranging programme of macro-economic stabilization and structural adjustment (including deregulation and privatization), with the goal of creating a more open, market-oriented, economy. By integrating the Indian economy into the mainstream of the international economy, these measures were expected to impart a new dynamism to it.

The policies advocated by the World Bank and the IMF are radical departures for India, where the economy has been largely centrally planned and closely regulated. The reforms would introduce major changes to trade, financial, and industrial policies, and the Indian currency has already been devalued. Resistance to these policies has come from all quarters of the political spectrum. Major opposition came from the communists and, leading their attack, the Chief Minister of West Bengal (a state under the control of the Communist Party of India [Marxist]) urged the Chief Ministers of all states to unite formally in opposing the reforms. In their opinion, the policies of the governing Congress(I) Party were imposed upon it by the World Bank and the IMF, and therefore constituted an infringement of India's economic sovereignty.[69]

The Janata Dal has been no less critical. Its leader in the Rajya Sabha (the upper house of the Indian parliament) has accused the IMF of being a political instrument of the G7 countries for trying to impose "non-economic" conditionalities on the Indian government, including insisting on defence budget cuts, human rights protection, and the signing of the NPT.[70] This would, he argued, lead to the loss of India's economic and political sovereignty, and hasten the process of India's "Latin Americanization." The Bharatiya Janata Party, which has its base of support in the north and which is the main opposition party, is also opposed to many aspects of the new economic policy. It is most critical of opening up the economy to multinational corporations since this would pose a threat to Indian industry, particularly to small-scale operations. The party has even staged demonstrations against the rising prices of foodstuffs, which it alleges are a direct consequence of the new policies.

Finally, even within the Congress(I) Party, there have been murmurs of protest. Many members are still not reconciled to what they regard as a clean break from the socialistic policies established by Nehru. The official party line, however, maintains that the new reforms do not represent a fundamental break with the past.[71] Rather, it argues that changing global economic conditions no longer afford India the luxury of pursuing isolationist economic policies and that, had Nehru been alive today, he would have done much the same thing.

The social obstacles to the acceptance of IMF and World Bank conditionalities are no less formidable than the political ones.[72] An emergent and assertive middle class is not likely to be willing to sacrifice an iota of its privileges, through inflation, curbs on salary increases, or similar developments. Similarly, wealthy farmers protest against the withdrawal of subsidies on fertilizer, electricity, and other agricultural inputs, and public sector workers can only fear privatization. These three groups are among the most articulate groups in Indian society, and know well how to protect their interests. They are unlikely to support the reform programme, as in their eyes it is the upper stratum of society that is responsible for the balance-of-payments problem, while the reforms will burden only the middle and voiceless impoverished classes. On the other hand, the change has been widely welcomed by business and industrial concerns. Freed from governmental controls, they can now plan expansion of their enterprises, firming up collaborative arrangements with international companies to acquire new technologies and obtain access to foreign capital.

Supporters of the reform programme maintain that the government had no option but to borrow from the IMF and the World Bank.[73] They see no need to be defensive and do not consider the reforms to be a surrender to the World Bank and the IMF, rather viewing them as "perhaps the last chance the nation has to move from the periphery of the global economy to its centre."[74] They argue that the Bank's and the IMF's recommendations only echo those of numerous government-appointed committees: "much of what the IMF is prescribing today has been on the country's agenda for a long time, but has fallen prey to reckless populism and driven the economy to its present state of crisis."[75] Prime Minister Rao has made it clear that the government is totally committed to the reform programme:

The economic liberalisation process is a logical continuation of the strategy of development adopted by India. It is a process necessary today for a new and higher level of growth. The decisions we took were well considered. It is not a one-time operation, not an inspiration coming overnight. It is an evolution. Thus, there can be no going back on it. The people of India have accepted these changes as necessary, and the results of the parliamentary elections in November last year remove all doubts on that score.[76]

He added: "The economic reform programme will continue and, in fact, will accelerate."[77]

In this debate, it is important to note that criticism of the new economic policies has focused on the government for its agreement to the conditions attached to the loan, rather than on the *idea* of a loan itself. Criticism of the World Bank and the IMF has been voiced, but has been largely secondary. This is consistent with the long-standing view that "on the whole, India retains its faith and interest in the Organisation. At no time has criticism of the working of the United Nations reached the level of fundamental opposition to it."[78] Thus the Indian commitment to the importance of multilateralism and the UN system has withstood the vicissitudes of time, and will likely remain unshaken in the future.

The non-aligned vision of India's role

The nations that united to form the United Nations themselves remained united only briefly. Within months of the signing of the Charter, the world was split into two hostile blocs, each determined to see the world ordered according to its ideological convictions and convinced that the other embodied the antitheses of peace, justice, freedom, and prosperity. India and the other newly independent nations were thus presented with a stark choice: both blocs actively sought their membership, and the price was involvement in the Cold War. It was, however, in the interests of the new states to remain independent of either bloc and retain the freedom to pursue independent policies so as to be better able to concentrate on the more urgent tasks of nation-building and economic development. By keeping out, they could also be in a better position to judge issues on their merits and, as independent observers, to play some part in promoting peace and security, freedom and cooperation.

India led the way in rejecting the ideological distinctions of the Cold War, as involvement with either bloc would have meant participation in a conflict at a time when India badly needed peace to further its development programmes for the benefit of the poor. India's decision to abstain from membership in either power bloc was, in short, made on the basis of its national interests.[79] This policy of non-alignment proved to be extremely attractive to other newly independent countries, which, following India's lead, began using non-alignment as the philosophical basis for their own external relations policies. Thus the Indian position served as the catalyst for the genesis of the Non-Aligned Movement (NAM).[80]

Non-alignment quickly became a potent force helping unite the third world in a common perspective on world affairs:

India and other nonaligned countries did something to show both the communist and non-communist powers that the world was not just made of colours that were black and white, that there were browns all over the place. The newly emerging countries need not be committed to one or the other block or ideology. There was room for a third ideology, the area of peace, to act as a bridge between the warring blocks.[81]

Apart from India, outstanding leaders of several other countries also contributed importantly to the development of the NAM, notably the leaders of Yugoslavia, Egypt, Indonesia, and Ghana. Nevertheless, India has always held a somewhat special position in the movement for a number of reasons: its history, geography, size, population, level of economic development, scientific and technological development, and leadership. India's leadership role was partially a consequence of favourable circumstances:

India's global leadership was made possible by peace and stability at home and the breakup of the great-power coalition of World War II that had dominated the international scene ... Nehru refused to become involved in this emerging conflict among power blocs. This policy – which became known as nonalignment – enabled India by the early 1950s to emerge as a significant mediator between power blocs and contributed substantially to India's ability to achieve the global recognition it sought.[82]

By the 1960s the non-aligned nations were a majority of UN members. Their growing impact effected "a profound transformation which quite transcends anything that framers of the Charter foresaw."[83] However, right from the beginning of the NAM, its leaders made it clear that they had no intention to form a third bloc, but rather that the NAM would be a collective force that would act through the United Nations.

In essence, the purposes and objectives of the NAM and the United Nations are similar, if not identical, and the functioning of each is intended to reinforce the other. Pointing out commonalities in the goals of the United Nations and the NAM, former Secretary-General of the United Nations Javier Pérez de Cuéllar noted:

The founding of the Nonaligned Movement more than two decades ago constituted one of the great acts of creative statesmanship in our time. Among the principal aims which inspired it was that of making the United Nations a more effective instrument for the maintenance of international peace and security and the promotion of justice in international relations ... the founders of the movement rightly felt that nothing would better accommodate the world's diversity and assure both the stability and the dynamism of a peaceful world order than a return to the basis of international relations laid down in the Charter of the United Nations.[84]

The NAM's staunch commitment to the United Nations is reflected in its conferences and summits, which have consistently upheld the primacy of the United Nations as the appropriate forum for addressing major world issues. Summit chairmen personally report the main recommendations of summits to the following session of the UN General Assembly.

But the vast changes that have occurred since the movement was launched have bred scepticism regarding the relevance of the NAM, especially in the 1980s. As a movement, concluded one observer, the NAM "has failed to make any meaningful impact," adding that "there is not a single issue on which the nonaligned countries have as a group taken initiatives in the United Nations" and "the so-called nonaligned states have as a group failed to cut much ice or to acquire a position in the political processes of the United Nations."[85] One reason for the decline in the role of the movement has been the perception among some member countries that the NAM is not strictly non-partisan, a perception that has affected its unity. As a Singapore diplomat observed:

NAM does not have the unity which the movement enjoyed during its early formative years. The main reason for this is the infiltration in the movement by a group of countries such as Cuba, Vietnam, Democratic Yemen, Ethiopia, Syria, Mozambique, Angola and others which are not nonaligned but which are allies of the Soviet Union. The presence within the movement of this group of countries is a constant source of friction and disunity, because they try, at every turn, to hitch the nonaligned train to the Soviet locomotive.[86]

Many believe that the passing of the bipolar world will mean a further reduction in the capability of the movement to accomplish anything significant. Some note that "to the nonaligned countries, bipolarity was not an unmixed curse as they were able to play one off against the other, had much room for manoeuvre and their support was avidly sought by both contenders."[87] For some, the role of the NAM has already been greatly diminished, since the NAM played no significant role in the 1991 Gulf War, and since Yugoslavia, in its hour of crisis, turned to the European Communities for assistance, rather than to the NAM, which it helped form.

In India, opinions contrary to traditional thinking on the NAM are now more openly expressed, particularly since the Gulf War. At the peak of the Gulf crisis itself, domestic constraints prevented India from playing an active role in attempts to resolve it peacefully: "India's failure to play a more substantial role in the Gulf Crisis can be attributed to its leadership preoccupations with the domestic situation, which made it difficult to focus on the crisis to assess its long-term impact and minimise its deleterious effects."[88] In pursuing political ends, Indian political parties missed an opportunity to promote a realistic view of the potential role in the crisis that India might have played as a leader of the NAM.[89]

Supporters of the NAM naturally claim some credit for bringing about the vast changes in world politics. Speaking before the UN General Assembly in October 1988, the Minister for External Affairs claimed that the transformation in the international climate was the culmination of the efforts that the NAM began:

the nonaligned movement, since its inception, has worked tirelessly for such an international climate. By taking principled positions on major issues of our times and by refusing to get entangled in the confrontation by competing military alliances, the nonaligned nations helped in containing conflict and thus contributed to the peace process ... Therefore, we, the nonaligned, could claim part of the credit for the improved state of affairs.[90]

However, the changing nature of global affairs and the domestic impulses to adjust to them have led to thinking in some quarters that perhaps the old formulas are indeed no longer relevant. Some observers perceive the shift to pragmatic policies as positive, "stemming from a realisation that championing anti-colonialism, nonalignment and Third World solidarity are not enough in today's world, guided as it is essentially by economic principles."[91] Changing world conditions, on this view, have forced India to modify its traditional positions in two crucial areas (South Africa and Israel), drawing it closer to the position of the United States, a country earlier viewed with much uneasiness because of its relationship with Pakistan. As a former diplomat is reported to have observed:

If you were writing a communique on the nonaligned movement earlier, you knew how topics like South Africa, Israel, colonialism had to be dealt with. Today, there are no such easy guidelines for reference.[92]

In the face of these challenges, some adjustments have been made to India's overall policy orientation, but India remains firm in its policy of promoting non-alignment. The policy continues to be based on broad consensus, and criticism (which has lately come from the communists) is predominantly against making adjustments to the NAM policy and moving India closer to the orientations of the Western powers on their own terms.[93] India's position is ultimately that the international scene has changed the context, but not the relevance, of the movement:

The essence of nonalignment is independence of judgement in foreign affairs as a mark of the sovereignty of nations, big or small, developed or developing, militarily strong or otherwise. Since that is the touchstone of nonalignment, the dissolution of one of the two power blocks makes no difference to its rationale for continuity.[94]

The official argument is that the NAM is now even more relevant, as the problems of poverty, inequality, and discriminatory practices in political, economic, and social spheres continue.

This is consistent with the view of other members of the NAM, which are overwhelmingly in favour of further strengthening the movement. An indication of its continuing relevance and vitality lies in the fact that some nations, including Guatemala and Honduras in Central America and Germany and the Netherlands, have recently decided to join the movement as observers and guests (and China has also expressed interest). In order to retain its relevance, however, the new objectives of the NAM must include the continuing pursuit of global disarmament, progress towards a just and equitable economic order, as well as the emerging priorities such as democratizing the United Nations, human rights, and the environment. The NAM will remain important to India, and there is a strong opinion that India should continue to play the leadership role in the movement:

The NAM platform magnifies India's voice on the world stage and the movement is a symbol to the Third World solidarity. India should provide the impetus for its revival and reinvigoration.[95]

Other multilateral affiliations

Two other multilateral institutions of which India is a member are the Commonwealth and the South Asian Association for Regional Co-operation (SAARC). Geographically, the Commonwealth has global scope, and SAARC, as its name suggests, is a regional organization. Initially, there were misgivings in some quarters about joining the Commonwealth. Having just won independence, any sort of connection with the United Kingdom was regarded as a lingering colonial mentality. Prime Minister Nehru argued, however, that joining the Commonwealth would not abridge India's status as a sovereign nation, but rather, that there were certain advantages in being a member. The decision finally to join the Commonwealth in 1949 was a major policy decision. Until the 1950s, the Commonwealth figured prominently in India's foreign policy, but it subsequently declined in importance. India continues to be an important member, but the Commonwealth is no longer the foreign policy cornerstone it was in the late 1940s and early 1950s.[96]

India's pre-eminent position in South Asia has long proven to be a hindrance to developing cooperation among states in the region. The smaller states have tended to view India as a protective, but often domineering, big brother, and have consequently looked beyond the region for counterweights. India also had its own apprehensions:

New Delhi in the past tended to view regionalism as a design to enable the other states to "gang up" against India. India has thus sought to deal with each country bilaterally and to discourage communication and contact among the nations on its periphery. For their part, the smaller countries have been reluctant to enter into regional cooperation for fear that India would inevitably dominate any association and that it would, in effect, institutionalise Indian hegemony.[97]

However, encouraged by the success of other regional groups (particularly the Association of South East Asian Nations), India took steps that resulted in the establishment of the seven-member SAARC in 1986.[98] As a nascent organization, the scope of its operation has been restricted to the establishment of economic cooperation among the seven member states, and all bilateral and contentious issues as well as questions of trade, finance, investment, and industry are excluded from its purview. Although its area of operation is restricted, and it has moved only slowly and cautiously, SAARC will eventually have to expand to include trade, since trade lies at the heart of all regional cooperation. Likewise, SAARC may in time also expand its limited agenda and realize its potential as a forum for promoting cooperation in the domain of peace and stability.

India in the new world order

Not surprisingly, given the unprecedented changes that are currently occurring in international politics, India's future role in the "new world order" has generated much discussion among the Indian press, policy makers, scholars, laymen, and others.[99] The collapse of bipolarity demanded some adjustment to India's foreign policy, and no doubt further changes will occur. One recent example would be India's support for the US-initiated resolution in the UN General Assembly in December 1991 to rescind its earlier 1975 resolution branding Zionism as racist.[100]

A clean break with the past, however, is neither possible nor desirable. Even changes that appear to be a drastic departure from established norms and practices are in reality mere adjustments necessitated by changing international conditions, in which India's national interest remains the most important criterion for formulating foreign policy. For example, non-alignment will remain an important Indian priority, even though there are bound to be changes in the NAM agenda to reflect the emerging concerns such as democratization, the environment, or human rights.

By virtue of its size, population, history, and geopolitical position, India has always felt entitled to play a significant role in international affairs. In the years immediately after its emergence as an independent nation, India did play a leadership role in the settlement of international disputes and in assisting the United Nations in its peacekeeping missions around the world.[101] The mid-1960s, however, marked the beginning of a period of low profile and reduced activity for India in the United Nations and other international forums.[102] But even though India opted to play a less active role on political questions, its diplomacy began to acquire a distinct economic dimension and its advocacy on issues concerning aid, trade, and development resulted in the creation of UNCTAD, IDA, and other multilateral innovations.[103]

During this time, the view that a high-profile involvement in global affairs was not in India's best interests and that it was better to give priority to domestic problems gained some currency, promoted mainly by intellectuals and academics. However, the view in favour of a low-profile international role does not enjoy much popular support today. The argument for giving primacy to the domestic economic situation is easily countered by pointing to what was achieved during the 1950s under almost identical constraints. What is needed instead, it is argued, is a forward-looking vision of the third world interest: "In the emerging multipolar world, India alone can be the leading spokesman in the Security Council for the nonaligned and the Third World."[104] Thus, on this view, India should invest greater energy in participating in the United Nations, and re-establish an activist role in world affairs.

It is in this context that India has from time to time raised the question of more equitable representation on the Security Council. The issue was raised as far back as 1979, but has since remained dormant. In the Indian view, the United Nations does not reflect the changes that have occurred in the world since its establishment half a century ago. In 1945, the criteria for permanent membership of the Security Council were based primarily on the military capabilities of the victorious allies, reflecting the international situation as it existed at the end of the Second World War. This cannot remain the criterion of permanent membership in today's totally changed context.[105] The Indian Prime Minister recently observed that, given the threefold expansion of UN membership, the size of the Security Council cannot remain constant any longer.[106] He argued that wider representation on the Security Council is necessary if it is to retain its moral sanction and political effectiveness, pointing out that the United Nations Charter gained its legitimacy from the collective will of the international community. India, he noted, also had a personal stake in the expansion of the Security Council.

India would also like to see effective changes to the current international economic order, which remains preoccupied with preserving the positions of the privileged nations and continues to neglect the interests of the poor. Protectionism continues to constrain the plans of developing countries to increase their exports. Decisions on global economic issues continue to be taken in forums where the developing countries are unable to provide any input.[107] Finally, the emergence of regional economic groupings poses new obstacles for the developing world. At the 1992 Security Council summit, India's Prime Minister called attention to these vital issues.[108] Emphasizing India's concern that development remain at the heart of any effort to restructure the international order, he pointed out that lasting peace and security required there be comparable levels of human well-being across the globe. It would be impossible to conceive of the United Nations functioning usefully or harmoniously while humankind continues to be plagued with ever-increasing economic disparities.

Notes and references

1. S. A. Kochanek, "India's Changing Role in the United Nations," *Pacific Affairs* 52 (1990), no. 1: 53.
2. M. S. Adiseshiah, "The Economic Agencies of the United Nations and Their Functioning," in M. S. Adiseshiah, ed., *Forty Years of Development: UN Agencies and India* (New Delhi: Lancer International, 1987), 14.
3. M. J. Priestley, "The UN and Economic and Social Development," in U. S. Bajpai, ed.,

Forty Years of the United Nations (New Delhi: Lancer International, 1987), 52.

4. Ibid., 51.
5. C. G. Boland, "India and the United Nations: India's Role in the General Assembly 1946–1957", Ph.D. dissertation, Clemont Graduate School, 1961 (Microfilm, Nehru Memorial Museum and Library, New Delhi), 3–4.
6. Kochanek, "India's Changing Role," 48.
7. *The Indian Annual Register: July–December 1946* (Calcutta: NN Mitra, 1947). Quoted here from: Indian Council of World Affairs, *India and the United Nations* (New York: Manhattan Publishing, 1957), 28. This was a report of a study group set up by the Indian Council of World Affairs (ICWA), prepared for the Carnegie Endowment for International Peace National Studies on International Organizations.
8. T. R. Reddy, *India's Policy in the United Nations* (Rutherford: Farleigh Dickenson, 1968). See also S. Rana, "The Changing Indian Diplomacy at the United Nations," *International Organization* 24 (1970), no. 1.
9. ICWA, *India and the United Nations*, 74.
10. C. Bowles, *The New Dimensions of Peace* (New York: Harper & Row, 1955), 189.
11. B. Vats, "United Nations Vital Role in Ending Apartheid," *World Affairs* 2 (June 1991), 75.
12. Statement by P. V. Narasimha Rao, Minister for External Affairs, at the 43rd session of the UN General Assembly, *Foreign Affairs Record* (October 1988), 335.
13. J. Djordjic, "India in the Contemporary World," *Review of International Affairs* 6 (February 1956), 4.
14. R. Singh, "India's Initiatives in the United Nations," *Indian and Foreign Review* 15 (November 1977), 13–14.
15. R. Berkes and M. Bedi, *The Diplomacy of India: Indian Foreign Policy in the United Nations* (Stanford, Calif.: Stanford University Press, 1958).
16. L. A. Viet, *India's Second Revolution: The Dimensions of Development* (New York: McGraw Hill, 1975), 175.
17. Statement by P. V. Narasimha Rao, *Foreign Affairs Record*, 336.
18. Viet, *India's Second Revolution*, 118.
19. J. Nehru, *India's Foreign Policy* (Delhi: Publications Division, Government of India, 1961), 28.
20. Viet, *India's Second Revolution*, 105.
21. J. Bandyopadhyaya, *The Making of India's Foreign Policy: Determinants, Institutions, Processes and Personalities*, 2nd ed. (New Delhi: Allied Publishers, 1980).
22. *The Hindustan Times* (New Delhi), 28 April 1992, 1.
23. S. S. Patagundi, *Political Parties, Party System and Foreign Policy of India* (New Delhi: Deep & Deep Publications, 1987).
24. R. L. Hargrave Jr., *India under Pressure: Prospects for Political Stability* (Boulder, Colo.: Westview Press, 1984), 138.
25. A. Vanaik, *The Painful Transition: Bourgeois Democracy in India* (London and New York: Verso, 1990), 242.
26. *The Statesman* (New Delhi), 11 October 1960, 1. Quoted here from A. Appadorai and M. S. Rajan, *India's Foreign Policy and Relations* (New Delhi: South Asian Publishers, 1985), 529.
27. R. Park, "India's Foreign Policy," in R. G. Macridis, ed., *Foreign Policy and Relations*, 5th ed. (New Delhi: Prentice-Hall of India, 1979), 324–325.
28. "Freeing India's Economy," *The Economist*, 23 May 1992, 21–23.
29. Appadorai and Rajan, *India's Foreign Policy*, 528.
30. Vanaik, *Painful Transition*, 263.
31. G. Ramachandran, *Nehru and World Peace* (New Delhi: Radiant Publishers, 1990), passim.
32. Ibid., 16.

33. M. Desai, "Disarmament: The Choice between Life and Death," *Indian and Foreign Review* 15 (7 June 1978), 11–14.
34. M. K. Rasgotra, *Rajiv Gandhi's Worldview* (New Delhi: Vikas Publishing, 1991).
35. Kochanek, "India's Changing Role," 66.
36. K. Subrahmaniyam, "Foreign Policy Planning in India," *Foreign Affairs Reports* 24 (January 1975), no. 1: 3.
37. J. Mohan Malik, "India's Response to the Gulf Crisis: Implications for India's Foreign Policy," *Asian Survey* 31 (September 1991), no. 9: 850.
38. T. Singh, "The Economic and Social Council in India," in Adiseshiah, *Forty Years of Development.*
39. K. B. Lall, "An Engine for Peaceful Change," in Bajpai, *Forty Years of the United Nations,* 65.
40. Viet, *India's Second Revolution,* 105.
41. J. Bandyopadhyaya, "Making of Foreign Policy," in S. P. Verma and K. P. Misra, eds., *Foreign Policy in South Asia* (New Delhi: Orient Longmans, 1969), 34–35. See also B. Prasad, *The Origins of Indian Foreign Policy: The Indian National Congress and World Affairs 1885–1947* (Calcutta: Bookland Private, 1962). See also N. K. Jha, "Cultural and Philosophical Roots of India's Foreign Policy," *International Studies* 26 (January–March 1989), no. 1: 45–67.
42. Vanaik, *Painful Transition,* 236.
43. Ravindra Nath Tagore, quoted in Ramachandran, *Nehru,* 43.
44. *Foreign Affairs Record* 12 (8 February 1966), no. 2: 16.
45. *India, Lok Sabha Debates* 38:7 (31 May 1967), Colo. 2164–5, New Delhi (MC Chagla).
46. N. A. Palkhivala, "Disarming the Unarmed," *Newsweek,* 19 June 1978, 45.
47. Hargrave, *India under Pressure,* 159–160. See also A. Kapur, *India's Nuclear Option: Atomic Diplomacy and Decision Making* (New York: Praeger, 1974).
48. *The Economic Times* (New Delhi), 1 February 1992, 1, 4.
49. Ibid., 14 February 1992, 4.
50. I. Malhorta, "Grasping the Nuclear Nettle," *The Times of India,* 20 February 1992, 8.
51. Priestley, "The UN," 55.
52. C. P. Bhambri, *World Bank and India* (New Delhi: Vikas Publishing, 1980).
53. See also C. H. H. Rao, *Technological Change and Distribution of Gains in Indian Agriculture* (New Delhi: Macmillan, 1975); F. Frankel, *India's Green Revolution* (Princeton, N.J.: Princeton University Press, 1971).
54. Bhambri, *World Bank,* 117.
55. Ibid., 118.
56. Ibid., v.
57. Ibid., 128.
58. *Indian Express* (Bombay), 13 January 1992, 10.
59. Ibid., 10.
60. Ibid., 1.
61. *Indian Express* (New Delhi), 2 February 1992, 6.
62. M. Lipton and J. Toye, *Does Aid Work in India? A Country Study of Official Development Assistance* (London and New York: Routledge, 1990); Government of India, *India and the United Nations* (New Delhi: Ministry of External Affairs, Publicity Division, 1985).
63. For a very informative account of the new development ideas that have been produced by the various UN agencies, see P. Harrisson, *The Third World Tomorrow* (Harmondsworth: Penguin, 1980), especially chap. 2.
64. Hari Mohan Mathur, "Experts of the United Nations in Third World Development: A View from Asia," in D. Pitt and Thomas G. Weiss, eds., *The Nature of the United Nations Bureaucracies* (London: Croom Helm, 1986).
65. P. M. Mathew, "International Bank for Reconstruction and Development in India," in Adiseshiah, *Forty Years of Development,* 71.

66. Ibid., 72.
67. C. Avares and R. Billorey, *Damning the Narmada: India's Greatest Planned Environmental Disaster* (Penang, Malaysia: The Third World Network / Dehra Dun: Natraj Publishers, 1988).
68. C. Kondpoi, "Indian Opinion of the United Nations," *International Organization* 5 (November 1951), no. 4: 709–721. See also S. C. Parasher, ed., *United Nations and India* (New Delhi: Indian Council of World Affairs, 1985).
69. *Indian Express* (New Delhi), 11 January 1992.
70. Ibid.
71. Ibid., 18 January 1992.
72. A. Kumar, "Into the Valley of the IMF, March the 800 Million," *Mainstream* 24 (24 August 1991), no. 44: 13–17.
73. As one writer argued:

    The present rate of inflation is 12 per cent, but had the IMF accommodation not been available, prices would have gone up by at least 30 per cent in six months, the economy would have ground to a halt, [with] industrial production declining by 20 per cent and transport costs skyrocketing as diesel would be limited. Ultimately it would have hurt the poor. The most essential goods would have disappeared from the shelves in the expectation of better prices and the limited fuel used only to transport elitist goods that could afford to bear higher transport charges.

    The Hindustan Times (New Delhi), 8 February 1992.
74. V. Bharati, "Reformers of the Retreat: A Minority within a Minority," *The Times of India* (New Delhi), 17 January 1992, 8.
75. Ibid.
76. P. V. N. Rao, "What Can Sustain Democracy?" *World Link* 5 (March/April 1992), no. 2: 41.
77. Ibid.
78. ICWA, *India and the United Nations*, 28.
79. M. S. Rajan, *Nonalignment and Nonaligned Movement* (New Delhi: Vikas Publishing, 1990), 79.
80. S. P. Verma, *International System and the Third World: A Study of Changing Perspectives* (New Delhi: Vikas Publishing, 1988).
81. V. P. Dutt, *India and the Third World* (New Delhi: Sanchar Publishing, 1990), 26.
82. Kochanek, "India's Changing Role," 49.
83. F. O. Wilcox, "The United Nations and the Nonaligned Nations," *Headline* 155 (September/October 1962), 3.
84. J. Pérez de Cuéllar, "Foreword," in M. S. Rajan, V. S. Mani, and C. S. R. Murthy, eds., *The Nonaligned and the United Nations* (New Delhi: South Asian Publishers, 1987), vii–viii.
85. K. P. Saksena, "Nonalignment and the United Nations," *International Studies* 20 (1981), 99–101.
86. T. T. B. Koh, "The Nonaligned and the Strengthening of the United Nations," in Rajan, Mani, and Murthy, *The Nonaligned*, 290.
87. A. S. Abraham, "Gulf War and the UN," *The Times of India*, 29 January 1991.
88. Mohan Malik, "India's Response to the Gulf Crisis," 861.
89. As one observer argued: "To the political parties, the Gulf War gave an opportunity to sling mud at one another with a scant regard to the foreign policy interests of the nation. Playing to the gallery seemed to be more important than conducting diplomacy" (P. S. Ghosh, "Post Gulf Foreign Policy: Need for Rethinking," *Mainstream* 39 (1991), no. 23: 27).
90. Statement by P. V. Narasimha Rao, *Foreign Affairs Record*, 333.

91. P. Chatterji, "Foreign Policy: Old Formulae Hold Good No More," *The Economic Times* (New Delhi), 1 January 1992, 13.
92. A. K. Damodaran, quoted in Chatterji, ibid., 13.
93. S. Maitra, "Emerging Multipolarism: It Is Nothing but Imperialism with a Vengeance," *Indian Express*, 10 January 1992, 8.
94. L. Mehrotra, "India's Foreign Policy Options in a Changing World," *World Affairs* 1 (June 1992), no. 1: 19–23. See also R. Thakur, "India after Nonalignment," *Foreign Affairs* 71 (Spring 1992), no. 2: 165–182.
95. M. Rasgotra, "Foreign Policy at Last," *The Hindustan Times* (New Delhi), 1 June 1992, 11.
96. N. Iyer, *India and the Commonwealth: A Critical Appraisal* (New Delhi: ABC Publishing, 1983).
97. Hargrave, *India under Pressure*, 161.
98. M. S. Adiseshiah, "The Regional Economic Arrangements: The What and Why," in M. S. Adiseshiah, ed., *Regional Economic Arrangements* (New Delhi: Lancer International, 1989). See also D. K. Das, *SAARC: Regional Cooperation and Development* (New Delhi: Deep & Deep Publications, 1992).
99. R. Jaipal, "A New World Order," *World Affairs* 2 (June 1991), 28–31; Ross Babbage and Sandy Gordon, eds., *India's Strategic Future: Regional State or Global Power* (Delhi: Oxford University Press, 1992).
100. *Indian Express* (New Delhi), 18 January 1992.
101. "Overall ... the period from 1947 to 1962 was marked by a major leadership role for India at the United Nations and on the global scene" (Kochanek, "India's Changing Role," 51).
102. M. Brecher, *India and World Politics* (New York: Praeger, 1968), 110–111.
103. Lall, "Engine for Peaceful Change," 60.
104. M. S. Rajan, "India Must Regain the Mantle of Third World Leadership," *The Pioneer* (New Delhi), 24 June 1992, 6.
105. S. Kumar, "The Gulf War: A Challenge to World Order," in S. Kumar, ed., *Year Book of India's Foreign Policy 1990–91* (New Delhi: Tate McGraw-Hill Publishing, 1991), 14. See also K. P. Saksena, *Reforming the United Nations: The Challenge of Relevance* (New Delhi: Sage Publications, 1993).
106. *The Economic Times* (New Delhi), 1 February 1992, 1.
107. C. Raghavan, *Recolonisation: GATT, The Uruguay Round & the Third World* (Penang, Malaysia: Third World Network, 1990), 107.
108. *The Economic Times* (New Delhi), 1 February 1992, 1.

Part II
Perspectives from the European periphery

3

Sweden and the United Nations

Ulrika Mörth and Bengt Sundelius

The relationship between state and society is a central theme of contemporary scholarship in comparative politics.[1] This analytical perspective can also be found in recent studies of international relations.[2] In this volume, the approach is used as the point of departure for several studies of states' relations with the United Nations during the post-war era. The editors want to push country surveys beyond traditional, intergovernmentally oriented examinations of the positions and activities of states in the General Assembly and the Security Council, towards an understanding of how the relationship between state and society in each country has influenced its approach to multilateralism, particularly the United Nations. Similarly, the editors are interested in how such multilateral engagements may have affected the domestic balance between state and society.

It must be clarified at the outset, however, that a sharp distinction between state and society fits poorly with the traditional view of the so-called Swedish model of consensus-based, corporatist political processes. The state–society divide, noted in the scholarship of many other nations, is in Sweden transcended by the institutionalization of organized interests into the state machinery. The classic conflict between the government authority and the governed elements of society has in this way been significantly diffused. The relationship "has to be thought of in terms of the division of shares and of distributing obligations and responsibilities and not as a matter of fundamental antagonism."[3] This corporatist domestic structure of interest accommodation also forms the basis for Sweden's relations with the outside world.

This chapter begins with an overview of Sweden's century-long tradition of support for multilateralism. Six profile areas of engagement with the United Nations are discussed to help identify the characteristics of the Swedish style of involvement in global affairs. Significant changes in orientation over time are noted, such as between the two periods of membership of the Security Council. The transitions are explained in terms of altered international and domestic structures and of the roles of prominent political leaders. The enduring features of the Swedish UN profile are rooted in its legacy of building a modern welfare society through a gradual and peaceful social engineering effort by reform-minded politicians and loyal, competent civil servants. The widely recognized intimate linkage between society and state has also shaped the national orientation toward global issues and international conflict.

The chapter concludes with a brief discussion of the recent fundamental changes in the European and domestic settings for Swedish policy. The established preconditions for the traditional posture of neutrality between East and West have been removed. Prevalent domestic structures have eroded, making for greater fluidity and open conflict among organized interests. Civil society has come to be recognized as something distinct from the organized state. Business and financial pressures to join the deepening and widening European Union have become strong. These domestic and regional factors will significantly shape the future direction of Swedish foreign relations. It remains an open question if the United Nations will be regarded as the central focus of Swedish engagement in, and support for, multilateralism in the next century.

Decades of multilateral involvements

Swedish support for multilateralism and international governance can be traced back to the inter-war period and Sweden's involvement in the League of Nations. During the early years of the League, the founder of the Social Democratic Party, Hjalmar Branting, and his associate, law professor Östen Undén, established the Swedish policy of support for peace, disarmament, and arms control, with arbitration as a primary instrument of conflict resolution. The high profile of

Sweden in the multilateral peace and security arena paralleled its inter-war record of peaceful domestic transition from authoritarian, élitist rule to a stable, consensual democracy based on mass parties and organized interests.

The Corfu incident of 1923 was the first major intergovernmental conflict faced by the League. Both Branting and Undén intervened actively in the proceedings "in their defence of the new principles of international morality embodied in the Covenant."[4] During the 1926 crisis over the entry of Germany into the League Council, Sweden, in a unique gesture, gave up its seat to facilitate the smooth inclusion of Germany in the collective security order. Even more unusual, Sweden accepted without protest a 1921 League ruling regarding the future of the Swedish-speaking Åland islands in the Baltic Sea. In a referendum, the islanders had requested a return to Sweden of this territory close to Stockholm. The Finnish government, on the other hand, successfully claimed the islands as a traditional part of its territory, and the League ruled in Finland's favour. These early decisions to give primacy to enduring systemic values over more narrowly defined and immediate national interests set precedents for the future Swedish orientation in other multilateral forums, such as in the United Nations.

Sweden was not a founding member of the United Nations, but joined the organization in 1946 following a brief domestic debate over the implications of this new commitment to multilateralism in the peace and security area. The public debate concerned the inherent tension between the traditional policy of neutrality in war and the logic of collective security, as mandated by the Security Council. Without much controversy, the government accepted the obligation to collective security of UN membership, backed by a national political consensus favouring membership as a natural continuation of the inter-war tradition of fostering international security through multilateralism. In contrast, the entry into the League in 1920 had caused some domestic opposition. In the public declaration upon applying for entry into the United Nations, Foreign Minister Undén cautioned, however, that Sweden would avoid entanglements with great power groupings should they arise from outside the organization.[5]

Sweden's immediate concern with potential bloc division became an acute political reality during the early 1950s. During the Korean conflict of 1950–1953, the government confronted the dilemma between supporting UN-mandated military action and the national aspiration to stay out of great power conflicts, adopting a cautious approach in this precedent-setting case. Sweden limited its direct involvement to the provision of a field hospital, and refused to support the US-led majority of the General Assembly on all the pertinent issues. At the war's conclusion in 1953, Sweden became a member of the UN supervisory team for Korea, and the government was for some time used as a communication channel between the combatants. Sweden's image, gained during the Second World War, as the "useful neutral" playing a positive role in international politics owing to its neutral position with respect to international power blocs was reinforced by its stand in this first post-war test of collective security. Sweden's reputation as the useful neutral has been further strengthened over the years through the many other service functions performed during occasions of superpower conflict. In the domestic setting, this positive contribution to world order has, over time, become perhaps the most central notion associated with Swedish neutrality. The role of a useful and valued participant in global peace endeavours has become a central feature of Swedish national self-identity, and the inherent tension between neutrality and the obligations of UN membership to collective measures to maintain international peace and security faded into the background during the many years of bloc divisions in the Security Council.

During the Persian Gulf crisis of 1990–1991, however, this fundamental policy problem re-emerged in domestic debate with some intensity, causing the government some concern over how to respond to the Security Council call for contributions to the collective military measures taken under US leadership. As in the Korean case, a field hospital was (after some delay) put together to care for Iraqi prisoners of war. Among the public at large, but also within the top political leadership, considerable confusion surfaced over the place of neutrality in this UN-mandated military action. Even the Prime Minister, Ingvar Carlsson, fell victim to the wide reluctance to give unequivocal support to one party in this conflict. He declared that the Swedish field hospital should be viewed "as a humanitarian act and not as taking a stand in the conflict." But this spontaneous comment by the head of government was criticized in some quarters as an inadequate articulation of Sweden's membership obligation to support UN measures on behalf of collective security.

Sweden's commitment to the financial well-being of the United Nations has been substantial and even exemplary. For 1991/92 the government budget included a direct allocation to the organization of SEK 242 million (US$40 million), representing 1.21 per cent of the

UN budget. In contrast to many other governments, Sweden also contributes substantially to the voluntary components of the UN activities, such as the peace-keeping missions. After the United States, Sweden has been the largest financial contributor to the United Nations Development Programme. During the 1970s, Sweden funded about 20 per cent of the UNICEF budget. UN refugee programmes, such as the UNHCR or the UNRWA, have received consistently high levels of funding, and several other specialized agencies and programmes of the United Nations are heavily dependent on Swedish financial and technical support. Sweden has also contributed to the operations and expertise of the organization by making available competent personnel, many of whom have come to occupy high positions within the UN community.

In these resource-related respects, the Swedish UN profile resembles that of the other Scandinavian countries, particularly Norway. The Nordic link has also been important with regard to the formulation of policy positions and joint representation in the various governing bodies of the UN community.[6] In many respects, one can find a shared Nordic perspective on global issues such as development, the environment, and human rights, or in often similar approaches to the role of the United Nations in multilateral governance of global problems. Considering the many shared domestic features of Nordic societies, these parallel international orientations are not surprising. This is a useful illustration of the importance of the underlying national cultural, social, and political factors for a state's overall orientation toward global multilateralism. The so-called national capacity for international cooperation may be more directly related to deep-seated domestic structures and traditions than to more readily observed external dependencies or partnerships.

During Sweden's first period of Security Council membership (1957–1958), the government, with Foreign Minister Undén at the helm, maintained a low profile on the politically charged issues on the UN agenda.[7] One reason for this caution could have been consideration for the position of the Swedish Secretary-General, Dag Hammarskjöld. He had been recruited in 1953 as a dedicated civil servant known for effective and discrete diplomacy. Soon after his appointment, he emerged as a leading public international figure, representing to many the conscience of the organization. One issue facing the Security Council at the time was the conflict between India and Pakistan over Kashmir. This problem had clear Cold War overtones and Sweden kept a low profile. In its view, a resolution of the dispute could be accomplished "by referring some of the legal aspects of the matter to the International Court of Justice."[8] Sweden's ambassador to the United Nations, Gunnar Jarring, also served as a mediator in this conflict, allowing Sweden to serve a useful purpose without taking sides in the inflamed controversy.

The Lebanon crisis of 1958 became the most difficult problem for the Social Democratic government during its first tenure on the Security Council. In the Cold War context, the Swedish position was confined to rather narrowly defined national security interests, with little of Sweden's later pronounced emphasis on upholding the primacy of the United Nations or long-term systemic objectives. In fact, a dispute developed within the Foreign Ministry over the positions taken in some key Security Council votes, with the head of the New York delegation, Gunnar Jarring, having argued for a position closer to that advocated by the Secretary-General, while the head of the political department in the Foreign Ministry, Sverker Åström, defended a more cautious position.[9] Östen Undén, then a very senior cabinet member, played a pivotal role as the final authority on Swedish government policy in this area.

During the next Swedish term on the Security Council, 1975–1976, both international conditions and domestic circumstances had changed dramatically from the late 1950s. Further, the composition of the Council had also expanded, making for different dynamics in the politics behind key votes and resolutions. This altered political and organizational context facilitated a more active role for Sweden in the deliberations of the Council. The Swedish role as an intermediary between the democratic and prosperous West and the South, in its quest for a New International Economic Order, became well established. On several key issues concerning international development, human rights, and disarmament, Sweden controlled the crucial ninth and deciding vote. Consequently, it was courted by both the West and the South and could use its strategic position to include some preferred language into the final texts. Often, Sweden served in a bridge-building capacity by modifying proposals by third world nations into more broadly based UN recommendations.[10]

While the character of world politics had changed between 1958 and 1975, the domestic setting was also very different in the "media decade" of the 1970s. The positions taken by Sweden in the Security Council in 1975–1976 cannot be understood in isolation from the wider context of domestic concern for, and active interest in, global issues. Olof Palme, since 1969 the charismatic but controversial leader of the Social Democratic Party, also affected Sweden's position in the Security Council, his extensive travels and personal involvement in foreign affairs helping shape at home and abroad its image as an active and globally committed small state. This heightened role for Sweden in international affairs did not, however, provide any direct domestic political payoff. In fact, during this tenure on the Security Council, the Social Democratic Party was (in 1976) voted out of government for the first time since 1936.

The Social Democratic tradition of promoting international solidarity, which emerged during the early years of the League, re-emerged as a core concern of Swedish foreign policy during the 1970s. Sweden's earlier image of the useful neutral was supplemented by the even grander notion of the "active neutral." In addition, the defining features of this new, resource-demanding foreign policy dimension were set more in North–South terms than along the traditional East–West axis. While this phase clearly represented something new in Swedish post-war foreign policy, it also built on the legacy of international leadership founded by Hjalmar Branting some 50 years earlier.[11] In this sense, the Swedish record in 1975–1976 on the Security Council had more in common with its service on the early League Council than with the Cold War-dominated 1957–1958 period.

In the public mind, Sweden's stance as a promoter of multilateralism and the peaceful resolution of international conflict has helped define its self-image. Sweden is thought to have a special destiny as a small but responsible, competent, and globally involved nation. The speeches of leading Swedish statesmen and senior diplomats in international service on the special character of the Swedish contribution to multilateralism have over the decades helped reinforce this image. To many in Sweden and elsewhere, Olof Palme symbolized the high profile of small Sweden at the centre of deliberations over international peace and security.

The Swedish profile in the United Nations

The Swedish record of involvement in the United Nations and its associated organizations can be discussed in terms of six spheres of activity:

- the emphasis on international law and the peaceful resolution of conflict;
- international mediation;

- participation in UN peace-keeping missions;
- solidarity across the North–South divide;
- support for human rights in Africa; and
- peace-building and disarmament initiatives.

These preferred areas of UN involvement are a manifestation of a national aspiration to project globally the domestic experience of the Swedish version of the "good society."

Without a colonial past, but with a heritage as a regional power, Sweden has yearned for international recognition and appreciation as an exemplary member of the global community. The UN community of agencies has provided one avenue for such aspirations, a global channel for diffusing Swedish ideas and values. Through its active and technically competent involvement in these global arenas, the distinctive features of the Swedish approach to social harmony, political stability, and economic prosperity have been introduced into other national settings. These distinctive features of national political life have also been a significant basis for multilateral declarations of principle and recommendations for policy. In this sense, the Swedish UN profile includes a clear normative element similar to the postures taken by other, more influential members of the organization. During the last 25 years, this aspect of its UN involvement has grown in importance. Certain national cultural preferences have been advocated in the global setting alongside the ideas emanating from other cultural or political settings, such as from the United States or the former USSR. In one sense, Sweden has through this type of normatively grounded activity behaved more like the larger member nations of the United Nations. Ironically, Sweden tends to criticize those states for imposing their culture-specific preferences on the world. It is also noteworthy that the once comparatively strong Swedish economic and technological base, which formed a justification for this advocacy position in multilateral settings, has eroded significantly in recent years.

International law and the peaceful resolution of conflict

The belief in the primacy of law over might in international affairs has been a trademark of Swedish policy both in the United Nations and in the League of Nations. During the leadership of Foreign Minister Undén (a former professor of law), Swedish foreign policy positions were generally justified by reference to legal precedent or some other judicial principle. The use of justifying arguments rooted in international law was particularly pronounced (in UN affairs and else-where) during the period between 1947 and 1965.[12] For example, a strict interpretation of Article 51 of the UN Charter was offered dur-ing the Lebanon crisis of 1958 that ran counter to the preferred American view and consequently was not adopted by a majority of the Security Council.[13] Although Sweden lost some prestige within the organization through its rather isolated position in this critical Se-curity Council vote, Undén believed a wider interpretation of this key article could have had implications as a precedent for Sweden itself. To critics, the Swedish legalistic argument was merely a pretext to hide its inability to reach a politically comfortable position in this po-tentially explosive East–West conflict.

A frequent Swedish approach to international conflicts has been to urge the parties to submit their dispute to the International Court of Justice or to arbitration, and to criticize states that do not abide by judicial decrees against them. Upholding international law and pro-moting a judicial resolution to disputes has been one of the centre-pieces of Swedish advocacy in multilateral settings. It is therefore cur-ious that the government has rarely submitted disputes in which Sweden is a party to such international legal procedure, the last in-stance being in 1921, when Sweden lost the Åland islands to Finland. The long-standing diplomatic praxis has been to safeguard the right of the Swedish government to solve disputes unilaterally or through direct negotiations with another state. It appears that the inter-national judicial system is viewed as a proper mechanism for other states, while Sweden prefers to rely on other means for protecting its national interests.

During the mid-1960s, the Swedish emphasis on the primacy of law over politics in international affairs was replaced by a more activist foreign policy orientation. The tendency in official statements to-wards ideological or morally based criticism peaked during the per-iod 1966 to 1976.[14] Support for symbolically important declarations of general objectives and norms for collective action also became a characteristic feature of Swedish behaviour in the United Nations. One illustration of this new profile was the support for the 1974 dec-laration on the New International Economic Order. Expressions of morally based demands upon other states took precedence over the traditional reliance on a more technical and legal orientation in pub-lic argumentation. To shape international opinion over the long run became a government objective on a par with more concrete contri-butions to the resolution of acute conflicts or topical global problems.

The domestic features of public advocacy, debate, and opinion formation were to be transferred onto the multilateral arena to create a parallel process of open debate among states.[15]

A comparison of Swedish behaviour during its two terms on the Security Council (1957–1958 and 1975–1976) dramatically illustrates this change in orientation. In 1957 Östen Undén was still at the helm, whereas by 1975 a new generation of diplomats and political leaders, such as Olof Palme, were creating government policy in the Council. The attentive public had by then become sensitive to global issues, in particular to the plight of the third world. "Gone was the time when Östen Undén almost single-handedly could shape the foreign policy direction and content. Something new and significant had emerged with civic actions, group-based demands, and a variety of manifestations of opinions."[16] Society and political debate had experienced a radicalization, which came to a symbolic high point in the heated Viet Nam protests. Sweden was in this respect merely part of a wider cross-national trend.

International mediation

The use of Sweden and Swedish diplomats as mediators in international disputes is a well-established tradition with its origins in the League of Nations. Judge Emil Sandström headed the UN committee responsible for the plan to divide Palestine, adopted by the General Assembly in 1947. Count Folke Bernadotte was assassinated in 1948 while mediating in the Middle East conflict. Gunnar Jarring mediated between India and Pakistan over Kashmir in 1957 and in 1967 in the Middle East. Between 1961 and 1975, Sweden undertook between two and nine UN mediating missions each annual session.[17] Olof Palme served from 1980 as a special representative of the Secretary-General in a mediation effort between Iraq and Iran. After his assassination in 1986, his mission was continued by his assistant (who later became Sweden's ambassador to the United Nations), Jan Eliasson. In 1992 Eliasson was appointed Under Secretary-General of the United Nations with responsibility for humanitarian relief efforts.

An important basis for the Swedish post-war tradition of mediation has been its status as a neutral state between the superpower blocs. During the 1950s, Sweden's aspiration to be recognized as a useful neutral became a reality as both superpowers relied on its impartiality and competence in this regard.[18] Its involvement in many UN peace-keeping missions since their inception in 1956 reflects this image of usefulness in difficult situations with Cold War overtones. Sweden has also played mediating roles within several East–West negotiating contexts (such as arms control) and in some crises in which success often depended on discretion and on the ability to grasp the complexities of the technical aspects of the dispute. Domestic critics have noted, however, that Swedish mediation efforts have served another, more political purpose in protecting from criticism a government unwilling to take sides in complex disputes, such as in the Middle East.

Although less well documented, Sweden has also served in a mediating capacity in the international economic arena during recent decades. One early effort, inspired by the hope for pan-European economic cooperation, was participation in the Geneva-based UN Economic Commission for Europe, headed from its founding in 1947 until 1957 by the acclaimed social scientist and Nobel laureate Gunnar Myrdal. As in the security arena, the combination of an independent political stature within the West and a high level of technical expertise facilitated a bridge-building function in this other major sector of multilateralism. The active profile of Sweden in the UNCTAD context as well as its role within the World Bank are also notable. Finally, the record of Sweden in the recent GATT rounds gives further evidence of its role as an independent and technically sophisticated negotiator outside the major trade blocs of the world.

Peace-keeping

United Nations peace-keeping missions have been able to draw on substantial Swedish support. More than 60,000 Swedes have served in these forces around the world, beginning with the United Nations Emergency Force (UNEF) contingent following the Suez crisis of 1956. Only Canada has a record of greater participation in such UN missions. The most comprehensive Swedish peace-keeping involvement was in the Congo crisis of 1960–1964 during which the Swedish contingent saw active combat. Swedish troops have served with the UN forces stationed on Cyprus since 1964 and well over 20,000 Swedes have served in the various Middle Eastern peace-keeping missions. The Swedish contribution to this high-profile UN activity has been highly regarded at home, helping accentuate the popular image of a peaceful nation unselfishly contributing, not without risk to the young people involved, to the resolution of major world conflicts. In a comparative perspective, however, the Swedish role in peace-keeping seems less unique than its role in many other, less widely noted UN involvements. A number of other small states, neutral as well as allied, have also participated in these missions. In particular, the other Nordic nations, Ireland, and Canada have equally distinguished records in this regard.

Solidarity across the North–South divide

During the 1970s, Sweden's independent position within the West became a platform for its aspiration to bridge the gap between the North and the South. At that time, the two groups were in sharp confrontation in several international forums over ideological and economic issues. Lacking a colonial past and already having an image of independence in the United Nations, a more active role for Sweden on behalf of the emerging third world majority in the United Nations seemed a logical step. The inequalities of the Bretton Woods-based world economic order became a target for criticism from the new states. Many joined the Non-Aligned Movement to stake their position outside of the two superpower blocs. Sweden frequently articulated support in the United Nations for reform proposals and acquired observer status at meetings of the Non-Aligned Movement. Contacts were not limited to these periodic conferences but also included cooperation and coalition-building in other UN activities.

In the disarmament field, the government did not hesitate to support resolutions directed against the prevailing practices and strategic doctrine of NATO. One observer has noted that "Sweden has, in its critical or even moralistic international posture, sometimes come so close to the style of the non-aligned that some analysts have labelled its policy neutralist."[19] The notion of a bridge-builder between the main antagonists in global politics was, during the so-called superpower *détente*, stretched beyond the traditional East–West axis to include a focus on the plight of the third world.

At this time, the so-called Palme doctrine was in vogue in Sweden. This thesis linked Sweden's foreign policy goals to the shared perspective and concerns of other small states in a dangerous world dominated by hegemonic superpowers. As a leading small state, Sweden would assist other small states in their search for independence, security, prosperity, and dignity in an unequally structured political and economic world order. The right to secure borders and the recognition of sovereignty became an important matter of principle shared by small states, a concern that helped manifest solidarity between nations with diverse cultural traditions. According to the Palme doctrine, the superpowers shared responsibility for the poor state of global affairs. At a Social Democratic Party conference in 1974, Prime Minister Palme argued that "one superpower is organized as a harsh capitalist society – social problems are major – its ideals have been corrupted by the Vietnam War – the other superpower represents – an excessive form of socialism."[20] This type of reasoning became a primary source of inspiration behind Sweden's official posture in UN affairs. The policy emphasis was more on long-term international opinion formation than on rationalistically based resolutions of technical disputes.

Much of domestic political debate over foreign affairs during the 1970s did not concern Swedish foreign policy *per se*. Rather, each party was expected to have a clear position on major global issues, such as regional conflicts, superpower interventions, development issues, or the South African situation. Vocal protest groups on the left of the political spectrum set the agenda of public debate on foreign affairs, while most established party leaders tended to follow their lead. One concern of the Social Democratic leadership (including Olof Palme) was to neutralize left-wing radicalism and keep the party united. "As Prime Minister and party leader, Palme was concerned that the cabinet and the labour movement be able to lead on the Vietnam issue and this controversy not be shaped by other forces."[21] Critics of Sweden's verbally activist line argued that Sweden had moved from its traditional position as an impartial mediator to a more controversial and exposed role as the international critic.[22] It is noteworthy, however, that the emergence of this new role did not occur at the expense of the more traditional mediating position, with both profiles having been prominent over the last 25 years. During the 1976–1982 period of non-socialist government, Sweden retained this distinctive style as a vocal international critic. South Africa, Israel, the Soviet Union, and the superpowers generally have remained consistent targets of Swedish criticism.[23]

As noted above, the high public profile of Swedish foreign policy, activist to the point of annoying leading Western governments, has emerged in large measure from domestic politics. The massive concern over the Viet Nam War was, as in many other societies, a manifestation of deeper societal forces. Viet Nam was more than a national foreign policy issue, and became a symbol of the youthful protest against the established and seemingly arrogant authorities of

113

the Swedish "middle way."[24] Olof Palme, more than any other politician of that era, grasped the importance of capturing this national
mood and steering it into the fold of the labour movement. It was
thought that any potential diplomatic risks of such a maverick course
would be well compensated for in the domestic setting.

During this period, Sweden's second membership of the Security
Council became the focal point of support for the demands of the
third world nations in the United Nations. The most critical issue
was South Africa, where Sweden had a long record of opposing
apartheid and of giving both verbal and financial support to the African National Congress and other opposition groups in southern
Africa. In the deliberations of the Security Council, in contrast to
most other Western states, Sweden supported sanctions against the
South African regime. It also favoured participation by the Palestine
Liberation Organization in Security Council meetings concerning
Middle Eastern questions. International irritation with the maverick
Swedish position on these and other high-profile issues has been
well documented.[25] In particular, US representatives found the
Swedes overbearing, and found it incomprehensible that a like-
minded, democratic, capitalist nation could choose to align itself on
global issues with proposals emanating from the USSR and its associates in the third world.[26]

On the other hand, the leading Western states could at times use
Sweden as a go-between in attempts to modify the most unrealistic
or offensive proposals of third world states. Sweden served in a useful go-between capacity in UN affairs because of its maverick status
in the West and its good relations with the South. In several instances, it was able to help pull together the different initial positions
of the major blocs into some mutually acceptable compromise.[27] In
this respect, the activist role of Sweden in the United Nations during
the 1970s was a continuation of the search for consensus-based formulas for international peace and security in the immediate post-war
period, the only difference being that the lines of conflict had shifted
from an East–West to a West–South axis. While still considered independent and annoying, Swedes were at the same time seen as useful
bridge-builders helping to advance the UN process.

Human rights in Africa

The South African problem has traditionally been a high-profile area
for Swedish UN policy, the South African government having been

the most frequently criticized international actor during the post-war era. The rejection of apartheid has been consistently pursued by both Social Democratic and non-socialist governments, and significant financial contributions have been made to the organizations leading the struggles for freedom in that region. In one significant controversy during its second tenure on the Security Council, the Swedish vote determined the outcome of a resolution condemning South African intervention in the Angolan civil war. According to the Swedish Foreign Minister, "If we had abstained and the proposal had failed, South Africa would have collected the greatest prestige gain ever received in the world organization."[28] Similarly, the government took a firm stand against the South African presence in Namibia. In its view, the situation in Namibia constituted "a threat to international peace and security."[29] The General Assembly, with Swedish support, made several attempts over the years to secure a Security Council resolution mandating sanctions against South Africa, all of which failed in the face of Western resistance.

In 1987, the Swedish government acted unilaterally to impose economic sanctions, including a trade embargo, against South Africa. This step was a significant deviation from the long-standing Swedish policy not to participate in economic sanctions unless they were mandated by the Security Council. For example, the Swedish refusal formally to join the US-led technology embargo of the USSR during the 1980s was justified in terms of this principle. Naturally, critics of the 1987 decision to impose an embargo on South Africa noted the symbolic significance of this step, arguing it would have grave consequences in the area of multilateral technology export control. Still, the government chose to undermine the justification for its restrictive position on sanctions, arguing that the flagrant and persistent violation of human rights in South Africa demanded an exception to established doctrine. In addition, any potential Security Council action on this question was blocked by a minority veto, while the majority favoured sanctions.

Without question, the Social Democratic cabinet was in 1987 under heavy domestic pressure to take a firm, visible stand on the South Africa issue, which had been on the national foreign affairs agenda since the early 1960s. Its image both around the world and at home was at stake in this matter of international solidarity. Vocal opposition to apartheid in Sweden was not only found on the left of the political spectrum. With a legacy of African missionary work and broad popular support for third world development efforts, it is not

115

surprising that liberal intellectuals and Christian groups were in the forefront of pressuring the government to act unilaterally. Business interests, on the other hand, emphasized the costs to the domestic economy and the futility of taking such action unilaterally. In 1992, the new conservative government came under pressure from industry to remove the trade embargo in view of the political reforms by the South African government, although no immediate action was taken.

Peace-building and disarmament

Disarmament issues have been an area of active Swedish involvement throughout this century. During the inter-war period, Sweden served in a leadership role during the long disarmament negotiations in Geneva. In 1925, parliament even drastically curtailed Sweden's defences as a gesture of good faith. Since 1945, the primary focus for Swedish multilateral disarmament initiatives has been on the reduction and control of nuclear weapons.[30] As a result of its neutral and independent security posture, Sweden had by the 1960s acquired considerable technical expertise in the field of nuclear weapons. It could offer sophisticated solutions to the technical problems faced by the negotiators in ways that were generally acceptable, such as suggesting the use of seismic monitoring of the testing activities of both superpowers as a compliance control mechanism.[31]

In 1962 Sweden was elected to the Eighteen Nation Committee on Disarmament, and has taken this assignment seriously over the years.[32] Two senior Swedish diplomats, Rolf Björnstedt (1971–1979) and Jan Mårtensson (1979–1986), have headed the UN Department (now Office) of Disarmament Affairs. Sweden initially took a leadership role in this Geneva-based forum in searching for a formula for agreement on a Comprehensive Test Ban Treaty. Sweden was also one of the first signatories to the Nuclear Non-Proliferation Treaty. This step was significant because Sweden was, by that time, on the technical threshold of acquiring nuclear weapons. Subsequently, in the periodic review sessions of these treaties, the Swedish delegation has offered proposals to strengthen these multilateral regimes for nuclear weapons control. More recently, Sweden has launched several initiatives to deal with the increasingly difficult problem of the proliferation of various types of weapons of mass destruction.

With the changing global agenda of the 1970s, international development issues became relevant to the disarmament initiatives of the

United Nations.[33] Much of the Swedish activity during the 1970s and 1980s on the UN Committee for Disarmament generated criticism from the NATO states and praise from the Warsaw Pact members and many third world nations. In 1978 Inga Thorsson was appointed to head a UN study on the relationship between disarmament and development. Over the next three years, 40 studies on this topic were produced, representing the most exhaustive UN investigation on the topic to that time. The initiative for this study came from the Nordic governments, which also made significant substantive and financial contributions to the reports. These UN studies were based on the assumption that significant progress on disarmament would release material resources for international development. Realizing the many obstacles to such a massive and complex transfer of capital, at least in the short term, the study was also an initiative to help foster an international awareness of the economic consequences of armaments and the potentially disastrous material and human effects of nuclear war. Although the international security context of the early 1980s was not receptive to the holistic perspective on disarmament and development presented in the study, the issue has resurfaced in the wake of the collapse of the Warsaw Pact under the rubric of the "peace dividend."

A number of regionally focused initiatives have also been launched in the disarmament and arms control area. The so-called Undén plan of 1961 proposed a nuclear-free zone in Central Europe. Although this initiative came to naught, similar proposals have since been made for other regions of the world. Throughout the 1980s, a Nordic nuclear weapons free zone was the subject of heated debate in Scandinavia. Similarly, Sweden in 1982 launched a plan for a nuclear-free zone along the East–West divide in Central Europe. During recent years, Swedish proposals have focused on naval arms control and the need for pledges to keep nuclear weapons out of certain territories. Most of these initiatives brought considerable criticism from the NATO member states, while they were generally supported by the USSR. In domestic debate, the Swedish proposals were by and large commended as proper expressions of the nation's long-standing commitment to international peace and security.

In part, the seemingly idealistic, even naive, Swedish positions on global peace issues can be explained as a pragmatic realization of the core, long-term security interests of the nation. Support for multilateralism in forums such as the United Nations is one important component of a comprehensive national security strategy (which, of course, also includes a credible military defence and economic and civil preparedness). In the annual foreign policy declarations to parliament, for example, the vital role of an active Swedish profile in the United Nations is always emphasized in national security terms. It is asserted that diligent and persistent work in multilateral forums toward complete nuclear disarmament, international development, and the protection of human rights in South Africa has a direct bearing on the future security of the nation. Further, the periodic security policy planning directives, issued by authoritative defence commissions working in a long-range perspective, include similar statements about the link between support for multilateralism and national survival.

It is a widely held belief in Sweden that small states are likely to be losers should great power conflicts occur in their vicinity. Therefore, the leaders of small states ought vigorously to support all efforts toward peaceful resolution of great power conflicts. Such activity would be a meaningful investment in national survival and a complement to more conventional national defence preparations. This is a highly realistic, not idealistic, national security strategy in view of the limited resources available to a small state exposed to the ever-changing character of great power relations. This is a long-standing policy in Sweden, and represents a conceptual departure from the mainstream emphasis on national adjustment strategies among security analysts in the West. It may therefore be relevant to the further conceptual development of the academic study of international security as well as to the national policy planning considerations of the major states in the post–Cold War era.

Domestic sources of the Swedish UN profile

Peter Katzenstein has shown that the "small European states differ from the large industrial countries in their centralized and integrated corporatist structures, which fuse state and society."[34] Sweden has been cited as an example of a small, corporatist state, where the spheres of government and organized interests are brought together in intimate policy networks at the élite level. Public policy, including international economic and security policy, is formed within such enduring domestic structures. Individuals tend to pursue their careers almost exclusively within their chosen sphere of economic or political activity. "Revolving door" career paths between positions in business and public service are rare, unlike the tradition in some other countries, but influence can be exerted across the range of societal interests, without changing careers, by acting through the policy networks. Although the corporatist policy-making structure aims to transcend class conflict, it nevertheless "produces a pattern of cleavage between those who are included and those excluded from the corporatist sector."[35]

This approach to policy-making can be traced back to the international economic pressures faced by Sweden in the 1930s. At that time, enduring cooperative arrangements were established among the representatives of the state, the business sector, and organized labour, and since then Sweden has pursued an economic policy encompassing a "commitment to liberal competition policies in the world economy sphere combined with domestic welfare protection."[36] The cooperative spirit has extended beyond economic matters into the area of national security policy in which the need to maintain a united public front against the rest of the world has been emphasized. Concern for maintaining the international credibility of Sweden's posture of neutrality has also served as a useful damper on the public debate over security issues, a tradition that has its roots in the grand coalition of 1939–1945, which acted to stifle public discussion of foreign affairs as a matter of national survival. The general consensus is that this type of social partnership has served the nation well in the postwar conditions of economic liberalism and alliance confrontation in Europe.

Similarly, the Swedish approach to the United Nations and other cooperative international ventures is also built upon the foundations of the corporatist domestic structure, such that diverse social interests have direct input into Sweden's multilateral efforts. The UN delegation, for example, is not only composed of government officials, but includes some 20 parliamentarians across the political spectrum. Five or six experts from the major interest group organizations are also included, serving approximately three-month terms on a rotating basis. The purpose of this approach is to gain their input on specific policy issues and more generally to broaden the understanding of the United Nations in the political parties and throughout society. Prior to the fall session of the General Assembly, and in preparation for major multilateral conferences on specialized topics, the Foreign Ministry spearheads a comprehensive review of the positions to be taken on upcoming agenda items. In this elaborate and confidential process, detailed consultations are held with the opposition parties and the major interest groups concerned. The final product of this

119

process is the government's written instructions to the official delegation. Relevant interest groups and business associations are also represented on official delegations to other multilateral organizations.
Swedish positions in international forums, therefore, not merely are
articulations of government views, but represent a national expression of a wide variety of interests and viewpoints. The corporatist
partnership in the formation of policy thus extends to international
issues, including Sweden's role in the United Nations.

One example of this is the domestic background for Sweden's multilateral leadership efforts on nuclear weapons-related issues. After
the war, it was thought that Sweden's uranium deposits (although of
low grade, some of the largest in Europe) could become the basis for
a domestic nuclear power industry as well as a self-reliant nuclear
force. Business interests, research planners, military officials, government leaders, and other parties joined in support of a large-scale industrial development project towards that end, and for most of the
1950s it was an open question whether Sweden would join the nuclear club, especially as this was advocated by the military leadership
and several political parties. This option was closed politically in the
early 1960s as a result of strong opposition to the acquisition of nuclear weapons from within the ruling Social Democratic Party, particularly from its leading female members. The ageing Foreign Minister,
Östen Undén, apparently joined the opposition, while other members
of the cabinet favoured the development of a nuclear capability. In
terms of technical capability, however, the nuclear option remained
open.

With the signing of the Non-Proliferation Treaty in 1968 the government foreclosed any such future possibilities. Instead, the considerable national expertise that had been acquired in this high-technology area, particularly by the National Defence Research Agency
(FOA), was able to be used as a resource base for its multilateral
nuclear disarmament and arms control initiatives taken under UN
auspices. Recently, for example, Rolf Ekéus was assigned as a UN
inspector to investigate Iraq's possession of weapons of mass destruction. Ambassador Ekéus previously served as the Swedish representative to the disarmament sessions in Geneva. The International
Atomic Energy Agency in Vienna has been under the direction of a
Swede since 1961, with scientist Sigvard Eklund serving for 20 years
until 1981, when he was succeeded by former diplomat and Foreign
Minister Hans Blix. Some of the activists of the successful opposition
to the acquisition of Swedish nuclear weapons in the 1950s later be-

came leading figures in the government delegation to the Geneva multilateral negotiations. Among others, Alva Myrdal, Inga Thorsson, and Maj. Britt Theorin have personified Sweden's high-profile stand against nuclear weapons over the last 30 years.

Sweden's national experience is also evident in other areas of multilateral activity. For example, Sweden has placed less emphasis on the free market mechanism in its international development programmes than have other Western states. Rather, programmes reflecting the Swedish tradition of state-led development have been advocated. Similarly, "freedom from want" has been as important to its development philosophy as the classical liberal notion of "freedom of opportunity." Human rights have been defined more broadly than in most other states to include the right to a decent life without fear of material or cultural deprivation by government or private business. The Swedish notion of "equal status" between the sexes was in 1975 accepted by the International Labour Organization (ILO) as the basis for action, supplementing the more traditional concern in many societies with gender "equality." Similarly, Sweden's impressive record of adult education, which many observers have found instrumental in ensuring the enduring political prominence of the labour movement, has inspired similar efforts in many other countries. The first UN conference on the environment, which took place in Stockholm in 1972, was the result of a Swedish proposal for greater UN involvement in this area, and the Swedish lead in this area reflected a long-standing domestic concern with environmental issues.

The character of Swedish involvement in resource-demanding multilateral arrangements, such as in the United Nations and other international organizations, seems to be based on the assumption that, for a small but advanced state, persuasion is a cost-effective means of influencing international events and opinion. Recognizing its limited capacity for resisting the direct demands of a superpower for policy changes, or for forcing any policy redirection upon a major state, a long-term indirect approach to influencing the actions of other states has been adopted. If multilateral organizations, issue-based regimes, and the international legal order could be infused with rules, norms, and decision-making procedures sympathetic to Swedish interests and values, its national security would be strengthened. Further, for a small state such as Sweden, politically independent but economically entrenched in the West, such normative and process-related aspects of the world order could serve to cushion the effects of direct great power pressure.

It is often assumed in Sweden that "international opinion" exists, can be influenced, and is worth influencing. During the Viet Nam War, for example, Sweden's persistent and unequivocal criticism became one element of a widening international and American domestic rejection of US military involvement in South-East Asia. However, in such cases of alleged Swedish influence, the critical analytical notions of international opinion and its formation process have never been fully defined or explored. The assumption that "international opinion" can shape the policies of major states in vital questions rests on the questionable premise that the processes of representative democracy also operate in the international arena. Nevertheless, the hope that an open, international democratic process in which small states, through solidarity and joint action, can outmanoeuvre the great powers has been the inspiration behind Swedish work in multilateral forums throughout this century, a tradition that draws on Sweden's domestic experience, classical writings, and the public service training of an entire generation of Swedish political leaders and government officials.

The pioneering work of Hjalmar Branting, and of Olof Palme years later, was influenced by their conceptions of democratic government and by a belief in solidarity across class and among nations.[37] In this view, the weak should seek protection against the mighty through collaborative arrangements, such as majority voting rules and the rule of law. The domestic experience of the Swedish Social Democratic Party pointed to the usefulness of these two principles, having ensured the success of the drive for improved living conditions for the weaker elements of Swedish society. In the first half of this century, the labour movement captured the state machinery as a result of reforms to the election process and the innovation of mass parties. According to the standard interpretation of the evolution of the modern welfare society, once in a position of power the dominant Social Democratic Party used the elements of law and legitimate rule to shape the nation according to its image of the good society, building the Swedish "people's home" through consensus-based and judicially legitimate political reforms. By extending this domestic logic into the international sphere, international society could be transformed through peaceful means to benefit its many weaker members.

This belief in the rule of law has been paralleled by a national heritage of reliance by the political leadership on a loyal and competent civil service. The former Uppsala professor Östen Undén and his younger associates, Dag Hammarskjöld, Gunnar Jarring, Olof Ryd-

beck, Sverker Åström, and many other prominent Swedish representatives to the United Nations, were influenced by a strong legal tradition that placed a high value upon an impartial civil service. The activist state, in the task of constructing the welfare society, had to rely
on a loyal corps of implementers. In a curious meeting of minds,
Social Democratic politicians and the civil servant élite, who were
recruited from very different socio-economic backgrounds, joined
forces in the complex task of social engineering. There was a distinct division of labour and political responsibility, in which civil servants offered technical solutions to the societal ills defined by the
political leaders. The role of the UN mission, in the context of this
civil service tradition, was to implement the policy directives formulated in Stockholm.

The intellectual underpinnings of this judicial approach to governance were based on the Uppsala philosophical tradition. The founder
of this school of legal reasoning, Professor Axel Hägerström (1868–
1939), advanced a view in which law was intimately related to the
surrounding social order and the role of sanctions was important.
The notion of an inherent "natural law" (found in many other legal
systems) was rejected by Hägerström, and never became an important element of the Swedish legal tradition.[38] Consequently, diplomats were trained in a public administration tradition that emphasized the importance of law, sanctioning rules, technical reasoning,
and the role of ombudsmen or arbitrators. By extension, the international order should be built on a legal framework that recognized the
surrounding political context but that constrained the inevitable vicissitudes of great power relations. The diplomat and the international
civil servant in pursuit of world order must be protectors of the judicial system governing the relations among states.

The emphasis on technical studies and the advancement of knowledge as an integral part of the process of resolving international disputes seems to be based on two assumptions of the Swedish social
scientific tradition. The first was that through increased technical
knowledge complex social systems can be managed and shaped in
a politically desirable direction. Particularly during the formative
1930s and 1940s, it was thought that all social ills could be removed
through rationally derived technical remedies. In its most excessive
form, this activist orientation would have included official guidance
for family life and child-bearing. Its admirable purpose was to "rationally plan society in such a way that a maximum of happiness and
a minimum of unhappiness would exist."[39] The belief in the power of

social science strongly influenced the labour movement. During the 1950s, Prime Minister Tage Erlander justified the activism of the state by speaking of the importance of science as the analytical foundation for the "strong society." It is not surprising, then, that the Swedish government has often promoted scientific enterprises as means for improving the plight of the world community. For example, the UN study initiative on disarmament and development was a technical enterprise whose political purpose was to reduce global inequalities and the threat of nuclear war.

A second assumption has been that the shaping of public opinion is an important element in the politically motivated task of social engineering at home, and hence Swedish government agencies have devoted considerable resources to it. The so-called "defence will" has been carefully nurtured since the Second World War, and public enthusiasm for international development assistance has been regularly measured. During the 1980s, several activist organizations received considerable government funding to stimulate public understanding of the necessity of global peace. The long-range impact of these publicly funded attitude-shaping strategies has been noted by their supporters as well as by their critics. When applied to the United Nations, the transformation of international opinion would eventually generate political demands for the desired changes in nuclear weapons and military spending policies of other states. In other words, it was assumed (with some oversimplification of the difficulties involved) that the success of the labour movement in shaping Sweden's predominant political values and defining social debates could be repeated in the wider global arena.

A primary reason for the impressive Swedish record of involvement in international mediation efforts has been the deep-seated belief in the possibility of peacefully resolving even the most intense conflicts. The domestic experience in labour–management relations during the last 50 years has underscored both the futility of unilateral action (such as striking) and the mutual gains that are possible through peaceful settlement. Often, a government-appointed mediator has worked through "quiet diplomacy" to find a mutually satisfactory compromise formula. The Swedish model of a labour–industry–government tripartite relationship is widely recognized as having been effective for handling industrial relations and the resolution of domestic disputes. Similarly, it is reasoned that mediation can facilitate the peaceful settlement of inter-state conflict. This approach to the accommodation of conflicting interests is essentially rationalistic, rather than ideological, and rests on a belief in the primacy of reason over passion, or pragmatism over ideas.[40] As with the traditional emphasis on law and adjudication, the mediating role fits well with the technical orientation of the traditional Swedish civil servant.[41] In the past, public administration was even seen as a process of objective mediation or arbitration among a myriad of interests within society, in which it was the obligation of the civil servant to find the judicially correct, as well as the politically astute, compromise for a particular government policy.

According to Arne Ruth, editor-in-chief of the largest Swedish morning paper, "The secret of Swedish social ethics is often said to reside in the word *lagom*; ... the word ... means just right, as well as in moderation; sufficient, as well as appropriate and suitable. It connotes not only a quantity, but a moral judgment on it as well."[42] The so-called *"lagom* code" served to lessen competition for resources and was used to integrate various sectoral interests into a holistic view of the good society. This mind-set has facilitated a mediation approach to political problem-solving in Sweden. In international affairs, the Swedish public official can bring to bear a similar ability to find the proper *lagom* reconciliation of competing viewpoints and interests in such a way that world peace and justice are served in the same way as equality and social harmony are at home. The limitations of this optimistic approach to international conflict resolution became evident during the Viet Nam War: as former ambassador Yngve Möller observed, the prevailing government position was that "a conflict, be it domestic or international, should be resolved through deliberations, compromise and agreement. But the Swedish model did not work in Viet Nam, neither did any other model."[43]

These examples demonstrate how particular national experiences and traditions become the foundation for government initiatives and involvements in multilateral issues and forums. In this case, certain features of the Swedish experience with the welfare state have been externalized to the global context. The normative framework within which the government pursues its initiatives influences the declarations and recommendations of the United Nations and other multilateral agencies. In turn, these statements of preferred policy, once they have gained legitimacy in the international arena, are reintroduced by the government into the domestic debate. For example, they can then be used as evidence of a binding treaty commitment, which must be ratified by the legislature. At other times, the international legitimacy of a particular policy line can be used as a supporting argument in domestic deliberations. Over the years, several international organizations have served as reference points in Swedish domestic policy debates. Recently, the primary focus for debate over the necessity for national policy changes has been the European Union. Regionalism, rather than global multilateralism, has come to dominate the national mood in an unprecedented way during the last few years.

Turning the perspective around, Swedish society and politics have been affected by Sweden's involvement with the United Nations community, and the growing number of issues on the global agenda has greatly influenced the topics of public debate inside Sweden. For example, in the early years of the United Nations, the government's focus on international development helped promote a public concern for this task. The recommendation of the United Nations that governments contribute 1 per cent of their GNP to the task of international development soon became the national standard in Sweden, as it did in a few other Northern nations. The notion of what constitutes the proper political–economic relationship with a third world nation has changed in response to shifting emphases in the leading multilateral organizations. Similarly, domestic debate on international security issues has to some degree been shaped by the work of the United Nations in the disarmament field, where the Swedish government has kept a high profile.

Critics have argued that too many of Sweden's foreign policy activities have not been concerned with issues relevant to Swedish national interests. Instead, public debate and official statements have focused largely on the various topical problems of global affairs. In most cases, Sweden's stake in the outcome has been marginal. However, having a well-articulated position on such issues has been regarded as important in demonstrating a political party's concern for foreign affairs. According to this critical view, the international solidarity advocated by many prominent political leaders, like the late Olof Palme, primarily served their domestically defined partisan ends. If one accepts this, it becomes clear how the activities and debates of the United Nations infuse Swedish political life with new ideas, normative guidelines, and arguments for further involvement in global affairs. In turn, local cultural and political conditions have facilitated a receptive public attitude toward such external influences.

Thus ultimately the flow of ideas between Sweden and the multilateral arena forms an endless cycle of back and forth diffusion between the domestic and international realms. Swedish national values and domestic experiences have had an impact on its profile in the United

126

Nations; similarly, a Swedish élite attentive to international affairs has helped inject issues of global significance into the domestic debate over foreign affairs. Also, internationally accepted standards of national policy in various sectors have been introduced through legislation or by government decrees. Such direct influence has been inspired less often by UN resolutions than by the more concrete policy guidelines by the many other organizations in the multilateral community, such as the ILO or OECD. The domestic importance of the United Nations has been primarily in its agenda-setting and debate-shaping functions.

Future prospects

Swedish foreign policy has been affected by the significant changes in the European political context of the last few years. Its traditional core doctrine of neutrality seems less relevant to its national security in the wake of the collapse of the antagonistic bloc structure. The conservative government that took office in October 1991, led by Carl Bildt, has emphasized in its official statements that the European arena will be the primary focus for Swedish foreign policy over the next decade. The application for membership in the European Union, filed in July 1991 by the previous Social Democratic government, was vigorously pursued. In the first declaration of the new government, the customary mention of the United Nations as a cornerstone of Swedish foreign policy was missing. However, in the 1992 annual foreign policy address to parliament the tradition was restored, and the government began actively campaigning for a seat on the Security Council for the 1993–1994 term.

Sweden's domestic context has also changed significantly over the last decade. A comprehensive and authoritative study of democracy and power in Sweden concluded that many of the traditional foundations of the so-called "Swedish model" of consensual politics have been replaced by new socio-political features.[44] The domestic structures associated with Sweden and other European small states no longer define the political landscape. Rather, the distinction between the state and civil society, common in many other Western countries, is increasingly prominent. Advocacy of privatization has replaced corporatism as a political virtue, and the state and its corps of civil servants are less widely seen as the enlightened guardians of the common good or the impartial mediators between conflicting sectoral interests.

127

Public support for internationalism has been rivalled by concern over the uncontrollable domestic effects of economic internationalization. The Social Democratic Party's celebrated economic policies of full employment and government control of investments and international financial flows seem to be in jeopardy as a result of Sweden's growing economic interdependence with the rest of the world, particularly Europe. A heavy influx of refugees has stimulated public concern over the future homogeneity of Swedish society, bringing home to the Swedish voter the international dimension of public affairs in a direct and often threatening way. Perhaps it was more comforting to the public when personal engagement in international affairs merely meant taking a stand on some remote, if burning, issue on the global agenda, such as the Viet Nam War or the South African conflict.

Thus, although the primary emphasis of Swedish foreign policy since the 1940s has been on the wider multilateral setting (including the United Nations), critics have argued that it is time for a fundamental redirection of this dominant foreign policy orientation in light of the altered regional and domestic environments. The current Prime Minister appears to be giving a higher priority to the European context than did his predecessors, and the domestic debate appears preoccupied with finding the proper place for Sweden in Europe. If Sweden were to join the European Union in 1995, its future latitude to pursue an independent and distinctive foreign policy would be somewhat circumscribed, thus perhaps muting the Swedish voice in multilateral affairs.

As part of its greater emphasis on Europe, Sweden will maintain its high profile in the Conference on Security and Cooperation in Europe (CSCE). At the July 1992 Helsinki summit, the CSCE enacted new provisions to strengthen its role in dispute resolution. With assistance from other regional organizations, such as the Western European Union or NATO, the CSCE may in the future shoulder a greater share of the peace-keeping burdens within Europe. With a membership of 52 states, covering a geographical area from Vancouver to Vladivostok, and with sharply differing cultural and socio-political traditions, the likelihood of conflict within the CSCE is high. In December 1992, Sweden assumed the position of chair of this regional multilateral organization, a task that has engaged Swedish diplomats in mediating conflicts between the territories of the former USSR. A Swedish diplomat, Nils Eliasson, has already served as head of the CSCE Secretariat in Prague, following the 1990 signing of the Charter of Paris. This active engagement in the work of the

CSCE demanded a considerable allocation of funds and expertise. Similarly, the obligations of membership in the European Union would draw heavily on the limited Swedish resource and talent base.

But, at present, no direct evidence can yet be found that Sweden is retracting from its established commitments to international development, the strengthening of the United Nations, and continued support for global multilateralism. Sweden's candidacy for a seat on the Security Council (which was unsuccessful) was taken seriously by the Foreign Ministry, the government, and the Social Democratic opposition. After the 1992 General Assembly vote, domestic disappointment was expressed both over the negative outcome and over the inability to draw on "Swedish global good will" in this matter of national prestige. No reduction in the large development assistance appropriation has been announced, and Sweden will continue its participation in the large and increasingly expensive UN peace-keeping missions. Former Prime Minister Ingvar Carlsson even heads a new Geneva-based organization charged with examining ways to strengthen the United Nations. It is thus reasonable to argue that the traditionally positive attitude towards Sweden's active UN profile has become so deeply entrenched in the domestic political context that any current government preference for a different priority between regional and global multilateral commitments will affect public opinion only slowly and marginally. It is equally clear, however, that Sweden's limited resource base, including its government machinery, can handle only so many areas of international involvement. For Sweden, the 1990s will be a period of scrutiny of established policy priorities and the making of hard choices, the most important question being to what extent this small state can maintain its active profile in both the European and the global multilateral arenas. In official statements this tension is not acknowledged, but it was asserted in 1993 that "our foreign policy is not a zero-sum game."

Time will tell if Sweden's traditional commitment to the development of international consensus and solidarity, which first manifested itself in the work of Hjalmar Branting at the League of Nations, will survive the present rush to join in the construction of a new, post-Cold War Europe. One sceptic, Arne Ruth, predicted a decade ago that:

the myth of Swedish internationalism is bound to deflate under the impact of the real conflicts of interest between the old and new industrialized countries, between traditionally rich and hopelessly poor nations in the North and South ... Swedish foreign policy stands the risk of going through a similar process of contraction such as occurred before 1939: from the solidaristic internationalism of the twenties, to an attempt to formulate a regional concept of security following the breakdown of the sanctions system of the League of Nations, and finally, in the neutral isolation of the war years, to an interpretation of the national interest so narrow that even Sweden's Nordic neighbours felt a sense of betrayal.[45]

Notes and references

1. See Linda Cornett and James Caporaso, "'And It Still Moves!' State Interests and Social Forces in the European Community," in James Rosenau and Ernst Otto Czempiel, eds., *Governance without Government: Order and Change in World Politics* (Cambridge: Cambridge University Press, 1992); Peter Katzenstein, "The Small European States in the International Economy," in John Ruggie, ed., *The Antimonies of Interdependence* (New York: Columbia University Press, 1983); Joel Migdal, *Strong Societies and Weak States: State/Society Relations and State Capabilities in the Third World* (Princeton, N.J.: Princeton University Press, 1988).
2. See Robert Cox, *Production, Power and World Order: Social Forces and the Making of History* (New York: Columbia University Press, 1987); John Ikenberry, David Lake, and Michael Mastanduno, eds., *The State and American Foreign Policy* (Ithaca, N.Y.: Cornell University Press, 1988); Stephen Krasner, *Defending the National Interest* (Princeton, N.J.: Princeton University Press, 1978).
3. Cox, *Production*, 170.
4. Shepard Jones, *The Scandinavian States and the League of Nations* (Princeton, N.J.: Princeton University Press, 1939), 254.
5. Alf Johansson and Torbjörn Norman, "Den svenska neutralitetspolitiken i historiskt perspektiv," in Bo Hugemark, ed., *Neutralitet och försvar: Perspektiv på svensk säkerhetspolitik 1809–1985* (Stockholm: Militärhistorika förlaget, 1986).
6. Åke Landquist, ed., *Norden på världsarenan* (Stockholm: LTs Förlag, 1968).
7. Ulrika Mörth, *Sverige i FNs säkerhetsråd* (Stockholm: FOA, 1991).
8. Ibid.
9. Ibid.
10. Ibid.
11. Sven Andersson, "Den rastlöse reformisten – En uppsats om Olof Palme och världen," in Bo Huldt and Klaus Misgeld, eds., *Social-demokratin och den svenska utrikespolitien* (Stockholm: Utrikespolitiska, 1990).
12. Ulf Bjereld, *Kritiker eller medlare?* (Göteborg: Nerenius & Santérus förlag, 1992), 66.
13. Mörth, *Sverige*.
14. Bjereld, *Kritiker*, 66.
15. Magnus Jerneck, "Olof Palme: en internationell propogandist," in Huldt and Misgeld, *Social-demokratin*, 128.
16. Yngve Möller, *Sverige och Vietnamkriget* (Stockholm: Tidens förlag, 1992), 360.
17. Bjereld, *Kritiker*, 82.
18. Harto Hakovirta, *East–West Neutrality and European Neutrality* (Oxford: Oxford University Press, 1988).
19. Ibid., 87.
20. Ingemar Dörfer, *Nollpunkten: Sverige i det andra kalla kriget* (Stockholm: Timbro, 1991), 32–33.

21. Möller, *Sverige*, 363.
22. Krister Wahlbäck, "Från medlare till kritiker," *Internationella studier*, no. 3 (1973).
23. Bjereld, *Kritiker*, 57.
24. Möller, *Sverige*, 360.
25. Mörth, *Sverige*.
26. Hakovirta, *East–West Neutrality*.
27. Mörth, *Sverige*.
28. *Utrikesfrågor* (1976), 41.
29. Security Council Official Records (1975), 1828th meeting.
30. Bo Huldt, "Svensk nedrustnings: och säkerhetspolitik frän tjungotal till åttiotal", in Hugemark, *Neutralitet*.
31. Ibid.
32. See Nils Andrén and Yngve Möller, *Från Undén till Palme: svensk utrikespolitik efter andra världskriget* (Stockholm: Norstedts, 1990); and Lars-Göran Stenelo, *Mediation in International Negotiations* (Lund: Studentlitteratur, 1972).
33. Huldt, "Svensk nedrustnings."
34. Katzenstein, "The Small European States," 114.
35. Cox, *Production*, 187.
36. Ibid., 224.
37. Torbjörn Norman, "Hjalmar Branting, Nationernas Förbund och naturrätten," in Huldt and Misgeld, *Social-demokratin*.
38. Staffan Källström, *Den gode nihilisten: Axel Hägerström och striderna uppsalafilosofin* (Stockholm: Raben & Sjögren, 1986).
39. Yvonne Hirdman, *Att lägga livet till rätta: Studier i svensk folkhems politik* (Stockholm: Carlssons, 1990), 10.
40. Åke Daun, *Svensk mentalitet* (Stockholm: Raben & Sjögren, 1989).
41. Anders Mellbourn, *Byåkratins ansikten: Rolluppfattningar hos svenska högre tjänstemän* (Stockholm: Liber, 1979).
42. Arne Ruth, "The Second New Nation: The Mythology of Modern Sweden," *Daedalus* 113 (Spring 1984), no. 2: 60.
43. Möller, *Sverige*, 361.
44. SOU, "Demokrati och makt i Sverige" (1990), 44.
45. Ruth, "Second New Nation," 75.

4

Romania at the United Nations, 1956–1993

Mircea Malitza

Introduction

Romania became a member of the United Nations in December 1955, along with 15 other states.[1] Its admittance to the organization was a significant political event for both the Romanian government and its public. Romania had requested UN membership since 1947, but was constantly denied owing to the politics of the Cold War. Moreover, it yearned to be recognized for the contribution it had made to the victory of the Allies during the Second World War. Given the great material and human loss suffered, Romania considered that it should have been treated as a major co-belligerent on the Allied side during the Second World War, but such an acknowledgement was not made.[2] While the Romanian authorities saw admission into the United Nations more or less as compensation for the long period of post-war isolation, its society expected that the country's entry on the world stage would result in an improvement of its living standards and an end to the systematic programme of internal class oppression that was being carried out in that country.

In any retrospective analysis of Romanian state–society perspectives on the United Nations system, the following points should be addressed or at least borne in mind:

- Romania did not simply enter the United Nations with an ahistorical or blank slate. It had historical memories, largely shared by the population, of a visible and active role in the League of Nations. During that time, Romania followed a well-designed philosophy that generally adhered to a "legalistic approach" and that allowed it to make a mark on the world system.

- The prevailing principle governing the creative and active phase of multilateralism was an attempt – also rooted in history – to carve out a distinctive space not entirely beholden to the polarity of the Cold War or to the Eastern bloc. An implicit conviction permeated its foreign policy, as was manifested in its UN activities: several parallel routes were taken in order to ease the grip of an exclusive alliance and enhance its security and development.
- Once this multilateral "space" had been created, it was captured by the personalist dictatorship of Nicolae Ceauçescu, who pushed the cult of personality to absurd levels and in so doing obscured the initial and genuine justification for this policy.
- The recent upsurge of multilateralism in Romania is rooted in the historical experiences of its activity in the UN system. This history should be critically examined if one is properly to apply its lessons to contemporary realities and trends. The fact that Romanian society at the present time is an integral part of a new and vibrant multilateral society is a positive sign.

One caveat is in order here: the subject of Romania's contribution to the United Nations is generally visited by Ceauçescu's ghost, whose label seems to have been imprinted, according to most authors on the subject, on almost all of Romania's foreign actions from 1965 until his violent death. A critical analysis of Romania's role in the UN system might go a long way in exorcising this ghost. But, to Romanians and the rest of the world, the Ceauçescu factor was not simply an ephemeral one. Analysts who try to explain everything via the personality ingredient in Romanian politics and foreign policy ignore a significant question that ought to be addressed: "To what extent can the policy of a particular country be attributed to the personality quirks of a leader?" It is ironic that in the former communist countries – supposedly ruled by strict determinism and faith in the objective forces of history – policy cannot be understood without first solving the mysterious riddles of the enigmatic personalities who find their way to the top of the hierarchy.

However, it would be incorrect to give the impression that Romania's foreign policy can simply be identified with, and attributed to, one single individual who appropriated it and ultimately abused it. An examination of the main events in Romania's foreign policy creation in the 1960s would demonstrate that it was designed before Ceauçescu appeared on the scene and that it developed largely without his participation. Once Ceauçescu came to power, he acted like a tenant who takes possession of a recently constructed but unfinished home, and who drives away the builders in order to place his name on the door as both builder and owner. The moment he achieved full control was the beginning of a flawed Romanian foreign policy. The music, as it were, turned into shrill noise; modesty was overturned by arrogance and bragging; caution was substituted by reckless action. The distortion brought about by one man resulted in the replacement of an otherwise quite soberly and rationally built edifice by an inwardly kitsch setting, and this in turn led to negative consequences. Through it all, the principles of sovereignty and independence, which were once used as safeguarding precepts, became a screen behind which to hide the actions of a tyrant and his total disregard of international norms. Relations with the third world were reduced to club meetings with other dictators from the South; discreet ways of mediation became mere occasions for photo opportunities and television appearances.

There is definitely a tragic side to the analysis of Romania's activity at the United Nations. A subject such as this, which deserves scientific research and analysis, runs the risk, owing to a historical accident, of becoming no more than a case-study in pathological psychology. Several contemporary authors, repulsed by the Ceauçescu dictatorship, have asserted that Romania's whole post-war policy was nothing more than a fake, that independence was but a pretext for serving Soviet interests and that the regime constructed a façade to conceal the internal terror that was being experienced in Romanian society. To the first assertion, a well-documented answer is provided by Robert Weiner, whose thorough analysis of the nature and dimension of the Romanian–Soviet disagreement at the United Nations provides us with a much more nuanced and sophisticated position on Romania's post-war role in the organization.[3] The second accusation is an oversimplification that, although partially valid, needs refinement. Despite the distortion and personal abuse of power in the making of Romania's foreign policy with respect to the United Nations, there were still some inherent merits to the Romanian perspective on the organization and to its contribution to international politics.

In examining Romania's presence in the United Nations and its interplay within the world system, or the relations of Romanian society at large with the international body, the following main periods can be distinguished:

- the apprenticeship years (1956–1961);
- the rise and plateau period (1962–1975);
- the era of erosion, decline, and decay (1976–1989).

These dates are not strictly delimited, since the passing from one period to another was gradual and spanned several years; for instance, the transition from the apprenticeship stage to the more dynamic one that occurred between 1962 and 1964. But the periodization can help one to organize significant facts and identify general trends regarding Romania's insertion into the multilateral arena.

Romania's activities within the UN system

The apprenticeship years (1956–1961)

At the time that Romania became a member of the United Nations, Bucharest was the stage of a struggle between Communist Party leader Gh. Gheorghiu-Dej and the "pro-Moscow" faction. One battle had already been won in 1952 when Ana Pauker and other leaders were expelled from the party. A second group, which supported Soviet policy unconditionally and was represented by Joseph Kishinevsky, arrived in Romania backed by Soviet troops. The conflict between "pro" and "anti" Moscow factions would later rear its head in the appointment of persons to key diplomatic positions. Although quite influential in the Ministry of Foreign Affairs, the Kishinevsky group could not manage to impose upon the ministry one of its members as ambassador to the United Nations. The position was instead offered to Athanase Joja, a cultivated intellectual who specialized in Aristotelian logic and who had been imprisoned with Gheorghiu-Dej. Joja was a very unconventional individual, who could discuss Romania's Latin affinities with the French ambassador, quite comfortably discuss St. John Perse with Dag Hammarskjöld, or organize contests with the Greek ambassador during official dinners in the recitation of Homeric verse memorized by heart. Athanase Joja hardly fitted the picture of an Eastern communist.[4] The instructions he received from Bucharest were, however, those from a country strangled by a military and ideological alliance that refused to take into consideration dissent or different opinions. "Consult the friends" was the leitmotif of these instructions, and this was followed almost religiously by a vote that was identical to that of the Eastern communist bloc countries in virtually all matters before the United Nations.

Romania's particular interests at this stage can be deciphered by examining the agenda items that it initiated, or by analysing the resolutions that were authored or co-authored by Romanian representatives. Among these, economic and social issues were most prominent. A sampling of the issues that occupied the Romanian UN representatives included: the "Possibilities of international cooperation in the field of oil industry in developing countries" (reflecting Romania's experience of cooperation with India in those years); a draft declaration on the "Promotion among youth of the ideals of peace, mutual respect and understanding between peoples"; and a resolution initiated with Mexico in 1957 devoted to the "bases of world economic cooperation."[5] The ECOSOC proceedings in particular were devoutly followed by Romania during this period, even though at the time it was only an observer of that body. Political issues were tackled cautiously, with an emphasis on maintaining consensus among the Eastern bloc group. As a contribution to fostering the notion of coexistence, Romania proposed an agenda item for the General Assembly entitled, "Action on the regional level with a view to improving good neighbourly relations among European States having different social and political systems."[6] This was followed in 1957 by a distinct Romanian government initiative to foster cooperation among the Balkan states – a policy goal of Romanian foreign policy to this day.[7]

Romania's UN membership gave it access to other intergovernmental bodies such as the FAO, ILO, and UNESCO.[8] Among these bodies, Romania exhibited special interest in UNESCO. Romanian intellectuals felt that through this forum they might make a significant contribution in the cultural and scientific area. An endorsement to Romania's admission to UNESCO on the ECOSOC agenda was obtained after much diplomatic insistence on the part of Romanian representatives in 1954, but at the UNESCO General Conference in Montevideo that year Romania's request for membership was turned down.[9] It took eight years before that goal was achieved: in 1962, at the twelfth session of the UNESCO General Conference, Romania's representative was elected as a member of the executive council.

This first phase of Romania's participation in the United Nations was devoted to "learning the ropes." Romanian representatives quickly learned that the tortuous path of moving an initiative from idea to resolution could take years of effort and consultation. They found ways to gain partners and allies in the pursuit of particular objectives, or of combining their interests with that of the alliance's group logic in such a way that it could be used to promote broader world causes. It is possible that their experience would have borne much more fruit, particularly in terms of advancing Romanian foreign policy, had it not been for the October 1956 popular uprising in Hungary, which was summarily suppressed by Soviet military might, or for the worsening of the international climate following the Suez crisis (October 1956). By 1957, Kishinevsky's group was banished, and in 1958 Soviet troops left Romanian territory. In 1960, Gheorghiu-Dej participated along with Khrushchev and other Eastern leaders in the fifteenth session of the United Nations General Assembly, but the Romanian deputy minister, who imitated Khrushchev's boisterous behaviour during the proceedings of the session and was complimented by Khrushchev, was soon disavowed by the Romanian people and (a few years later) was totally repudiated and eventually lost his position.

Rise and plateau (1962–1975)

At the start of the 1960s, Romania used its presence in international circles to establish more contacts and to involve itself in a vigorous campaign towards "normalization."[10] This campaign included the liquidation of its financial debts owed to Western countries, the upgrading of diplomatic offices from legations to embassies, and the establishment of new diplomatic and bilateral economic ties. It was primarily through its membership status at the United Nations that Romania was able to accomplish this. This period of Romania's insertion into the United Nations was a time for exercising a certain measure of autonomy. As a member of the Security Council in 1962, and in the absence of directions from home, since the President, Prime Minister, and Foreign Affairs Minister were away at the time on a visit to Indonesia, the Romanian delegation recorded a distinctly different position from the Soviet bloc on the Cuban missile crisis. The delegation failed to comply with Zorin's request to support the thesis of the non-existence of Soviet missiles in Cuba. They also encouraged Secretary-General U Thant to draw up his now-famous appeal to the USSR and the United States of America. The delegation's expression of support for Cuba was done strictly on legal grounds with respect to the problem of the maritime quarantine.[11] On their way back home from Indonesia via Moscow, the Romanian leadership were made fully aware of the great risks involved in not playing along with Khrushchev's political game.

It is undisputable that Romania's policy in vital matters and its activity at the United Nations were closely connected. The conflict between China and the USSR was well known to Romanians, since it had been revealed at a Congress of the Romanian party in June 1960. Throughout this conflict, which worsened over the years, Romania chose to occupy an intermediary position. It was not accidental that Romania's delegation to the United Nations stood actively in favour of acknowledging Chinese rights and supported this for a decade until mainland China gained its place at the United Nations in 1970. It was also during this period of "rise and plateau" that Romania's relations with the United Nations steadily improved. In 1963, U Thant visited Bucharest, and that same year Romania, along with the developing countries, started to reap benefits from UN technical assistance. In 1964 and 1965 it concluded a number of technical assistance agreements with the UNDP and other UN specialized agencies. The projects accomplished in the following years covered a variety of areas: cereal growing, land-use planning and irrigation, the development of the Institute of Polytechnics in Bucharest, air and water pollution control, the development of the tourism industry, and modern technology.

In 1963, at the eighteenth session of the UN General Assembly, Romania for the first time voted differently from the other socialist countries on an essentially political matter. The issue was the adoption of a resolution endorsing the denuclearization of Latin America. This action was consistent with its desire to win support for its own initiative for the denuclearization of the Balkans.[12] As if to test further the waters of autonomy, a year later the Romanian Communist Party issued a declaration that rejected the notion of supranational planning over the countries of the Council for Mutual Economic Assistance (CMEA, i.e. COMECON), and asserted that "nobody can decide what is and what is not correct for other parties."[13] In that same year, at the UNCTAD I session in Geneva, Romania's voting pattern demonstrated again that it did not feel compelled to side with the Eastern bloc countries. In 10 important resolutions Romania's vote was more in line with that of developing countries than with its communist allies.[14] Moreover, the delegation obtained the consent of the Group of 77 developing countries (G77) to be accepted into its ranks and began preliminary negotiations for admission into GATT. In both cases, Bucharest refused to give final consent. When the Romanian government later tried to resume these negotiations, it had to wait until 1976 before these goals could be attained.

Other circumstances illustrate the character of Romania's activity at the United Nations during that period. Following up on the item placed on the UN General Assembly's agenda in 1960 – "Coexistence in Europe" – the Romanian delegation focused its efforts on trying to gain support for the idea of European cooperation. Following consultations with A. Stevenson, K. Waldheim, M. Jakobson, P. Harmel, and other influential UN diplomats, a resolution signed by nine countries was passed in 1965 that foreshadowed the European agreement that was to be concluded later during the Helsinki CSCE process.[15]

Although much of the Romanian political literature considers 1965 (the year Ceauçescu took over the reins of the state) as the initial moment of an active phase in Romanian foreign policy at the United Nations, examination of the facts reveals that the dynamism of the Romanian presence in the international system started long before that date and independently of Ceauçescu's contribution. This second period evinces a striking continuity, which is accounted for by Romanian Prime Minister Ion Gheorghe Maurer's role in the conduct of foreign policy; by the quasi-autonomy allowed the Ministry of Foreign Affairs by its minister, Corneliu Manescu, who protected it from the interference of other institutions eager to control it in the 1961–1972 period; and simply because, at the time, Ceauçescu did not feel confident enough in his own ability to deal adequately with foreign policy matters.

The 1960s can be considered the apogee of Romania's activity on the world stage. During that time, at the UN General Assembly sessions the Romanian Foreign Affairs Minister regularly met with Dean Rusk of the United States to discuss ways to bring an end to the Viet Nam war, and Romanian emissaries subsequently made frequent trips to Hanoi in an effort to play a constructive part in the peace efforts.[16] At the UN General Assembly's special session on the 1967 Arab–Israel war, Romania surprised everyone by refusing to break diplomatic ties with Israel – a move that was in contrast to the position taken by neighbouring countries. That same year, Romania was the only Eastern country to establish diplomatic relations with Bonn.[17] In the autumn of 1967, the Romanian Foreign Affairs Minister, Corneliu Manescu, was elected president of the twenty-second session of the UN General Assembly, and used his office to play a considerable and constructive role in resolving several difficult and seemingly intractable problems, including his contribution to the Security Council's efforts that eventually led to Resolution 242. But Romania's most dramatic stand of the period was recorded in 1968, when it decided not to be part of the invasion of Czechoslovakia by the USSR and the Warsaw Pact. Romania was subjected as a result to severe criticism and denunciation from the alliance. At the twenty-third session of the UN General Assembly, the Romanian delegate responded with a series of severe criticisms of the USSR-led action and in the process repudiated the Brezhnev doctrine.[18]

There were numerous other occasions on which Romania departed from the common positions of the Eastern alliance on a number of major issues of importance (the Soviet–China conflict, the Middle East war, attitudes toward Germany and other European matters, North–South confrontation, etc.). Its attempt to play an active role in conciliation or mediation aroused the interest of many authors who speculated on the motivating force behind this policy.[19] Some investigated psychological temperamental factors and history for clues; others placed great emphasis on the economic element as an overriding stimulus for policy deviations (K. Jowitt); yet others began with a mix of domestic variables and political leadership factors (R. Weiner), coming close to the thesis that foreign policy is an exercise to enhance the personal prestige of leaders. Although it is difficult to extract one factor as the explanation for any foreign policy strategy (which is usually a mix of several objectives and means), one particular event or factor may help to reveal what underlies the dominant position in a country's foreign policy. Such is the case with the 1964 declaration by Romania on the right to independent economic development, which implied that it considered that it had the right to make independent political decisions. This position must be placed in the context of the real and considerable fear of being an essentially marginalized Soviet province in a regionally centralized supranational system, relegated to a position of being an economy heavily dependent on primary products. To take an independent posture in foreign policy-making meant challenging a superpower. How did Romania get away with this while other East European countries did not do the same? First, unlike the other Soviet satellites, Romania did not have Soviet troops on its soil. Also its defiance was never of an ideological nature but remained within the parameters of ideological orthodoxy, carefully avoiding any pretext of a doctrinal conflict with Moscow. Less well known is the fact that the Ministry of Foreign Affairs succeeded in avoiding the direct and daily control of the Foreign Section of the Central Committee, submitting all matters to the top only where details were presented in as technical and non-ideological a manner as possible.

For Romanian diplomats, multilateral diplomacy became one of the most fertile fields in their institutional laboratory of ideas. Pursuing initiatives, drafting resolutions, obtaining co-sponsors, interacting with various countries and groups, were all part of the experiment in winning friends and as a consequence gaining the international support that was perceived as needed to enhance Romania's security. In fact, one can make the general argument based on Romania's experience that multilateral activity bestowed a certain degree of immunity upon the countries that engaged in it. With two opposing blocs, each requiring absolute fidelity of its members and imposing the logic and the discipline of an alliance, the only way successfully to resist attempts to be brought in line was to have a foot in the other camp or to manufacture strong links with neutral countries. These kinds of ties were seen as an insurance against, or at least an element to discourage, punitive measures. It was not enough for Romania to seek visibility at the international level through speeches, visits, contacts, or even the aid of good press coverage. There was a perceived need among the foreign policy establishment for the creation of a Romanian "space" on the international stage that could be considered in some sense as an extension of the cultural identity of the state/society in the realm of international politics. Such a space could be carved only by inserting the country on to the multilateral stage (i.e. through its membership in the UN system) and by performing a mix of roles combined from the available projects of international society.

Parallel with these "great policy" attitudes was Romania's quiet but steady activity in UN working bodies. In 1965, Romania became a member of ECOSOC, in which it presented a resolution on "The use of human resources in development"; this issue was also debated in the ILO for several years thereafter.[20] Other issues proposed by Romania at the time were directed towards what were perceived as relevant state/society objectives, such as issues dealing with science and engineering in the service of development, the application of data-processing techniques, and the role of modern technology in development.[21] In each case the topics reflected Romanian society's aspirations for Western-style modernization and indicated that the United Nations was being looked upon as a possible vehicle for achieving this goal. The crowning achievement of Romania's efforts in these areas was the attraction of UN institutions to that country: a Centre for the Specialization of Personnel (CEPECA) – a modern institution of management that could be attended by students of other countries as well – was set up in Bucharest in 1967, a UN Information Centre was established in 1970, and a UNDP office in 1971; 1972 marked the creation of an office of the Common Centre (ONUDI) in Romania, and that same year UNESCO's European Centre for Higher Education (CEPES) was opened in Bucharest in the presence of René Maheu, the Director-General of UNESCO. The placement of UN institutions in Romania was facilitated by the energetic negotiations undertaken by the Romanian diplomats, who spared no effort to ensure a strong UN presence in their country; these efforts were rewarded.

In the 1960s, the Ministry of Foreign Affairs hosted several international meetings on the UN system in the Romanian capital. In 1968, the UN Administrative Committee on Coordination and the Committee for Programmes and Coordination of ECOSOC brought together the heads of the specialized agencies as well as UN Secretary-General U Thant in a session held in Bucharest. Under the auspices of the Association of International Law and Relations (ADIRI), three international seminars on European cooperation and security were held (in 1968, 1969, and 1970), which came at the start of the pre-negotiations around the CSCE process.[22] In April 1974, the UN Economic Commission for Europe held its first session outside Geneva in Bucharest. The same year, Romania's capital hosted the World Conference on Population, which was attended by several thousand participants.[23]

Disarmament issues have been a special focus of Romanian diplomacy since 1960, when it became a member of the Committee of Ten, followed by membership of the Committee of 18 in Geneva in 1962. One of its major initiatives during this period was to place on the agenda of the twenty-fifth session of the UN General Assembly the item entitled "Economic and social consequences of the armaments race and its extremely harmful effects on world peace and security," an item that subsequently became a routine topic in the Assembly.[24] A still more interesting Romanian proposal came in 1972, related to the agenda item "Strengthening of the role of the UN with regard to the maintenance and consolidation of international peace and security, the development of cooperation among all nations and the promotion of the rules of international law in the relations between states."[25] The idea cross-cut another project aimed at bringing about reforms in the UN Charter, an issue supported by a number of developing countries. The same year Romania formulated several proposals aimed at strengthening the role of the United Nations in the peaceful settlement of disputes. One proposal called for the creation of a permanent commission of the General Assembly, which would have functions of mediation, aid distribution, and conciliation, among others. The committee did not record significant progress and in 1979 Romania revisited the issue by placing on the Assembly's agenda another related item – "The peaceful settlement of disputes among states." With respect to this, a Declaration was carried in 1982 by the Assembly, based on a draft prepared by Romania, the Philippines, Egypt, Nigeria, Tunisia, and five other states.[26]

It is in the 1970s that the gradual deterioration of the resources that nourished the dynamism of the 1960s became apparent. After reaping the personal prestige that followed Romania's stand against the Soviet invasion of Czechoslovakia in 1968 and, particularly, after having visited China in 1971, Ceauçescu took full control over Romanian foreign policy and in the process eliminated two statesmen.[27] He thus followed the practice of dictatorship by ensuring his absolute control over every aspect of Romanian policy. Subsequently, there would be no delegation of power or attributions to others who helped to make Romanian foreign policy. All negotiations with other states would be carried out by the dictator himself. The only valid diplomacy would be that which occurred at the very top level. Foreign policy contacts were limited to his discussions with heads of state. Romania was the only Warsaw Pact state with political ties to both the Arab world and Israel, and Ceauçescu used this position to play an intermediary role between the two sides. He visited Egyptian President Anwar Sadat in May of 1977 and Sadat returned his visit in October of that year. Israeli Premier Begin also travelled to Bucharest in 1977, and, in the wake of Sadat's dramatic journey to Israel, Ceauçescu was credited by Begin with having been helpful in facilitating the dramatic breakthrough.[28] Going against official Soviet Middle East policy, Ceauçescu praised Sadat's initiative. However, a total disregard was shown by Ceauçescu for the part played by several highly qualified men who had served as Romanian diplomats in the past and for the contribution they made to the settlement of certain conflicts (e.g. Middle East and Viet Nam) or in some *rapprochements* (United States–China) in an earlier period.

Illustrative of the way in which a permanent role in foreign policy was attributed to Ceauçescu was a publication released in 1976 called the *Political–Diplomatic Romanian Chronology 1944–1974*. In it, Ceauçescu's name was the only one to appear; any quotes not made by the dictator were anonymously attributed to a function rather than the name of the official. The climax was reached in 1982, when the speech of the Minister for Foreign Affairs to the thirty-seventh General Assembly appeared in the press under the rather bombastic title: "President Nicolae Ceauçescu fights with perseverance completely to eliminate force from inter-state relations, to defend the right of nations to live in peace and understanding."[29]

The decision-making mechanism in Romania was guided by the Political Bureau (later named the Executive Committee) of the Romanian Communist Party's Central Committee. Position papers prepared by the Ministry of Foreign Affairs went to Prime Minister Maurer, who introduced them to the Political Bureau. But in the 1970s, and especially after Maurer's sacking, these papers on foreign policy first had to be accepted and personally approved by Ceauçescu, whose dual position as State President and Secretary General of the Party underlined his supremacy over the party and country. The loss of authority by the Ministry of Foreign Affairs can be illustrated in the following case. In the late 1960s, a law expert had to be appointed to a UN Commission, and he was selected by the ministry from the University of Cluj on the basis of his merits and his excellent interpretation of Hugo Grotius' work on war. But in the 1970s, when another lawyer was required by a UN Conference, a professor of scientific socialism and former security officer was picked by the Central Committee because he was particularly trusted by the party's top brass. There were many other examples of the unprecedented concentration of power: essentially, the party machinery took over the state machinery, and was in turn taken over by the power-hungry Ceauçescu. The end result was that the Foreign Ministry was downgraded as a distinct influence on foreign policy.

In 1971 a campaign for the primacy of ideology put the existing groups of experts and specialists, including those from the diplomatic service, in an awkward situation. The postgraduate school for diplomats, which had functioned since 1963 at the Bucharest University Law Faculty, as well as at the CEPECA autonomous management school established by the UNDP and ILO in Bucharest, was transferred to the Academy of Party Political Studies. Staff purges proliferated within the Ministry of Foreign Affairs.[30] The new and ideal type of diplomat became the party activist with practical training in production fields and with a "worker mentality." One cannot begin to enumerate the far-reaching consequences of these measures on Romanian foreign policy.

Erosion, decline, and decay (1976–1989)

During the late 1970s and early 1980s, three major subjects were prominent as concerns for the international community: the armaments race, human rights, and ecological concerns. But Romania chose to deal with only the first of these. The other two topics were downgraded by the government primarily because it was one of the major violators of international human rights and ecological norms, and hence Romanian diplomacy gradually found itself flowing against the tide of international meetings and multilateral regimes.[31] As far as ecological matters were concerned, despite the fact that Romania was the only country from Eastern Europe to participate in the Stockholm Conference on the environment in 1972, it continued to be a reckless disseminator of toxic chemical products pollution. The primary reason for this was the fact that the dictator's wife had elevated chemistry to the rank of a "sacred science"! Romania thereafter gradually withdrew from international debates dealing with this issue. With respect to human rights, the principles of independence, sovereignty, and non-interference in domestic affairs that had been emphasized in the 1960s as a means of shielding Romania against the attempts to integrate it into the communist bloc were now being invoked to block international scrutiny. The Romanian leader showed extreme irritation whenever Romania was criticized for violating civil and political human rights in CSCE or UN debates. Most of these attacks came from Western industrialized states and, whenever they occurred, Romanian diplomats were instructed to launch a strong offensive by exposing human rights abuses in capitalist societies and to emphasize the collective rights "to work and education."

The seemingly insignificant incident that had the greatest repercussions in terms of destroying Romania's position in the world system revolved around a Romanian citizen from the international staff of UNESCO who was retained at home and pressed to resign. The individual, Professor Sorin Dumitrescu, was an expert in hydrology and a director in the Division of Natural Sciences in the UNESCO headquarters in Paris. The charges laid against him were ridiculous, and indicated unequivocally that this was a purely arbitrary action. The international press, the UN International Civil Service Commission, several other international bodies, and many important individuals (including former state presidents) stood up for the man concerned and went to Bucharest to remind the dictator that Romania was under obligation to observe international commitments. This forced Ceauçescu to reconsider the issue in 1976. However, by this time Romania's international credibility had been irretrievably damaged. A similar case of obstinate self-destruction by a despotic leader was recorded in the nineteenth century, when Theodorus, emperor of Abyssinia, refused to release the Queen of England's consul.

While in the earlier period Romania's leader regarded the international system with increasing suspicion and discomfort, in the 1980s he began to think of it as a stage where plots were hatched against "independent and sovereign countries," and he came to mistrust the multilateral arena and its players. In particular, Ceauçescu considered two international institutions as the embodiment of evil: the International Bank for Reconstruction and Development (IBRD) or the World Bank, and the International Monetary Fund (IMF). The reasons for this become clear once one understands the predicament that the Romanian government faced during the decade leading up to the 1980s. Romania had to declare bankruptcy immediately after Poland found itself on the brink of insolvency. By 1980, foreign banks refused credits to these countries. It was at this point that the World Bank and the IMF entered. During the discussions on rescheduling debt payments Ceauçescu accused the IBRD and the IMF of "veiled imperialism." These types of accusations reached an apogee in 1986, as the enormous sacrifices imposed on the population to repay the debts rapidly mounted. Romania's reputation was further tarnished by the fact that its debt burden forced it to default on its assessed contributions to the UN regular budget and to the budgets of the specialized agencies. This placed it in the awkward position of losing its franchise in the organization that was once perceived as its ticket to autonomy.

Desperate attempts were made by the dictatorship to restore Romania's prestige abroad. In 1984, a decision was made to participate in the Los Angeles Olympic Games – games that were boycotted by the other Eastern bloc countries. However, the country's credibility was further questioned by the world community after another embarrassing international incident. In 1986, another UN official who was in the highest position held by a Romanian at the time (Director of the Institute for Disarmament) was detained in Romania and forced to resign. The case produced a scandal greater than the previous one.

It was even placed on the UN General Assembly agenda for discussion. The affair dragged on for almost two years until the UN official was eventually released. The ignominy of Romanian policy during this period was capped by the two negative votes it cast during the CSCE process. Given the consensus rule in operation, this amounted to casting a singular veto, which had the effect of hindering the adoption of important international agreements on human rights and environmental protection.[32] These incidents demonstrate the extent to which Romania had fallen in terms of its international reputation over 15 years. It had gone from making constructive contributions to becoming an obstructionist actor in the multilateral arena. All this, combined with the criticism by most member states of the international community of Romania's human rights record, did much to stymie any effort on its part to play a meaningful role within the international system.

The historical bases of Romanian multilateralism

The analysis of Romania's activity within the UN system and the propensity towards multilateralism that it implies requires an understanding of its historical tradition. Romania had an intense training in multilateralism as a result of its participation in the League of Nations. The diplomat who represented Romania in the League Assembly at Geneva was Nicolae Titulescu, Romania's Foreign Minister between the two world wars. The acknowledgement of his personal contribution was manifested by the fact that he was the only diplomat to hold the chairmanship of the General Conference for two consecutive years, in 1929 and 1930.[33] Romanians had a sense of pride in this diplomat, who launched their country into the international orbit and was at the heart of the negotiations aimed at creating a new international order after the First World War. In 1963, when Haile Selassie visited Romania, he recalled positively and glowingly the personality of Nicolae Titulescu – the man who had defended him in Geneva during the Italian aggression in Abyssinia in 1936. The emperor's testimony produced such a strong impression upon the Romanian leadership that, shortly afterwards, the Ministry of Foreign Affairs reclaimed Titulescu's home in Bucharest and decided that it would house the Association of International Law and International Relations. It was also around this time that the work of Titulescu began to be reconstructed and published. It was quite extraordinary for a communist regime to acknowledge the worth of someone who was a former minister of the royal cabinet, a member of a conservative party, and (what is more) a landowner. All of Titulescu's ideas on peace and security, good neighbourliness, subregional arrangements and agreements, and the promotion of culture or law over force were revived by Romanian proposals at the international level in the 1960s. Even Titulescu's method of establishing special ties with certain countries or groups of countries became a model for Romanian diplomacy, and his works were quoted on occasion by Romanian representatives at the United Nations.[34] It is clear that respect for this diplomat is alive today: a European Foundation for Nicolae Titulescu was established in Bucharest in 1990 and his remains were brought back to Romania in 1992 from France, in accordance with his will. Romanian diplomacy also inherited Titulescu's outlook on international relations, the hallmark of which was legalism and the importance attached to international organizations.

Between the two great political philosophical trends of his day, realism and legalism, Titulescu clearly chose the latter, opposing the use of force in preference for an international relations that revolved around adherence to legal principles and norms. This fact is underscored by the name given to the association created in the 1960s in honour of Titulescu, which brought together the concept of international law and international relations.[35] Thus, drawing on the Titulescu legacy, Romanian diplomacy was inclined towards the creation of, and adherence to, principles, norms, declarations, charters, and the codification of rules of conduct in an effort to foster a climate of international legality and to show a clear preference for a world system of states rather than a world carved up into regional groupings or alliances. This position served the primary purpose of thwarting any attempt to integrate Romania further into the Eastern bloc of communist countries or at least providing shelter from it. By stressing these principles at every bilateral or multilateral meeting in which Romania was involved, its representatives were deliberately creating a "space" in which Romanian autonomy could be preserved. Romanian politicians were nevertheless aware of the decisive role that armed force and economic power were playing in post-war events. That is precisely, however, why they persisted in espousing legal principles and the importance of working within the multilateral arena, and why they were so resolute in their positions on disarmament and on the dismantling of military blocs.

Romania's diplomacy has a rich historical record, with influences that are discernible over centuries. Encircled by the Ottomans, Russians, and Austrians, Romanian territory was coveted by all three empires. This complicated situation actually offered the Romanians who practised diplomacy an opportunity they did not miss: it took a special blend of skill and strategy to be able to assert Romanian independence while at the same time not arousing the kind of suspicion among the surrounding empires that would lead to a situation of insecurity for Romanian society.[36] This tricky tightrope did not ultimately guarantee Romanian security, and its leaders opted to try to enhance their country's security by being integrated into a collective security system of regional pacts and alliances. Despite this, Romania still lost three large portions of its territory in 1940. The Warsaw Treaty proved also not to be the answer to Romania's security dilemma. The Warsaw Pact turned out to be a guise under which the Soviet Union sought to control the smaller allies. It was perceived by Romanians as little more than an instrument that could be used for expansion or confrontation that could easily draw the country into conflicts that were alien to its interests.

Regional and global multilateralism as a counterweight

When Romanian delegates first entered the United Nations, they found Romania labelled a "satellite." Being in the Soviet orbit may have been unavoidable, but Romania was determined to find ways of giving itself other identities as well. Thus in the 1960s, as a result of the diplomatic and political links it had made, Romania gradually became known as a European, a socialist, and a developing country. In some circles it was also referred to as Latin, Balkan, Danubian, and riparian to the Black Sea. It was regularly invited to participate in meetings of the non-aligned countries. In UNCTAD, Romania was sometimes present in meetings of the Latin American caucus. And in the Disarmament Committee in Geneva, it became the twenty-second country to be admitted to meetings of the 21 non-aligned states. Romania's historical experience taught it to resist the idea of polarization (and to avoid it in its own relations) and also convinced Romanian diplomats to adhere simultaneously to as many groups and coalitions as possible.[37]

Romania's first major international initiative – the Balkan initiative – deserves some attention here. It was hardly a coincidence that it was conceived and announced in 1956, the year of Romania's admittance to the United Nations. In 1957 a message was sent by the Romanian government to the governments of Albania, Bulgaria, Yugoslavia, Greece, and Turkey that set forth its views on the development of broader collaboration among the Balkan states. The idea was picked up from Romania's pre-war experiences in two subregional alliances: the "little Entente" (Romania, Czechoslovakia, Yugoslavia) and the "Balkan Entente" (Romania, Yugoslavia, Greece, and Turkey), both of which were born as anti-revisionist fronts, the first in early 1920 and the second some 10 years later. The language in 1957 was cautious – it was just an exercise in "coexistence," taking care not to arouse the suspicions of the Soviet Union, which made clear its dislike of the coalitions of states on its south-east flank. In 1959 the idea became a little bit more ambitious: to create a zone of peace and good-neighbourly relations. Next came the objective to build up a weapons- and missile-free zone; an aim that corresponded with other zonal initiatives being debated and encouraged in the United Nations at the time. However, the Balkan initiative never materialized in an institutionalized form (i.e. with the creation of a permanent secretariat). Although bilateral communiqués always seemed to support it, at ministerial meetings there was always some country absent in protest at some crisis between that state and one of the others. Nevertheless, there were several successful non-governmental functional organizations that were either revived or created as an indirect result of the Romanian initiative. For instance, the Balkan Medical Union (created in 1932) and the Balkan Union of Mathematicians (created in 1934) were revived in Bucharest. Other non-governmental civil bodies were created: the Permanent Conference of Engineers in South East Europe (Athens, 1972), the Conference of Red Cross and Red Crescent Societies (Belgrade, 1972), and new forms of cooperation between architects, scientists, athletes, and so forth (the Balkaniads). This fact is important because it demonstrates the role of societies within a state/society complex. In this case, one can argue that governmental multilateral action was reinforced by a parallel participation of the civil society in the multilateral process. In fact, the non-governmental and transnational groups that developed proved to be more immune to the vagaries of official politics and seemed to have had a greater chance of being efficient and durable.

Balkan solidarity was no substitute, from a Romanian perspective, for the larger multilateral game. While a country may seek regional and subregional associations so as not to be swamped in the huge pool of multilateral relations, it was always considered important to have ties with other groups and alliances outside of the regional group of countries with which Romania shares some basic historical interests. Romania sought to do just that when it decided to form a relationship with the Group of 77, as a reprieve from the burdens of the Eastern bloc alliance. One can make the case that the first real approach for membership in the G77 was made *not* in 1968 at the UNCTAD II meeting in New Delhi, but rather in Geneva in 1964 at UNCTAD I. At that time consent was given by the Committee of Ten that was responsible for the agenda of the G77. In any case, as noted earlier, the Romanian government failed to ratify the action of the delegation, fearing that this political step would further aggravate tensions in Romanian–Soviet relations, already strained by Romania's 1964 Declaration of Economic Independence. It took 12 years before Romania finally became a member of the Group of 77.

Romania's linkage to the group of developing countries provided it with a new and useful identity. It opened up the possibility of developing mutually advantageous relations with a group comprising over 125 countries. It did not take long, for instance, before Romanian universities started to receive a large number of students from those countries. Agreements on trade and economic cooperation were concluded, and a number of collaborative ventures sprang up in the areas of raw material extraction, fishing, and transportation. Romanian firms received contracts to build ports, roads, and public buildings, particularly in North Africa and the Middle East.[38] The soldiers of several developing countries wore uniforms made in Romania, and military armaments from Romania found their way into those countries. Romanian-made jeeps were put to test in the Sahara. A great number of Romanian technical experts opted to work in developing countries since this provided them with a rare opportunity to get a passport and travel abroad. The use of a barter system of payments made trade attractive for both Romania and its partners, since they both lacked hard currency. With the exception of some copper mining projects in Peru and diamond production in Central Africa, the experience overall was mutually profitable and helped to establish the high reputation of Romanian technical specialists. This latter point was confirmed in 1991 when Romanian specialists played a role in extinguishing the fires in the Kuwaiti oil wells.

The conceptual basis for Romania's relationship with the third world was its normative quest for revisions in the global economic order and its adherence to the ideas accepted by the United Nations and its specialized agencies. The New International Economic Order (NIEO) was perhaps the ideological trend that had the greatest impact on Romania's foreign policy. Its elements of distributive justice were indeed close to the socialist ideal of equality; likewise, the view of the state as a main agent of development corresponded with the credo of the planned economy. These elements did not, however, fully persuade Moscow, which, while embracing the NIEO in official texts, did so with great reservation, clinging to the idea that "the new economic order" would have to be based on its version of socialism. Romania, in contrast, wholeheartedly supported the claims of developing countries. Because the G77 was divided into geographical areas and since there was technically no European area, the few European developing countries sought to be placed under the umbrella of other regions (Yugoslavia with Asia, Romania with Latin America). In international bodies, the Romanian delegates usually dealt with the practical side of relations with the developing countries such as generating long-term agreements, joint ventures, means of financing, or barter payment arrangements. These contacts with the developing world provided the Romanian economy with some resilience (at least until the 1970s) and in a sense also presented world-scale opportunities. For example, Romanian-made diesel engines were traded in developing countries all round the world for cotton, oil, and ore. An idea that was never fully achieved (primarily because it arose on the eve of the dark period in Romanian foreign policy) but remains of some interest to this day concerns triangular operations: adding Western capital and supplementary technology, plus Romanian technology and technicians, to local labour and resources in order to process raw materials and to develop industry and agriculture in developing countries.

Likewise, the process of decolonization in the 1950s and 1960s touched a nerve in Romania, particularly because it was congruent with the Romanian need to avoid all forms of foreign domination. It is no wonder then that Romanian society supported the liberation movements of the third world and immediately established diplomatic and economic relations with those countries that won their independence from their colonial masters. Unlike other countries (e.g. the Scandinavian ones), Romania's lines of technical assistance tended to be bilateral rather than multilateral, although most of the contacts were made within the multilateral forums of the UN system. But, essentially, the bottom line for Romanian diplomacy was the need to distance itself from practices that could be construed as neo-colonial.[39]

Finally, Romania also pursued relations with other great powers.

152

Among these, its contacts with China can be singled out because of the high level of cordiality and consistency. Romanians followed with interest each stage in the Sino-Soviet rift from the start (which can be traced to June 1960 when Khrushchev clashed with the Chinese delegate at the Congress of the Romanian Communist Party). From 1964 on, the Romanian party took a noticeably neutral position in this quarrel. One commentator wrote at the time that the "effects of the Sino-Soviet conflict are most obvious in Romania. Bucharest very skilfully exploited the conflict to improve its position vis-a-vis Moscow and to resist Soviet demands."[40] For more than a decade, there was a flurry of visits to Moscow and Peking by members of the Romanian Communist Party leadership that were not arranged through governmental channels. Despite the fact that the discourse was highly ideological (debating various interpretations of Marxism–Leninism), the essence of Romanian political strategy was the pursuit of the interests of the state. As proof, one needs only to establish that while the Romanians were engaged in friendly dialogue with orthodox anti-reformist China an almost parallel form of *rapprochement* was being pursued with the overtly reformist Eurocommunist movement.[41] On the multilateral stage, Romania was one of the most active advocates of the recognition of the right of the People's Republic of China to occupy seats in UN bodies.

Owing to strong historical and linguistic traditions, Romania has enjoyed a privileged link with France. Perhaps it is because of this relationship that some analysts have made the observation that Romania's concern with autonomy was not unlike that of France. In fact, one can draw parallels between both countries' attempts to maintain a degree of independence from their respective blocs, although Romania did not go as far as France did when it withdrew from the NATO command. Romania, however, did act similarly when it refused to allow the Warsaw Pact to hold military exercises on its soil, and when it refused to accept the idea of supra-statal control from the alliance's high bodies. The explanation for both countries' moves lies in a similar adherence to, and understanding of, the notion of independence (and of other common views regarding the global balance) as was demonstrated by President de Gaulle on the occasion of an official visit to Bucharest in 1968.[42]

Relations with the United States became more positive, particularly after the Limited Test Ban Treaty was signed in Washington in 1963. Thereafter, American economic agreements and licences allowed the development of the Romanian petrochemical industry, which was considered a high priority at the time and an important pivot of the country's attempt at modern industrialization. The difference between Romania and the Soviet Union with respect to the United States became obvious when, in 1967, Richard Nixon was warmly welcomed to Bucharest whereas in Moscow he had been received with aloofness. When Nixon returned in 1969 in an official capacity, Romania became the first Eastern communist country ever visited by an American President. But when President Carter came to office, he and his National Security Advisor, Zbigniew Brzezinski, shifted US priorities away from Romania towards Poland, and the Republican administration of President Reagan redirected its attention to Hungary and then to Czechoslovakia. Romania, the country that had managed to acquire the status of "most favoured nation" in 1957 (followed closely by China and Hungary), gradually lost its privileged position with respect to its relations with the United States.[43]

There was also an evident attempt on Romania's part to utilize the United Nations as a forum in which to diversify its cooperative ventures with the West. Good examples of this are collaboration with Western countries like Germany and Switzerland for machines and equipment, with the United Kingdom for aviation, with France for computers and cars (e.g. Renault and Citröen), and with the United States for chemical and oil equipment. Romania's trade steadily leaned towards the West until the 1970s, when a rough balance between Western and Eastern countries was recorded.[44] But, at the same time, Romania practised pragmatic bilateralism with countries whose main activities were performed outside the United Nations, based on the idea that such links might protect it from Eastern accusations of being manipulated by the West.

The societal basis of multilateralism

The identification of societal trends is usually more difficult to accomplish in closed and non-transparent societies like those of the socialist Eastern countries. Theoretically, only the activities of the monolithic state, with one party at the top or at the centre, could be considered. Even then information would be difficult to obtain without an insight into developments. However, a thorough examination reveals that in Romania's case there was some evidence that the perception of public opinion played a role in the leadership's creation of foreign policy. Foreign observers have noted the large internal support given to Romania's leadership during the Czechoslovakian invasion in 1968. It is also noteworthy that the reasonable and independent policy of the 1960s was perceived as such and supported by the public. Nevertheless, support for Romania's leadership decreased in the 1970s and was transformed into hostile opposition in the 1980s. Public opinion was therefore an important factor and its expression could not be attributed to any single faction, although the intellectuals were its most articulate element.

In a society kept under very tight control, where only a few creative (writers, painters, musicians) or professional (mathematicians and other scientists, engineers, physicians) associations were allowed to operate within a framework of limited freedom of movement, the relations established in the framework of foreign policy offered individuals in the society a chance to breathe and to obtain (in some cases) the much desired passport that allowed them some freedom of movement outside the country. For the teacher who went to Algeria or Congo, for the construction worker who built roads, hospitals, dams, irrigation equipment, or parliament houses in the Middle East or in the heart of Africa, for the mining experts who went to Latin America, multilateralism embraced by official policy meant the chance to live a meaningful existence. Many specialists did not return, resulting in a brain drain. But those who returned put to use their mental acumen for a new purpose, particularly in the creation of new civic attitudes. In the intellectual field, for instance, there was a tremendous amount of interest shown in the global studies of the Club of Rome, whose reports started to be translated and commented on in the 1970s.[45]

On the basis of the Romanian experience one is tempted to argue, as one analyst of the tendencies recorded in Eastern Europe has put it, that civil society is no longer made up of distinct social groupings (and their affiliated parties, seeking to promote special interests) but is rather clustered around problems that transcend social cleavages. Instead of being part of conspiracies and underground organizations, these movements have now set up a society of their own.[46] They have in essence come to full maturity. Through their internal political experiences and related external ones, these societal forces in the Eastern countries, including Romania, slowly evolved towards the creation of an underlying civil society that coexisted with a state impaired by its corrupt and ineffectual party and ideology. This "parallel polis" voiced in turn its approval, its support, its indifference to, and, finally, its rejection of the policies that the state offered to it.

The most significant instance of the influential role of the UN system on Romanian policy came in 1964 when an internal amnesty resulted in the release of almost all political prisoners.[47] Soon after Romania's admittance into the United Nations, it was hoped that the harsh period of detention and forced labour for those accused or suspected of counter-revolutionary activities in the 1950s would come to an end.[48] It probably would have happened then had it not been for the events in Hungary in 1956, which resulted in a new series of incarcerations. Many of those released in 1964 had been detained in the 1956 round-up. The opposition political parties in Romania, particularly the liberal one (restored after December 1989), have made the case that the amnesty in 1964 was due in large part to the visit to Romania by UN Secretary-General U Thant.[49] During the visit, he received petitions from individuals who took the risk of breaking past the militia's cordons in order to pass the petitions to the Secretary-General. It is well established that in discussions with members of the political élite U Thant raised the general issue of political prisoners and mentioned specifically the petitions that were handed to him. It was simply a matter of time before Romania, a country whose delegates participated year after year in the process of drawing up the Covenants on Human Rights at the United Nations, would be held up to close scrutiny for the apparent divorce between principles and conduct in the human rights area, at least in the matters that were most glaring. Another possible reason for the 1964 amnesty can be linked to the need for the political élite in Romania to generate internal support for its confrontation with the USSR over the well-known economic issues.[50]

Political life after the Second World War was dominated in Europe by the outbreak and unfolding of the Cold War. This climate was responsible for isolation and suspicion, a strangulating control of individual life, political persecution, the strengthening of the state's repressive role in communist countries, the interdiction of travel outside these countries, the limiting of personal contacts, and witch-hunts. These phenomena were only too well known in Romania, and it is safe to say that Romanian society's greatest hope was for the removal of East–West tension. During the Cold War a vast literature was devoted to its genesis and description, but, until the 1960s, less emphasis was placed on the attempts to put an end to it. Although its attempts were time and again overturned by crises, Romanian diplomacy played a significant role in pushing the notion of a thaw in the East–West Cold War environment. Its own conceptions of *détente* and "peaceful coexistence" differed from Moscow's understanding. While "peaceful coexistence," for instance, was a term intermittently proclaimed by the Soviet leadership, it was a relatively static and non-progressive concept of a coexistence between blocs. The Romanian conception, on the other hand, aimed at cooperation among countries and across blocs. From that standpoint, the Romanian outlook went beyond the static character of coexistence and the Soviet position that cooperation with the West should be limited to the economic and technological spheres. The Romanian position was based on defusing the ideological conflict and competition between the two blocs, and Romania's steady rejection of bloc logic was manifested on many occasions.[51] One such instance came in 1972 when the negotiations that eventually led to the Helsinki Final Act were launched: Romania proposed the modification of the rules of procedure and called for a rule that would allow each state to speak in its own name.

Conclusion: Romania's stake in future multilateralism

Many analysts refused to accept that there were "shades of difference" between socialist countries and argued, in some instances, that a system that was basically flawed could produce only negative results. These analysts are wrong. Likewise, based on the same Manichean argument, one would hardly be able to find merits in any of the stages of Romania's diplomatic past. But no one can say for certain what would have happened if Prague's spring had been successful, or if Romania's multilateral undertakings in the 1960s had not been appropriated and denigrated by Ceauçescu. Although I subscribe to the view that, because of certain built-in flaws, the most enlightened reformism could not have stopped the eventual collapse of the system, it is possible that, if some basic truths had been recognized, and fanaticism and paranoia had not reigned free instead, many people could have been spared the pain and affliction that accompanied the Ceauçescu regime. Likewise, the gap between the former socialist countries and the West would not have been so wide, their agitation for reintegration into the international system would not have started from the status of a pariah freed from isolation, and their present torments might have been avoided.

In order to speculate on Romania's future position in the world system one must place its experience at the United Nations within the context of the events that have occurred since the collapse of the communist system in Eastern Europe. All of the great global processes that helped in some way to establish Romania's position on the world stage – decolonization, disarmament, and development – have evolved into completely new forms. The end of the Cold War and of the confrontation between rival blocs has meant that the ideologies that fuelled the machines of totalitarian repression have at least subsided for the moment. The ideals of democracy and the market economy now seem predominant across Europe and many other parts of the world.

Once it became clear that the Cold War was ending, the general concern of all ex-socialist countries was to be integrated as quickly as possible into the institutions of Western Europe – basically to "re-enter Europe." In this respect, between globalism and regionalism the emphasis is clearly being placed on regionalism by these states. The current working agenda of these countries includes contacts with the European Union, the Council of Europe, and NATO, and within the CSCE process. This also encompasses a concern for regional and subregional groups (trilateral, pentagonal, and then hexagonal) aimed at bringing about a more rapid *rapprochement* with the West. In this respect, the UN system offers little support for these desiderata. Hence, for the moment at least, the UN system does not figure prominently in the focus of these East European countries, including Romania, and may even be considered less relevant and efficient than regional multilateralism in Europe.

However, these countries' "entry into Europe" has proven to be a much more problematic, difficult, and protracted process than most East Europeans expected. In the Romanian case, it became clear by 1993 that the European institutions, which divided the Eastern countries into those that were making a quick transition to a Western-style market economy and those whose progress was much slower, were treating it with reservation. Only NATO, operating on the principle of non-differentiation, made an exception.[52] The situation, however, began to change in 1993 when Romania was included among the eight Central European states with which the Western European Union established relations of close cooperation, through the signing of the agreement of association of Romania and the European Economic Community, and with the conclusion of an agreement with the member states of the European Free Trade Association.

Given Romania's propensity for "two-track multilateralism" (i.e. regional and global), one should expect that it will be considered an advantage to balance the regionalistic tendency with active participation in the UN system. Even if Romania becomes successfully integrated into the European system, it is likely, like many poorer East European countries whose economic development has lagged behind, to face serious marginalization. Also, the recent enhancement of the United Nations' prestige around the world, and the possibility that it might be reorganized into a more effective organization, are likely to remind Romania of the present topicality of its earlier concerns for improving and reforming the United Nations and strengthening its role in the peaceful settlement of disputes. One special circumstance recently singled out Romania on the UN agenda. As a member of the Security Council, and holding the chairmanship of that body in June 1991, Romania adopted a clear position on the Gulf War. Although it had considerable investments in Iraq, Romania unequivocally supported the actions of the Security Council. The role the Romanian chairman played brought praise from several Council colleagues.[53]

There is another reason why continued activity in the UN system will be important to Romania. North-east and south-east of Romania, battles of considerable proportion are being fought over the principles of unity versus fragmentation. The primary actors in this conflict are former members of two federations – the USSR and Yugoslavia – whose prevarications are clearly evident. In spite of the political influence that Western Europe has exerted upon the course of events, its impact was little perceptible, and, in the final analysis, it was United Nations' forces that were called upon to stop the situation from deteriorating further. Regardless of the end result, whether a protracted war or new flexible solutions, the United Nations stands out as an active agent in situations in the region to which Romania belongs. Although European institutions have treated Romania as unstable, its situation certainly appears stable considering the dramatic instances of fragmentation that surround it. Perhaps Romania might even find itself in a position to contribute to the process of stabilizing this region.[54]

Romania has been trying to define its new roles and its own space in terms of contemporary realities. This was expressed by its Foreign Minister in 1993, who made the following geo-strategic statement about Romania:

As is known, we hold the longest strip of the Western coast of the Black Sea and also the most important harbour facilities. Thus, through its connections with the Mediterranean Sea, Central Asia, and the Middle East, the Black Sea becomes, especially in the context of the post-cold war, a most important link. At the same time Romania controls a sizeable part of the navigable run of the Danube, all this river's mouths, and the Danube–Black Sea Canal. All these acquire new dimensions with the inauguration of the Rhine–Main–Danube canal, opening the prospect for this symbolic river of our continent to become a privileged waterway to all the cardinal points of Europe.[55]

One can gather from this that Romania wishes that the current tendency towards global polarization into antagonist economic blocs should not develop unimpeded, and that competition among these regional economic groupings should not be conflictual. This may be achieved both by accepting the realities of overlapping structures and by acknowledging the norm-setting and arbitration role of world institutions. The tragedies of the former Yugoslavia are being observed in Romania with feelings of empathy, pain, and sorrow. Romania never waged war against its neighbour and now has to pay a high price for implementing the relevant Security Council resolutions that (as in the case of UN sanctions against Iraq) will result in great economic losses for Romania.

The question that most Romanians are asking, along with the rest of the world, is: "Why are crises such as this one not prevented and why is a solution so difficult to find?" One conclusion is that the ligaments supporting international society are found not in the legal documents, the agreements, or the treaties – these can be destroyed in a single night – but in the sound interaction of the parts, held together in the pursuit of a common project of which everyone feels a part. The second lesson seems to be that the search for cultural identity that is the driving force of the process of fragmentation of mankind has to be tempered by the heavy-water of universalism.[56] Cultural relativism untempered becomes an explosive material.

Finally, ways must be found to ensure that the United Nations is not utilized only after the outbreak of a crisis. Here, many of the ideas in current circulation, such as UN "green helmets" (an army of young people who are at the age to qualify for military service but who would be dedicated to pre-emptive peace-building missions), are also articulated within Romanian non-governmental organizations (NGOs). Peace corps, volunteer corps, physicians of the world, ecological world movements, could all be good models for such international contingents, which would combine military discipline with a set of peaceful operating ideas to assist in emergencies, the eradication of diseases, or development projects, and which would inaugurate a new UN international preventive presence.[57]

160

As these issues are debated in Romanian NGOs, it is apparent that some of the elements of the multilateralism that Romanian society would like to practise are articulated by these non-governmental organs. Multilateralism for Romania and others in the future should be based on tangible projects in a world visited by scarcity and deprivation. It should put more weight on the unifying power of civilization and dampen the divisive aspects of culture, and in so doing offer new forms of preventive peace-building around the globe.[58]

Notes and references

1. See UN Resolution [Res.] 995 (X), 14 December 1955. It admitted the following as UN members: Albania, Austria, Bulgaria, Cambodia, Ceylon, Finland, Hungary, Ireland, Italy, Jordan, Laos, Libya, Nepal, Portugal, Romania, and Spain. This was in essence the first concrete step towards universality in the UN system, and it increased the membership from 60 to 76.
2. See Message of the Minister of Foreign Affairs of Romania to the Secretary General of the UN, Security Council Documents S/411, 10 July 1947.
3. Robert Weiner, *Romanian Foreign Policy and the United Nations* (New York: Praeger, 1984), 206. After two introductory chapters, "Domestic and External Sources of Romanian Foreign Policy" and "Romania and International Organization," the author scrutinizes the position of Romania towards arms control, Europe, the NIEO, the Middle East and Africa and decolonization, the specialized agencies, and international law. This book is an excellent source of documentary references on Romania's policies with respect to the United Nations but, for obvious reasons, there are not many insights about individuals inside the system.
4. Mircea Malitza, "Athanase Joja, diplomat," in *Athanase Joja in Romanian Culture* (Dacia: Cluj Napoca, 1989).
5. On the oil industry, see GA Res. 1425 (XIV), 5 December 1959, and ECOSOC Res. 1319 (XIII) and 711 (XXVII). The item on youth was included on the agenda of the GA XV (1960) and the resolution was carried with 25 co-authors five years later: Res. 2037 (XX), 7 December 1965. On economic cooperation see GA Res. 1157 (XII), 26 November 1957.
6. Explanatory Memorandum of the Romanian Government for the inscriptions of the European item on UN General Assembly agenda (19 August 1960).
7. For instance, note the Message of the Romanian Government to five Balkan governments to convene a summit conference for the transformation of the region into a zone of peace and friendship in 1957. The message of 7 June 1959 adds the objective of a nuclear weapons free zone.
8. Romania was also one of the founding members of the IAEA (1956).
9. ECOSOC Res. 554 (XVIII), July 1954.
10. Fred. C. Iklé, *How Nations Negotiate* (New York: Harper, 1964), divides agreements into several categories: extension, normalization, distribution, and innovation, categories that also cover the negotiations aimed at these types of agreements.
11. Documents of the Security Council meetings of 23–25 October 1962.
12. Roll-call in Meeting 1341 of the First Committee, 19 November 1963. Resolution on Denuclearization of Latin America, GA 1911 (XVIII), 27 November 1963. See also Alfonso Garcia Robles, *El Tratado de Tlatelolco* (El Colegio de Mexico, 1967).
13. Jonathan Steele, ed., *Eastern Europe since Stalin* (London: David & Charles, 1974), 125–127.

14. UNCTAD I, Geneva, 1964.
15. GA Res. 2129 (XX), introduced by Romania with Bulgaria, Hungary, Yugoslavia, Austria, Sweden, Denmark, and Belgium. See also A/6207.
16. On Romania's role in the USA–China reconciliation, see Tom Wicker, *One of Us: Richard Nixon and the American Dream* (New York: Random House, 1991), 468, 577, 582, 590.
17. The German Federal Republic and Romania established diplomatic relations and opened embassies on 31 January 1967. This initiative produced irritation among the other members of the Warsaw Treaty, which convened a meeting of the foreign ministers between 8 and 10 February to discuss the situation and to stop the spread of the Romanian action.
18. Armand Bernard, *L'ONU, oui ou non 1959–1970* (Paris: PLON, 1979), 351.
19. The following list is not exhaustive: Aurel Braun, *Romanian Foreign Policy since 1965: The Political and Military Limits of Autonomy* (New York: Praeger, 1978); Mary Ellen Fischer, *Nicolae Ceausescu: A Study in Political Leadership* (Boulder, Colo.: Lynne Rienner Publishers, 1989); Stephen Fischer-Galati, *The New Romania: From People's Democracy to Socialist Republic* (Cambridge, Mass.: MIT Press, 1967); Stephen Fischer-Galati, *Twentieth-Century Romania* (New York: Columbia University Press, 1970); David Floyd, *Romania: Russia's Dissident Ally* (New York: Praeger, 1965); Vlad Georgescu, ed., *Romania, 40 years (1944–1984)* (New York: Praeger, 1985); Trond Gilberg, *Modernization in Romania since World War II* (New York: Praeger, 1975); Ghita Ionescu, *The Reluctant Ally: A Study of Communist Neo-Colonialism* (London: Ampersand, 1965); Kenneth Jowitt and Ian Matley, *Romania: A Profile* (New York: Praeger, 1970); Ken Jowitt, ed., *Revolutionary Breakthroughs and National Developments: The Case of Romania, 1944–1965* (Berkeley: University of California Press, 1971); John Michael Montias, *Economic Developments in Communist Romania* (Cambridge, Mass.: MIT Press, 1967); Daniel Nelson, ed., *Romania in the 80's* (Boulder, Colo.: Westview Press, 1981); Edgar Rafael, *"Entwicklungs-land" Rumänien* (Munich: Oldenburg Verlag, 1977); Michael Shafir, *Romania: Politics, Economics and Society: Political Stagnation and Simulated Change* (Boulder, Colo.: Lynne Rienner Publishers, 1985); Andreas Tsanlis and Roy Pepper, *Romania: The Industrialization of the Agrarian Economy under Socialist Planning* (Washington, D.C.: The World Bank, 1979); Robert Charvin and Albert Marouani, *Les relations internationales des états socialistes* (Paris: PUF, 1981).
20. See ECOSOC Res. 1090 (XXXIX), 31 July 1965; ECOSOC Res. 1274 (XLIII), August 1967. Also Res. 4, 20 June 1965, at the 50th General Conference of the ILO.
21. ECOSOC Res. 1083 (XXXIX), 30 July 1965; GA Res. 2804 (XXVI), 7 December 1971; ECOSOC Res. 1571 (L), 14 May 1971; ECOSOC Res. 1824 (LV), 10 August 1973; ECOSOC Res. 1826 (LV), 10 August 1973.
22. Le développement de la coopération entre les Etats européens, premisse d'un climat de paix et de sécurité. Colloque européen, ADIRI, Bucharest, June 1969; Problèmes de la Conférence pour la Coopération et la Sécurité, 2e Colloque européen, ADIRI, Bucharest, June 1970.
23. E/CONF 60/19, Fifth Resolution. See *Report of the UN World Conference on Population*, Bucharest, 19–30 August 1979.
24. See GA Res. 2667 (XXV), 7 December 1970, Res. 2831 (XXVI), 16 December 1971, and Res. 3075 (XXVIII), 6 December 1973.
25. GA Res. 3073 (XVIII), 30 November 1973.
26. The Declaration on the Peaceful Settlement of International Disputes was adopted by the General Assembly in 1982; see Res. 37/10, 15 November 1982. The guidelines for the commission proposed by Romania were adopted in December 1989; see UNGA 44/415, "Resort to a commission of good offices, mediation or conciliation within the UN."
27. Ceauçescu returned from his trip to China with special admiration for "permanent revolution."
28. *New York Times*, 27 November 1977.
29. *Scînteia*, 30 November 1982.

162

30. In December 1989, Romania had about 400 diplomats in the Foreign Affairs Ministry and abroad, as compared with 1,200 in 1968.

31. There was one case that can be considered an exception: in the area of science and technology, a Romanian representative was elected president of the Fourth Committee of the UN Conference on Science and Technology for Development in Vienna (1979).

32. Upon instructions from the highest level, the Romanian delegation blocked the consensus of the concluding documents of the CSCE Cultural Forum in Budapest (12 October – 25 November 1985) and the CSCE Meeting on the Protection of the Environment (Sofia, 16 October – 3 November 1989).

33. Jacques de Launay, *Titulescu et l'Europe* (Byblos: Strombeck-Bever, 1976).

34. For example, note the intervention of Adrian Năstase, Romania's Foreign Affairs Minister, during the general debates of the 47th General Assembly (23 September 1992).

35. The Association of International Law and International Relations (ADIRI) functioned without interruption from 1964, publishing the *Revue d'études internationales*. ADIRI encouraged research on the UN system. Among the books published in Romania on its activity are: A. Bolintineanu and M. Malitza, *Carta ONU* (Bucharest: Ed. Politică, 1970); M. Malitza, *Diplomatia* (Bucharest: Ed. Didactică si Pedagogică, 1970); Tanase Negulescu, *Romania la Organizatia Natiunilor Unite* (Bucharest: Ed. Politică, 1975); Romulus Neagu, *Organizatia Natiunilor Unite* (Bucharest: Ed. Politică, 1983); Romulus Neagu, *L'organisation des Nations Unies. Un point de vue roumain* (Bucharest: Ed. Meridiane, 1981).

36. R. W. Seton-Watson, *A History of the Romanian* (Cambridge: Cambridge University Press, 1934).

37. Ronald Haly Linden, *Bears and Foxes: International Relations of the East-European States, 1965–1969* (Boulder, Colo.: East European Quarterly, 1979).

38. By the mid-1970s, 20 per cent of Romania's trade was with developing countries and it remained at that level until 1990 (*Statistical Yearbook*, Bucharest, 1992).

39. Romania's historical experience was one in which it witnessed – not merely in a passive way – the disintegration of three neighbouring empires. This rendered it particularly sensitive to the decay of empires. After the Second World War, Romania never accepted the Soviet thesis that argued that the population of the former Bessarabia (about 4 million inhabitants) would speak languages other than Romanian and that the Moldovans could never be Romanians. These statements were considered by the Romanians as being the rhetoric of a colonialist.

40. E. Majorica, *East–West Relations: A German View* (New York: Praeger, 1969).

41. See Roy Godson and Stephen Haseler, *Euro-Communism* (New York: St. Martin's Press, 1978). The authors observe: "The Romanian Party has been the most forthright in defending the Western Parties' claims to independence from Moscow. Poland and Hungary have both revealed guarded sympathy for Eurocommunism" in their propaganda. The Czechs and the Bulgarians, at the other extreme, have taken the lead in denouncing "Eurocommunism" (p. 103).

42. André Fontaine, *Un seul lit pour deux rêves: Histoire de la "détente" 1962–1981* (Paris: Fayard, 1981), 82, 134, 138, 140, 164, 174.

43. A well-documented book on this subject is Joseph F. Harrington and Bruce J. Courtney, *Tweaking the Nose of the Russians: Fifty Years of American–Romanian Relations, 1940–1990* (New York: Columbia University Press, 1991).

44. In the 1970–1974 period, the percentage of Romanian trade outside the COMECON rose from 50.7 to 65.3, the highest among the members of COMECON (Charvin and Marouani, *Les relations internationales*).

45. An international conference on "future studies" was hosted in 1973 in Bucharest.

46. See the special issue of the *Journal of International Affairs* 45 (Summer 1991), no. 1: 1–275, entitled "East Central Europe: After the Revolutions."

47. The first decree of the amnesty of political infractions was issued on 24 September 1955

163

(D.421), and the main decree to pardon the same political category was issued on 16 June 1964 (D.310).

48. This period is retained in the collective memory of Romanian society as the time of the "Canal," after the Danubian Black Sea Canal was built with Romanian political prisoner labour.

49. Note statement by Amadeo Dan Lazarescu, Liberal representative in the Romanian parliament and editor of the newspaper *Liberalul* (1991).

50. J. P. Saltiel, "L'attitude de la Roumanie vis-à-vis d'une planification supranationale," *Cahiers de l'ISAE*, 168 (December 1965).

51. See Fontaine, *Un seul lit*, passim.

52. Special address by Manfred Wörner, Secretary General of NATO, "Perceptions and Concepts of Security in Eastern Europe," in *Report of the Bucharest Symposium of 4–5 July 1991* (Bucharest: ADIRI, August 1991).

53. See Security Council meeting, 5 December 1991, S/PV 3021.

54. It is also noteworthy that Romania adhered to an organization initiated by Turkey and comprising the riparian countries of the Black Sea, which allows it to capitalize on its experience of cooperation with the Middle East. The first summit of the countries of the area took place in Istanbul in June 1992.

55. Teodor Melescanu, speech made at the Academy of International Law, Mexico City, 20 April 1993.

56. By "culture" I mean those beliefs and peculiarities that come from a heritage that discriminates and separates.

57. M. Malitza, *UN Peacekeeping Operations and How Their Role Might Be Enhanced: The UN and the Maintenance of International Peace and Security* (Dordrecht: Martinus Nijhoff Publishers/UNITAR, 1987), 253–262.

58. See Robert W. Cox, "Programme on Multilateralism and the UN System 1990–1995," unpublished paper, United Nations University (April 1991).

Part III
"On the receiving end": Small state perspectives

5

Chilean multilateralism and the United Nations system

Roberto Duran

The backdrop to Chile's multilateral policy

Global and regional multilateralism has been a long-standing feature of Chile's foreign policy. Once the structure of the Chilean state had been consolidated under the 1833 Constitution, from approximately 1840 to 1870 one of the nation's highest foreign policy priorities was the creation of a regional defence organization in anticipation of an eventual attempt by the Spanish Crown to reconquer the South American continent.[1] Between 1870 and 1873 these regional multilateral efforts were slowly transformed into a set of competitive "power political relations." The highlights of this era were the War of the Pacific, a successful military campaign against Peru and Bolivia, and political and economic expansion into the Pacific basin (particularly Polynesia, the Philippines, Australia, and California). The Civil War of 1891 signalled the end of this period, and in 1895 Chile resumed its more multilateral foreign policy focus, playing a significant role in the 1899 Pan American Conference held in Washington D.C. When the League of Nations was founded in Geneva after the First World War, Chile was an active participant and was perhaps a leading Latin American member.

Before the Second World War, increasing commercial competition among South American economies and the global economic crisis of 1929–1936 affected Chile's terms of trade with developed countries.

One consequence of this crisis was a reorientation of domestic economic priorities, favouring industrialization and an increased role for government in the allocation of resources in the Chilean economy as a whole. Because of the disruption to international trade in the 1930s, the crisis also affected Chilean commercial links, particularly those with the United States and Europe. The outcome was a shortage of resources, which denied Chile the ability to pursue unilateral policies based on strategic interests and balances, as it had been able to do during the second half of nineteenth century. It was therefore necessary to adopt a pragmatic approach to foreign affairs.

In this context, multilateral approaches were particularly appealing because they represented an open space for negotiations between powerful and weak countries. Because of its nature, multilateralism enables and encourages the existence of negotiating networks in which diplomatic skills prevail, making formal equality the basis of the relationship between members of the international community. This perspective on multilateralism has informed Chile's foreign policy and diplomatic style since the 1930s.[2] Thus Chile had considered the League of Nations to be the ideal forum for international political cooperation, and therefore believed it deserved strong support from all members, and particularly the Latin American countries. At the same time, the League provided an opportunity for lesser powers to represent their interests *vis-à-vis* the more powerful nations, as well as participate in certain global political issues.

The creation of the United Nations in 1945 was another important landmark in the history of Chilean foreign policy.[3] During the Second World War, Chile and other Latin American countries suggested the creation of a new world organization, whose purpose would be to resolve international conflicts and promote peace and cooperation among states. In 1944, Chile argued for the creation of an international system capable of enforcing peace and of dealing with the political problems that give rise to international conflict, at both the global and regional levels.[4] At this time, several Latin American governments were worried about the implications for inter-American security relations of the American entry into the Second World War, and the differing security interests between the United States and South American nations came to a head some years later during the negotiation of the Rio de Janeiro Treaty in 1947 (the Inter-American Treaty of Reciprocal Assistance, TIAR).[5] This concern over the role of the United States in the region in part helps explain the Chilean interest in global multilateralism.

In response to a Chilean government proposal, the so-called Committee on Neutrality (later the Inter-American Legal Committee) prepared a report that set forth the basic framework for a global cooperative system, to be vested with the political and legal power to resolve conflicts and, most importantly, provided with the institutional mechanisms sufficient to guarantee international peace. Chile's contribution to the final report was significant, since it included suggestions from the Chilean Ministry of Foreign Affairs, which had gathered the opinions of members of Congress, scholars, and international legal experts. It is important to note that, during the Second World War, policy makers relied heavily on the opinions and recommendations of a small cadre of former staff of the League of Nations who had gone on to Princeton University. These officials had a remarkable influence on the select group of Chilean diplomats who went on to dominate Chilean multilateral policy-making for the next 25 years.[6]

It is also worth pointing out that the principles of "functionalism" influenced Chile's contribution to the creation of the United Nations system. A number of drafts and documents prepared by Chilean and other Latin American scholars and officials in the 1940s were inspired by David Mitrany's functionalist perspective on such issues as "international security," "the protection of human rights," and "international equality."[7] This can be clearly seen in light of two of the basic assumptions of the Chilean multilateral perspective:

- the new world organization should be based on the principle of universality;
- the new organization should play a leading role in international social and economic development.

According to the Chilean government's approach, the universal character would prevent, or at least neutralize, manipulation of the main decision-making bodies and mechanisms by the more powerful nations, the dangers of which had been made plain by the bitter experience of the League of Nations. From a strictly conceptual viewpoint, the universality of an organization reduces the potential for monopolization of the decision-making process, and conversely increases the opportunity for participation by less developed countries, such as Chile. Secondly the purpose of this new institution would be not only to achieve global security, but also to foster international cooperation in the fight against poverty and underdevelopment. This was the most clearly functionalist aspect of the Chilean position, a view shared, furthermore, by all Latin American countries.

Chile's participation in the UN system

The record of Chile's participation in the United Nations between 1945 and 1992 divides itself naturally into three stages, marked by the beginning and the end of military government. The first, between 1945 and 1973, was undoubtedly the most active and successful period of Chilean multilateralism. Chile's multilateral activity was in part driven by economic motives. The disappointingly meagre trade between Latin America and the main European and North American markets on the one hand, and the enormous political and commercial limitations of economic bilateralism on the other, led to the conclusion that the strengthening of global multilateralism was acceptable as a rational and gradual means of pursuing a solution to underdevelopment. This was the understanding implicit in Chile's multilateral and foreign policy orientation from the early 1940s until the beginning of the 1970s.

Chile's multilateral activism was also manifest in the Economic and Social Council (ECOSOC), particularly in 1947, which was a crucial, pre-Cold War year for the United Nations. Discussions were focused on very sensitive issues surrounding international trade, and the importance most governments placed on enhancing their positions and securing the attention that they felt their resolutions deserved was reflected in the high status of the delegation members. In a previous ECOSOC meeting, the Chilean delegation had been among those charged with organizing an international conference on trade and development, for which purpose a preparatory committee made up of 19 countries was created. This committee prepared a report for the fourth meeting of the ECOSOC, which scheduled the conference to be held at the end of 1947 in Havana. As is well known, the ill-fated Havana Charter failed to create an international trade organization and resulted in the twin-track development of global economic institutions within the GATT/Bretton Woods system and in the United Nations. On the UN track, a first step was taken towards the UNCTAD, which was created in 1964 and in which Chile assumed a high-profile role among the Latin American and Group of 77 (G77) countries.

Also in 1947, the General Assembly set up an ad hoc committee to study the creation of an Economic Commission for Latin America under the aegis of the ECOSOC, with the purpose of assessing underdevelopment and poverty in the region. Chile, elected to this committee along with three other Latin American countries, suggested the preparation of the first regional survey of the Latin American economy. Following the recommendations of the survey, Chile proposed the creation of a regional organization to deal specifically with the problems of Latin American social and economic development. The following year an agreement was reached in the United Nations to support the creation of the Economic Commission for Latin America (ECLA). ECLA, supported by the work of academics and professionals, has played a major role in developing a theoretical and policy-relevant regional perspective on the chronic problems of underdevelopment – including poverty, illiteracy, unemployment, pollution, and many other issues connected with underdevelopment. ECLA's distinct doctrine of "dependency" (developed under the leadership of director Raúl Prebisch) played a special role among high-ranking Latin American officials, particularly in the foreign service, in central banks, in financial and trading organizations, and in organized labour and other non-governmental organizations. In this way, during the first attempts at regional cooperation in the period from the 1950s to the early 1970s, the various actors were "indoctrinated" or socialized into ECLA's views. The Chilean political élite was no exception.

Between 1960 and 1973, Chile's relationship with the United Nations remained generally stable. The nation's permanent delegations to New York and Geneva, as well as the additional delegates attending the annual General Assembly meetings, were staffed by highly qualified personnel, including officials from the Ministry of Foreign Affairs and members of Congress. During this period, two matters on the international agenda were of particular interest to the Chilean government: world disarmament and nuclear testing, and decolonization.

With respect to disarmament, Chile was particularly active in two fields. It supported negotiations between the superpowers to secure an effective agreement on limiting nuclear weapons, in full agreement with the spirit of a decade that saw the international community engaged in the task of achieving a strategic-political balance between the superpowers in the wake of the 1962 Cuban missile crisis. In fact, Chile's position *vis-à-vis* nuclear weapons was consistent with the global attitude with respect to the arms race. Chile also promoted disarmament among Latin American countries in order to free resources devoted to defence for investment in projects aimed at reducing social marginalization, unemployment, and extreme poverty. In 1972 and 1973, Chile increased its participation in disarmament matters as a member of a 31-nation committee charged with organizing a world conference on disarmament. It also expanded the scope of its participation to deal with issues such as youth and women's equality, in general taking a renewed interest in the many matters related to international social development. The speech delivered by President Salvador Allende to the General Assembly in 1972 marked the close of the most active period of Chilean multilateral participation.[8]

Regarding the issue of decolonization, the Chilean government strongly adhered to the principle of self-determination of peoples. Aside from being in accord with the spirit of the San Francisco Charter, this principle had been a traditional element of Chilean diplomacy since the middle of the nineteenth century. Further, the Chilean position on decolonization was strongly informed by two perspectives:

- the understanding that independence or political autonomy automatically brings with it the status of sovereign equality with other states in the international system, a view that was particularly relevant to the African and Asian decolonization process;
- solidarity with other Latin American states (Chile, for example, has supported the legitimacy of Argentina's long-standing claim to sovereignty over the Malvinas/Falkland Islands).[9]

Between 1970 and 1973, Chile reinforced its presence in the UN Commission on Decolonization, assuming the chairmanship of the council on Namibia. A strong supporter of the anti-apartheid movement, Chile's human rights activism dated from its participation in approving the Universal Declaration of Human Rights in 1948. When this position is compared with the strange alignment between the Chilean military regime and the South African government from 1976 onwards, it is easy to understand the impact that ideology has had on the foreign policy-making of developing countries, and the extent to which ideology is decisive in the evaluation of national interests.

Finally, another significant characteristic of Chile's multilateral policy between 1945 and 1973 was its solidarity on certain issues with the other Latin American countries. There were two explanations for this. First, the 1960s and early 1970s were a "belle époque" in world politics from the Chilean perspective, with an international climate that fostered a great deal of optimism among Latin American countries over the prospects of regional integration. Secondly, Chile's democratic tradition promoted a world-view in which the benefits of solidarity were readily apparent. In general terms, Latin American cooperation and/or integration has been considered possible or desirable only when Chile has been under a democratic regime. Thus, after 16 years of authoritarian rule, Chile has since mid-1990 again joined in several regional networks.

The second stage of Chilean multilateralism refers to the authoritarian period, from September 1973 to March 1990. Chilean diplomatic performance between 1960 and 1973 cannot be explained solely with reference to the governments in office. The documentary record demonstrates that all foreign policies achieve maturity and consistency through years of practice and "trial and error" experiences, and the case of Chile is no exception. These experiences were particularly taken into account within the foreign service, and it was within the foreign service that competence in the design and implementation of Chilean multilateralism resided. In that sense, Chile's multilateral accomplishments of the 1960s and 1970s would have been impossible without the experience accrued since the days of the League of Nations, and this experience could not have been accrued without a bureaucratic establishment capable of passing it on to the next generation of young diplomats. A diplomatic tradition and specialized diplomatic institutions are basic features of the foreign services of developed nations. These features are all the more important in developing nations because of their tendency to unstable political rule, and the consequent irregularity of public, particularly foreign, policies.

One of the traits of the foreign policies of autocratic regimes is their disregard of multilateral issues when these cannot be dealt with through a direct, bilateral, diplomatic style. Authoritarianism exacerbates nationalism and makes paternal conceptions of the national interest pre-eminent. The prospects for foreign policy initiatives are limited by what may be accomplished through bilateral relations, and the perceptions and misperceptions between countries are a result of this peculiar "face-to-face" diplomatic style. Perhaps nowhere is this more clear than in the human rights issues record of the authoritarian government. The paramount importance that human rights had enjoyed, at both the regional and global levels, in Chilean foreign policy since the 1950s came to an end in 1973. Instead of confronting the political consequences for Chile's image and interests caused by international sanctions after the coup, the military government between late 1973 and early 1990 maintained an uninterested attitude, limiting itself to trying to refute the charges levelled annually against it. This scenario was replayed with varying degrees of emphasis at other levels in the UN system, further diminishing Chile's multilateral presence and influence.

With respect to the voting behaviour of member countries in the Human Rights Commission in Geneva, three cases are worthy of comment. First, Pakistan, which in those days also had an autocratic military government, voted in 1982, 1983, and 1984 against imposing sanctions on the Chilean regime. In the second case, the Argentinian delegation adopted a similar position, opposing sanctions against Chile between 1980 and 1983. Argentina's attitude must be assessed in light of the long-standing border dispute between the two countries, which by late 1978 had developed into such a serious crisis that it almost resulted in a war. By opposing sanctions against Chile, Argentina hoped to avoid adding further complications to the difficulties it already had with its neighbour. Because Argentina was, until 1983, also governed by the military, a particular sort of bond was created among these three countries that were in the spotlight at the Human Rights Commission. The third and last case, occurring between 1981 and 1985, was the result of the American government's attempt to establish closer ties with the Chilean military government. In order to foster these ties, the United States also refused to support sanctions against Chile, although on three previous occasions (1977, 1978, and 1980) it had voted in favour of them.[10] In 1977 and 1978 the American delegation had sponsored a motion against the Chilean government, but this approach did not contribute to improving bilateral relations between the United States and Chile, nor did it curb the human rights violations by the military regime.

Domestic factors and Chilean multilateralism

It is important to bear in mind that Chilean political actors have always considered it worth while to participate in the multilateral arena when national interests were at stake, particularly when the limitations of bilateral approaches had become readily apparent. During the 1950s and particularly the 1960s, therefore, multilateralism was a major issue for political parties, as evidenced by the countless debates and hearings in Congress.[11] Latin American integration, disarmament and collective security, economic and social development, international scientific and technological assistance, and many other matters were extensively discussed in plenary sessions and/or foreign affairs select committees of the Senate and the Chamber of Deputies (the Chilean legislature). These activities, of course, came to an end with the closure of the Congress by the military in September 1973. Until that point, however, Chilean delegations to the UN

General Assembly were invariably composed of foreign service staff and Congressmen, and were more than once headed by a Senator or a Representative. From 1965 until their proscription at the beginning of 1974, almost every political party maintained departments and/or ad hoc foreign affairs commissions to keep representatives, members, and partisans informed about the nation's foreign affairs. Between 1930 and 1973, the Congress also played a small direct role in foreign policy, as the appointment of ambassadors, for example, had to be approved by the Senate.

Although political parties did a great deal to promote an informed understanding of international affairs, only a small part of every political organization was clearly interested in foreign affairs subjects.[12] By about the mid-1960s the major parties had each established a "brains trust," which, when viewed collectively, constituted Chile's foreign affairs intelligentsia. This group actively participated in the design of Chilean foreign policy during the tenure of President Frei (1964–1970) and the prematurely terminated administration of President Allende (1970–1973). With respect to UN issues, the stances of different party élites and leaders (e.g. between Christian Democrats and Socialists) did not differ in their essentials. The administrations of President Frei and President Allende, for example, offered a similar perspective on disarmament and decolonization, and both held to a common position in promoting new rules for the international trading system. After 1974, discussion of international matters was restricted to the parties' intellectual élites and some outstanding leaders.

It is also worth highlighting the relative autonomy the foreign service enjoyed in multilateral pursuits, in both the formation of its basic assumptions and the implementation of specific policies. Most of the embassies related to multilateral forums (those in Geneva, New York, Washington, Brussels, and Vienna) were led during this period by officials of the foreign service. Even though the President formulated (as he does today) the general contours of foreign policy, the implementation and administration of foreign affairs were the exclusive preserve of the Ministry of Foreign Relations, even during the first few years of military rule. To some extent, this was a consequence of the efficiency of the Chilean diplomats and their virtual monopoly of foreign policy-making powers, as is indicated by Chile's multilateral activism in the 1970s (e.g. organizing the UNCTAD III conference held in Santiago in 1972). Even during the period of relative quiescence under authoritarian rule (especially in the 1980s),

175

Chile continued to participate in some activities considered important to Chilean interests, such as the UN Conference on the Law of the Sea. In such cases, the foreign service acted autonomously, both in establishing the basic assumptions of the foreign policy and in specifically implementing its multilateral dimension. The foreign service's autonomy must of course be understood in relative terms, as for any bureaucratic entity, particularly in a presidential regime such as the Chilean one.

The reasons for this autonomy of the foreign service and its emphasis on multilateralism are best understood in the context of the Chilean public bureaucratic tradition, of which two aspects are relevant. First, the institutional form of the Chilean public administration was shaped during the second half of the nineteenth century. The Constitution of 1831, the judicial structure of the Chilean state, and the style of the Ministry of Foreign Relations (created 40 years later) were all heavily influenced by the Hispanic and French Napoleonic traditions, which contributed to the establishment of a highly professional public service tradition endowed with great autonomy. The second point is related to Chile's geographical and historical context. Chile's remoteness from European and North American markets, as well as the experience of being involved in three international conflicts during the nineteenth century, reinforced a centralized conception of the management of international affairs. Simultaneously, the improvement in some South American economies and the stagnation of Chile's domestic economy affected its status within the region, pressing Chilean diplomacy to explore alternative foreign policy directions.

Since then, an intense involvement in multilateral affairs has been the hallmark of Chile's foreign policy and diplomatic style.[13] This professionalization of the foreign service allowed Chile to maintain an acceptable international image during the first four years of authoritarian rule, until the military decided to play a more direct foreign affairs role. Between 1973 and 1980, nearly one-third of the foreign service staff were dismissed for political reasons.[14] Those who remained managed to preserve some of Chile's multilateral expertise and maintain links with the various organizations of the United Nations system.[15] As it became increasingly apparent that the military was not about to relinquish power, these links gradually faded, mainly owing to the overt hostility of the regime towards the United Nations, its specialized agencies, or any form of multilateral expression whatsoever. The government conscripted the news media in its campaign against the United Nations, which reached its climax in 1977–1978 with the call for Chileans to "pronounce themselves against the intrusion of supranational organs in Chile's internal affairs." In January 1978, the military regime sought public support in a plebiscite ("consulta nacional") in response to the General Assembly resolution of December 1977 condemning Chilean human rights violations (and calling for sanctions) and the Human Rights Commission finding of confirmed human rights violations between 1973 and 1977. Not surprisingly, the results of the plebiscite solidly supported the government, which used them not only to maintain domestic legitimacy but to justify denying entrance into Chile of a General Assembly special investigative group on human rights.[16]

By contrast, the alleged *Realpolitik* and bilateralist orientation of Chilean foreign policy under the authoritarian regime did not go far beyond the mere expression of intentions, since the diplomatic, political, and economic resources to exercise much power within the region, much less at the world level, were not available. Regardless of its capabilities, the anachronistic anti-communist ideology of the military regime was at odds with the prevailing spirit of the international system during the 1970s: while the superpowers practised *détente*, Chile insisted on being confrontational. Although the government offered various rationalizations for the deterioration in Chile's international status, Chile's anti-multilateral reaction must be understood as merely the expression of a blind foreign policy that had been stripped of its former energy and restrained by authoritarian rule. Consequently, Chile's participation in world politics became disoriented and defensive, and its attitude, with very few exceptions, extremely passive. The Chilean foreign service was allocated very few resources, although it was encouraged to engage in political and trade negotiations both with the major Western states and even with the socialist world.

In the period between 1978 and 1983, Chile adopted what could be called a pragmatic approach in its multilateral diplomatic efforts. The military government tried to minimize the effects of Chile's political isolation by strengthening its diplomatic ties with some African and Oceanic countries, while making some tentative overtures to the People's Republic of China. These efforts failed to produce the desired results, while the annual censures from the General Assembly continued to tarnish Chile's image still further, particularly between 1981 and 1983. In response, a new approach to foreign policy that concentrated on the opening of the economy to the world was adopted, primarily for pragmatic reasons. With the government controlling monetary and fiscal policies, this dual strategy proved a boon for the domestic economy, succeeding in stimulating foreign investment, controlling inflation, keeping the budget deficit low, increasing productivity, and improving the competitiveness of Chilean goods on the world market.

By the early 1980s it had become apparent that the military regime believed it had finally found the correct formula, as the political costs to its international reputation of its human rights abuses were compensated for by its burgeoning international commercial linkages.[17] By 1984, Chile had earned a high reputation in the international market since almost all of its macroeconomic indicators compared favourably with those of the rest of Latin America. In multilateral terms, Chile's economic policies signalled the start of a growing participation in the GATT, and approval from the IMF and the World Bank. Nevertheless, Chile's international political problems persisted, as sanctions continued in protest against the human rights abuses and domestic political restrictions. The European Communities and European Parliament maintained a critical attitude towards the Chilean government (particularly between the first protest demonstrations of 1984 and the plebiscite of 1988), advocating a return to democracy along with registering their disapproval over human rights abuses. In fact, these formal diplomatic measures were part of a complex process in which, arguably, the pressures coming from international partisan organizations (such as the international organizations of Christian democratic, socialist, social democratic, and even conservative parties) were more effective than overt international diplomatic pressure. Each of these groups financed and supported their Chilean counterparts until the electoral defeat of the military regime in the plebiscite of October 1988.

Adding to the pressure already coming from Western Europe, the United States between July and September 1986 threatened to scuttle a US$250 million structural adjustment loan scheduled to be given to Chile by the IMF in November. This loan was part of an agreement to reschedule Chile's external debt payments, and was intended to aid in the structural transformation of the Chilean economy in order to promote an increase in both exports and investment. The threatened American actions were a response to bureaucratic and media pressure, although the US government finally abstained in the IMF vote, allowing the loan to be approved.[18] Nevertheless, the continuing diplomatic and political costs of authoritarianism were apparent.

In brief, there were two dimensions to Chile's multilateral activities during the 1980s. The first was political, and on this dimension Chile's reputation and policies were extremely discredited. The persistent condemnations by the General Assembly (and other bodies) of Chile's human rights abuses created a formidable obstacle to the achievement of Chile's international objectives. The second dimension was economic, and here Chile's successful multilateral economic and trade policies resulted in sustained growth from 1984 onwards. Of the two, the economic dimension has had the more profound impact on Chilean society. Opening Chile's trade relations and economic policies to global market forces has enhanced the competitiveness of Chilean goods on the world market, increased the growth rate of the domestic economy, and reduced unemployment. As a consequence of this success, the neo-liberal economic stance has become an entrenched feature of Chile's multilateral perspective. The transition to democratic government has not resulted in substantial changes in economic policy, and it is unlikely that there will be any change in the near future, since the policy appears to have gained the consensual support of the most influential social and political actors: political parties, businesses and financial holding groups, members of Congress, and labour unions. This has in effect widened the social basis of support for official multilateralism. Not surprisingly, there is a reluctance on the part of the current administration actively to support regional organizations promoting purely Latin American regional integration, since these measures are seen as relics of the 1960s, when a more utopian conception of multilateral cooperation prevailed.[19]

Chile's position regarding funding and organizational issues of the United Nations

The positive attitude of successive Chilean governments towards the United Nations and its specialized agencies remained relatively unchanged between the 1950s and the beginning of the 1970s. During this time, Chile's position was close to that of the majority of underdeveloped countries, although it guarded its right to act autonomously. After 1973, this attitude shifted towards a general aversion to multilateral processes, primarily as a result of the United Nation's isolation of Chile for the military regime's human rights abuses and, to a lesser extent, because of the general crisis of global multilateralism during the 1970s. In general, one can argue that, during periods of political (multilateral) isolation (as Chile experienced in the 1970s and 1980s), nations tend to compensate by adopting a pragmatic approach to foreign policy. This explains Chile's ambiguous stance towards several issues on the UN agenda during this time, in particular towards the UN financial crisis of the 1970s and 1980s.[20]

The reaction to the US-sponsored motion presented during the 1964 session of the General Assembly recommending the application of Article 19 of the Charter to nations that had not honoured their commitment to finance peace-keeping operations in Africa and the Middle East illustrates Chile's pre-1973 attitude towards the United Nations.[21] Although Chile and the Latin American delegations (except for Cuba) supported the American suggestion, Chile reminded the Assembly that denying voting rights to the Soviet Union and the other socialist countries might jeopardize the existence of the organization itself. This argument moderated the strong support the American motion had initially received, and the General Assembly eventually decided to postpone final pronouncement on the matter. Chile's main concern, in other words, had been the preservation of the universal character of the United Nations, and its reservations over (as well as its support of) the motion were an expression of concern over actions that might undermine the organization's legitimacy.[22]

Despite the military government's official reluctance as regards global multilateralism, Chile was moderately active in the Fifth Committee (on financial and budgetary matters) between 1977 and 1979, and participated in drawing up the agendas and organizing committee meetings for the 1980 and 1981 sessions. Nevertheless, Chile's overall UN policy was at odds with the positions of most third world nations. For example, the United Nations was, during this period, in serious financial trouble because of the depreciation of the US dollar and a net decrease in the financial support from the largest contributors. Chile sided with the United Kingdom, the United States, and other Western countries in supporting a tight and balanced UN budget, and was therefore viewed with suspicion by the third world members for whom the organization's financial woes were a result of a lack of commitment on the part of Western governments.

Chile maintained this fiscally conservative attitude throughout the 1980s for two reasons. The first was ideological. The military regime perceived danger in the increasing politicization of the organization's debates, arguing there had been a "notorious infiltration of international communism in[to] the United Nations," and offering as evidence of this the United Nations' continuing allegations of Chilean human rights abuses.[23] By limiting the financial resources of the United Nations, the military government hoped to undermine the primary source of international criticism of Chilean domestic policy. Perhaps more to the point, Chile hoped to deny Fifth Committee funding to send a special investigator to Chile to report on the human rights situation. The second reason was strategic. Since the military regime provoked animosity in most UN member countries, its ability to garner support for its actions and policies was severely limited. Its options were therefore few and, by supporting the Western nations in their crusade for a balanced UN budget, it hoped to find new and more powerful allies in the multilateral system, even if this meant abandoning its traditional allies of the 1960s.

As has already been noted, during the mid-1980s the United Nations was going through difficult financial times, owing mainly to the fact that the United States, its largest contributor (providing almost 25 per cent of its budget), had held back part of its 1986 financial obligation and the entire amount due for 1987. The fiscal crisis hindered the implementation of Resolution 41/213, which set forth a series of already approved reforms that could not be implemented until the huge number of pending contracts for programmes (with more than 150 states) were completed, along with the institutional and physical reorganization that was necessary before the reforms were introduced. However, the tactic of withholding funds to force other member states to modify their policies had not been effective in the past.

Chile could not understand, therefore, what the American motives were for triggering confusion. Since the United States justified its actions on the basis of what it considered to be the United Nations' over-funding of left-wing agenda issues, some delegations thought the Reagan administration made this move to appease American conservative groups, who considered the United Nations to be a puppet of the Soviet Union. While it was true that the Soviet Union's presence in multilateral forums was formidable, from the Chilean viewpoint this did not justify the unilateral demand for modifications to an organization created and maintained by the universal consent of all sovereign states. Even from the pragmatic perspective of the Chilean military regime, the most effective means for resolving international disputes was to negotiate in a spirit of flexibility and accommodation. In any case, the United States was, in relative terms, far less powerful in 1986 than in the immediate post-war period, and it could no longer command the influence it once did. This was confirmed by the tacit admission of the United States in 1988 that its initiatives had failed.[24]

In this puzzling UN maze, Chile today plays a modest but nevertheless important role. In general, it identifies most closely with the interests of the developing world, particularly the Latin American and Caribbean countries. The latter group does not share an ideological position, much less a dogmatic one, but rather has adopted a pragmatic approach aimed at defending and furthering its collective interests. In administrative and budgetary matters, the group's objective is actively to defend all programmes benefiting the development of the countries in the region, as well as encouraging the adoption of the most appropriate strategies to rationalize the UN system. In this context, Chile's role has been to try actively to instill a sense of pragmatism into the Latin American and Caribbean group, in order to better form realistic means to achieve collective objectives. The Chilean delegation has, moreover, stressed to member states the importance of meeting their financial contributions to the United Nations, since internal difficulties of member states, regardless of their nature, are no excuse for not honouring multilateral obligations. Chile has also supported the institutional reforms recommended by the organization and the Secretary-General. It has also deplored the fact that many of the proposed reforms are threatened by the budgetary restrictions faced by the United Nations, and noted that the consequent emergency measures have to a certain extent distorted the whole process of administrative improvement.[25]

Chile's future options

Since 1990, Chile has been engaged in a major effort to reinsert itself into global and regional multilateral networks. At the regional level, Chile has joined the "Rio Group," which includes most Latin American nations and whose primary objective is to formulate common regional trade and security policies. A second, and equally important, objective is to consolidate democratic rule in the region, under the assumption that regional cooperation must be built on a solid political as well as economic foundation. As in the European experience, Latin American regional stability is seen to depend on a system of regional cooperation or integration that will guarantee economic and social development and will not undermine cultural diversity or basic human rights.[26]

Much effort will be needed to overcome the effects of the multilateral crisis of the 1970s. The crisis served to frustrate many of the expectations for Latin American cooperation and integration. First of all, the crisis struck at the legitimacy of regional institutions, particularly because of the meagre results they had achieved in promoting regional trade. The widening gap between expectations and results increased the lack of confidence in multilateral organizations on the part of both governments and non-governmental actors. Secondly, the predominance of authoritarian rule in Latin America during that period resulted in a reorientation of priorities away from regional co-operation, so that the multilateral networks that had existed tended to wither. The democratization of the region during the 1980s did not automatically translate into the establishment of cooperation as a regional priority. Thirdly, the new style of multilateralism – more pragmatic and less ideological – will take time to develop the technical and bureaucratic expertise needed to manage the complex task of regional cooperation and integration, as most Latin American foreign services are currently inefficient and lacking in the requisite resources for negotiation and so forth.

In line with the current political and diplomatic resources available for multilateralism, Chilean foreign policy has opted for an "adaptive" rather than a "counter-hegemonic" approach.[27] Two reasons account for this. The first stems from Chile's reinsertion into the international community in the wake of its return to democratic government, and its need to re-acquire the professional skills needed to take advantage of and contribute to multilateral processes. This will be no easy task given the imprint left on Chilean diplomatic expertise by 17 years of military rule. On the other hand, the neo-liberal development model adopted by the military regime has left Chile with expertise in multilateral economic and trade issues, as well as entrenched relationships with the World Bank, the IMF, and GATT. In other words, the coming task of Chilean multilateral policy is to make maximum use of its strengths while mounting a sustained effort to overcome its weaknesses.

The second reason for Chile's adaptive stance is that currently its foreign policy is clearly oriented towards a particular type of multilateral activity. Chile will not attempt to adopt an overt leadership role in the process of Latin American integration, but will contribute to more global multilateralism by maintaining its high profile and effective participation in GATT, the IMF, the World Bank, and other organizations that promote the liberalization of the global economy. Chilean policy is therefore determined to keep a certain distance from potentially risky and inflexible new regionalist attempts in South America, such as MERCOSUR, a regional organization created in 1990 to promote trade and cooperation among its members

(Argentina, Brazil, Paraguay, and Uruguay). Chile's present economic condition, as well as the past and anticipated future growth in its external trade, reinforce an apprehension about inflexible and risky integrationist attempts, which were not satisfactory in the past. This, however, does not imply that Chile will stop supporting regional integration, but merely implies that Chile will assume that such attempts will not entail the creation of new organizations but rather improve the efficiency of existing ones.

Chilean multilateral policy faces three immediate challenges. First, Chile will have to construct a stable domestic state/society consensus framework within which Chilean foreign policy can operate. A strict devotion to "pragmatism" may not be the ideal way to promote this consensus, as it too can become dogmatic and politically inflexible. Secondly, the internationalization of the Chilean economy (in 1991, 34 per cent of the country's GNP was accounted for by exports) poses tremendous problems for domestic modernization policy, since it affects not only the economy but also traditional values and the entire social stratification of Chilean society, which is undergoing rapid transformation. Thirdly, despite official and unofficial efforts to join the North American Free Trade initiative (as manifest in the Canadian–Mexican–American agreement) and to establish links with the European Union and the Pacific basin, regional cooperation will continue to be crucial to Chilean policy makers. Thus circumstances may dictate that Chilean policy in the 1990s will have to combine a flexible diplomatic style at the regional level with a "long-term perspective" at the global level.

Notes and references

1. See Mario Barros, *Historia Diplomatica de Chile* (Santiago: Ed. Universitaria, 1970), chaps. 1 to 4. This work discusses Chilean regional multilateralism during the first half of the nineteenth century. See also Ivan Lavados, Raimundo Barros, et al., *Manual de integracion LatinoAmericana* (Caracas: Universidad Simón Bolívar, 1988), 123–146.
2. Lavados, Barros et al., *Manual*, 151–155.
3. See the Chilean Ministry of Foreign Relations, *Chile y la conferencia de San Francisco*, Official Report on Chilean participation in the conference of the United Nations Organization in San Francisco (Santiago, 1945), 188–190.
4. See *Official Record of the Ministry of Foreign Relations [ORMFR], 1944* (Santiago, 1944), 163–180, 182–185, and 203–228. See also Enrique Bernstein, "La creación de las Naciones Unidas," *Diplomacia*, Chilean Diplomatic Academy, ed. (Santiago, 1985): 21–30.
5. See G. Pope Atkins, *Latin America in the International Political System* (London: Macmillan, 1977), 138–153.
6. This period in the history of Latin American participation in international organizations remains largely unexplored. The interest of Latin American officials in the League of Na-

tions (particularly after 1920) is, however, widely acknowledged by scholars. See, for example, Warren H. Kelchner, *Latin American Relations with the League of Nations* (Boston: World Peace Foundation, 1930), 1101–1211.

7. The influence David Mitrany's framework had on the formation of the United Nations system is well known. See David Mitrany, *The Functional Theory of Politics* (London: St. Martin's Press, 1975), 171–205. The basic assumptions of functionalist thought also influenced the theory and practice of Latin American regional cooperation and integration. See A. J. R. Groom and Paul Taylor, *Theory and Practice in International Relations: Functionalism* (New York: Crane & Russak, 1975), 2–73. For a Chilean perspective, see Roberto Duran, "Chilean Participation in Global Multilateralism: The U.N. Case 1945–1989," paper presented at the ACUNS/IPSA/ISA/IPRS symposium, "The Future of the United Nations," Ottawa, 1990, 4–8. Functionalist assumptions are also implicit in many government documents; see *ORMFR, 1948* (Santiago, 1948), 120–148.

8. See *ORMFR, 1970* (Santiago, 1970), 48–52; *ORMFR, 1971* (Santiago, 1971), 67–69; and *ORMFR, 1972* (Santiago, 1972), 78–94. See also Humberto Diaz Casanueva, "Política multilateral del Gobierno del Presidente Salvador Allende en sus aspectos politicos y de derechos humanos, a laluz de las experienciasde un Embajador," in Jorge Vera Castillo, ed., *La politica exterior Chilena durante el gobierno del presidente Salvador Allende 1970–1973* (Santiago: Instituto de Estudios de las Relaciones Internacionales Contemporáneas, 1987). Jorge Vera Castillo's book also offers a compilation of Presidente Allende's official pronouncements on multilateral policy (pp. 359–407).

9. Chile, however, maintained a low profile in the Falklands/Malvinas affair because of its conflict with Argentina over the Beagle Channel, which lasted from 1977 until 1984. Since the Chilean–Argentinian Treaty of Peace (ratified by both governments in 1985), Chile has strongly supported Argentinian claims, despite the reservations of the Chilean navy.

10. Voting by the General Assembly on motions condemning Chilean human rights violations, 1974–1985:

	In favour		Against		Abstentions		Total	
	No.	%	No.	%	No.	%	No.	%
1974	90	72.6	8	6.4	26	21.0	124	100
1975	95	73.6	11	8.5	23	17.8	129	100
1976	95	71.9	12	9.0	25	18.9	132	100
1977	96	71.1	14	10.3	25	18.5	135	100
1978	96	68.1	7	5.0	38	27.0	141	100
1979	93	73.2	6	4.7	28	27.0	127	100
1980	95	66.9	8	5.6	39	27.4	142	100
1981	81	57.4	20	14.2	40	28.4	141	100
1982	85	59.4	17	11.9	41	28.7	143	100
1983	89	61.8	17	11.8	38	26.3	144	100
1984	93	64.5	11	7.6	40	27.7	144	100
1985	88	60.2	11	7.5	47	32.1	146	100

Source: Heraldo Muñoz, *Las relaciones exteriores del gobierno militar Chileno* (Santiago: Ed. PROSPEL-CERC, 1985), 192.

11. See, for the 1950s, *Hearings of the Chilean Senate* [*HCS*] (March–May 1953), 1–542; *HCS* (June–September 1954), 1–390; *HCS* (June–August 1955), 873–1988; *HCS* (January 1956), 1–181; *HCS* (May–July 1957), 887–2174; *HCS* (May–June 1959), 1009–2024. On the 1960s and 1970s, see *HCS* (May–July 1961), 405–1390, 1394–2294, 2298–3321; *HCS* (December

1961–March 1962), 1104–2189, 2193–3224; *HCS* (May–August 1962), 1–547; *HCS* (May–June 1966), 618–1762; *HCS* (October 1966–January 1967), 1042–2068; *HCS* (June–August 1967), 1584–2611; *HCS* (May–July 1972), 1–812; *HCS* (December 1972–January 1973), 1022–2115; *HCS* (June 1973), 1–83.

12. For statements and studies relating to Chilean multilateralism, see Gabriel Valdés, *Consciencia Latinoamericana y realidad internacional* (Santiago: Editorial del Pacifico S.A., 1970), 205–277. Valdés was the Minister of Foreign Relations in the government of President Frei (1964–1970). See also Manfred Wilhelmy, "Chilean Foreign Policy: The Frei Government, 1964–1970," unpublished dissertation, Princeton University, 1976. Both studies reflect the Christian Democratic Party point of view. For the perspective of the left, see Heraldo Muñoz, "La política internacional del Partido Socialista y las relaciones exteriores de Chile," paper submitted to the workshop "Politicas exteriores Latinoamericanas: enfoques comparativos" sponsored by the Institute of International Studies (University of Chile) and the Institute of Latin American Studies (University of North Carolina), Viña del Mar 1982, 15–36. Concerning the basic assumptions of Chile's multilateral policy, there is no substantial difference between the accounts offered by Muñoz, Valdés, and Wilhelmy. However, Wilhelmy emphasizes a realist perspective, whereas Muñoz and Valdés focus their analysis in a historical-functionalist perspective.

13. Mario Barros, *Historia Diplomatica*, 212–256.

14. Grupo Técnico, *La verdad sobre el Ministerio de Relaciones Exteriores durante el gobierno militar* (Santiago, 1990), 15–88. This is a study prepared by former Chilean diplomats.

15. See Roberto Durán, *La politica y la diplomatica multilateral de Chile entre 1934 y 1984* (Santiago: Ediciones Universidad Católica de Chile, forthcoming).

16. For the official view of the military regime on the General Assembly resolutions, see *ORMFR, 1977* (Santiago, 1977), 583–616 and *ORMFR, 1978* (Santiago, 1978), 507–522.

17. See Merrill Lynch Economics, *The Outlook of Latin America*, March, June, and September 1985 reports. See also Morgan Guaranty Trust Co. of New York, *World Financial Markets*, April, June, and August 1986 reports.

18. See Joanne Omang, "U.S. Said to Be Planning Abstention on Chile Loan," *Washington Post*, 17 November 1986. See also editorial section, *Wall Street Journal*, 7 November 1986.

19. Carlos Portales, "La política exterior chilena en el nuevo contexto política y económico internacional," *Cono Sur* 9 (January–February 1992), no. 1: 1–11; Francisco Rojas Aravena, "De la reinserción a los acuerdos: la política exterior chilena en 1992," *Cono Sur* 9 (January–February 1992), no. 1: 12–18.

20. An interesting theoretical framework for understanding this phenomenon has been offered by Deon Geldenhuys, "International Isolation: Toward a Framework for Analysis," *The Jerusalem Journal of International Relations* 10 (1988), no. 2: 1–25.

21. Article 19 of the Charter states. "A Member of the United Nations which is in arrears in the payment of its financial contributions to the Organization shall have no vote in the General Assembly if the amount of its arrears equals or exceeds the amount of the contributions due from it for the preceding two full years. The General Assembly may, nevertheless, permit such a Member to vote if it is satisfied that the failure to pay is due to conditions beyond the control of the Member."

22. See the Chilean Ministry of Foreign Relations, *The Official Report of the Chilean Participation in the Fifth Committee of the General Assembly* (Santiago, 1987), 24–36.

23. See *ORMFR, 1986* (Santiago, 1986), 216–218.

24. See *ORMFR, 1988* (Santiago, 1988), 64–68.

25. Ibid., 71–75.

26. Statement of the Chilean Minister of Foreign Relations, Mr. Enrique Silva Cimma, in *El Mercurio*, 15 June 1991, 4.

27. See the discussion of these two concepts in the Introduction to this volume.

186

6

Social forces and world order pressures in the making of Jamaican multilateral policy

Randolph B. Persaud

Introduction

By world standards Jamaica is a very small state.[1] The island was first settled by Arawak Indians around A.D. 1000. Columbus landed there in 1494 and systematic Spanish occupation began in 1509. With the rapid elimination of the indigenous population by overwork and European diseases, the Spanish turned to African slave labour.[2] The Spanish themselves were driven off the island in 1655 by an English expeditionary force, thereby setting the stage for making Jamaica into a British colony. Jamaica remained a British colony from the mid-seventeenth century until its independence in August 1962.

Although Jamaica is a typical third world country in terms of its colonial past and structural dependency, it does have some characteristics that justify the claim by some government officials of being a "middle-level" state.[3] With half the population living in urban areas, a literacy rate of 87 per cent, a relatively low infant mortality rate of 17 per 1,000, a high life expectancy of 75 for men and 78 for women, and a per capita GNP of US$1,100, Jamaica does indeed stand apart from most African, Asian, and even Latin American countries.

Jamaica's multilateral diplomacy

Since its independence in August 1962, Jamaica has pursued a particularly active role in multilateral institutions, quite often in a leadership position. This is perhaps best reflected in its membership and activities in the Non-Aligned Movement, the Caribbean Community, the Organization of American States, the Commonwealth, and most of all the United Nations and its specialized agencies. The breadth and depth of Jamaica's participation demonstrate the faith that the country's leadership has in multilateral diplomacy.

Support for human rights and liberation movements

The issues most vigorously pursued by Jamaica in virtually all international forums have been human rights, an end to racial discrimination, with special emphasis on dismantling apartheid in South Africa, the liberation of southern Africa, and a restructuring of the global political economy so as to facilitate a more equitable distribution of the world's wealth. Regionalism has also been of considerable importance, although more so to the People's National Party (PNP) than to the Jamaican Labour Party (JLP).[4]

Jamaica has pushed the issue of human rights in the United Nations more than in any other international forum. In fact, in the first year of its membership of the United Nations, Jamaica proposed that the United Nations declare an International Year of Human Rights. In delivering Jamaica's policy statement to the seventeenth session of the General Assembly, Foreign Minister Hugh Shearer stated: "it is apparent that one of the great unsolved problems of this age is the translation into actual practice of the democratic ideal of fundamental concern for individual rights and for the basic freedoms which man has been endowed by the creator."[5] Jamaica's commitment to human rights and especially to the International Year of Human Rights was so strong that one commentator remarked that Jamaica "has done more to promote this event than any other member of the United Nations."[6] Because of its record, Jamaica won a seat on the Human Rights Commission.

Jamaica has also espoused the liberation of southern Africa and the end to apartheid in South Africa. This issue has been pressed in virtually all multilateral institutions of which Jamaica is a member. Apart from a perfect record in supporting resolutions pertaining to the liberation of Africa in the United Nations, the Jamaican government has also supported the use of force to free South Africa, Namibia, Rhodesia/Zimbabwe, Angola, and Mozambique.[7] In 1965 a government paper, approved by the House of Representatives, outlined a policy *vis-à-vis* Rhodesia that was indicative of government policy toward the liberation of southern Africa as a whole. In part the paper stated:

Jamaica will support any action taken by the United Kingdom, including the use of force to remove the illegal government in Rhodesia. The cabinet also decided that Jamaica will cease to trade with Rhodesia ... passports issued by Mr Smith's government will not be recognised.[8]

Support for the liberation of southern Africa intensified during the 1970s. This was because of not only the heightened intensity of the conflict in the region itself but the accession to power of the PNP under Michael Manley in 1972.

In addition to giving financial assistance to the liberation movements in the region, the Jamaican government was instrumental in organizing broader economic support for the front-line states (FLS). Soon after Mozambique won its independence from Portugal, Samora Machel decided to close his country's border with Rhodesia in order to increase the pressure on Salisbury, even though this had deleterious consequences for Mozambique's economy. In these circumstances, Mr. Manley, at a Commonwealth Heads of Government Conference in Kingston in 1975, used his position of conference chairperson "to secure a commitment by the Commonwealth of material support for Mozambique."[9] This was achieved despite the fact that Mozambique is not a Commonwealth member. Two years later, the Jamaican Prime Minister was able to persuade Commonwealth members to extend this support to all the FLS – Botswana, Tanzania, Zambia, Angola, and of course Mozambique. According to Manley, the principle for such support lay in the "tremendous economic price" these states paid as a consequence of helping the freedom fighters of Zimbabwe and Namibia.[10] Further, Manley was part of the negotiating process that resulted in Namibia's freedom.[11]

In another act of solidarity with the people of southern Africa, the Manley government allowed Cuban troops to land in Jamaica on their way to Angola in 1975. Although Jamaica did not itself send soldiers, the diplomatic and political ramifications were clear. In fact, the United States viewed Jamaican complicity with such seriousness that Secretary of State Henry Kissinger reportedly promised Manley US economic aid if he broke off relations with Cuba and withdrew support from the Popular Movement for the Liberation of Angola (MPLA).[12]

Jamaica, the Non-Aligned Movement and international economic relations

In the area of international economic relations Jamaica has a record of sustained participation in multilateral institutions. Although more pronounced during the 1970s under Manley and the PNP, the country has been strident in its efforts to secure structural changes in the global political economy, which have been pursued through all institutions of which Jamaica is a member, but especially via the Non-Aligned Movement (NAM) and the United Nations system.

During the 1960s the issues most often raised by the government in the United Nations pertained to the terms of trade between developed and developing nations, improving commodity prices for tropical products, the establishment of a United Nations Capital Development Fund, and more access to the markets of developed countries. With respect to the latter, the country gained membership in the International Sugar Agreement in 1963, and, as Donald Mills points out, not only did Jamaica get a voting position on the International Sugar Council, it also took a leadership position in the negotiation of the International Sugar Agreement in 1968.[13]

It is also significant that during the 1960s the JLP government took pride in pointing out that Jamaica was not a typical third world country. As far as the JLP was concerned, Jamaica was set apart from other developing countries by its stable democracy and relatively well-developed economic infrastructure, ready for industrial "take-off." This unique category of the middle-range third world state demanded special recognition, such as trade and investments instead of foreign aid. Delivering the first Jamaican policy statement to the General Assembly in 1962, Shearer challenged the stigma of foreign aid. He stated: "I fail to see why the outflow of capital funds from one advanced country to another should be called investment, but the outflow of capital from an advanced country to a less developed one should be called economic aid."[14] Although decidedly pro-Western and conservative, the JLP government remained critical of the unjust economic relationship between developed and developing nations.

The criticism of the unbalanced and exploitative economic relations between North and South heightened during the 1970s. Whereas in the 1960s Jamaica was satisfied with mere observer status in the Non-Aligned Movement, in the next decade it became not only a full-fledged member of the movement but also one of its leading advocates. The Manley government saw the East–West conflict as secondary to the problems of the third world, claiming "that it was our duty to avoid its entanglements and our duty to resist hegemonic pressure wherever and by whomever it was exerted."[15] But non-alignment meant more than simply staying clear of the Cold War rivalry.

After the Algiers Conference in 1973, the Non-Aligned Movement increasingly focused on global economic questions. In the language of regime theory it may be said that the NAM sought to change the principles, rules, norms, and decision-making procedures of those regimes that underpinned the post-war global political economy.[16] In its broadest terms, the challenge of the South was articulated within the parameters of the New International Economic Order (NIEO). The Jamaican government and Prime Minister Manley himself took a leading role in this venture. Essentially, the government's contribution lay in political mobilization on the domestic and international scene and in negotiations. At a formal level Jamaica had a seat on the Coordinating Bureau of the NAM. This allowed it to act as a broker between countries with divergent perspectives and to reconcile their positions with the objectives of the NAM. Often this meant working outside the purview of the NAM itself. For example, at the Commonwealth Heads of Government meeting in Jamaica in 1975 the main items on the agenda were all pursuant to the NIEO. In 1978, Manley took the initiative to invite several high-level officials to Jamaica to discuss the NIEO. Participants included the heads of state or government of Canada, Venezuela, Nigeria, Norway, the Federal Republic of Germany, Australia, and Guyana. As a former Jamaican ambassador to the United Nations has stated, this was in fact the first North–South summit.[17] Domestically, the political mobilization was so highly showcased that "many in Jamaica thought the NIEO was Michael Manley's idea."[18]

As is well known, NAM meetings, among other things, were used to prepare the Group of 77 (G77) bloc for negotiations in the UNCTAD and elsewhere. Jamaica assumed considerable responsibility in this process, especially in its capacity of chairperson and chief negotiator of the G77 countries. Its ambassador was also chief negotiator on behalf of the G77 on major issues such as the establishment of a common fund for commodities. Given its reputation at the negotiating table, it not surprising that Jamaica was one of a small number of countries invited to the Conference on International Economic Cooperation held in Paris between 1976 and 1977. According to Mills, the meeting was instrumental in clarifying issues that had presented major difficulties at previous UN negotiations. More importantly it cleared the way for the common fund for commodities, an issue over which the North and South had hitherto been dead-locked.[19]

Jamaica's role in the Law of the Sea negotiations

Jamaica also played a major role at the Third United Nations Conference on the Law of the Sea, which led to the UN Convention on the Law of the Sea. In fact, one of the rapporteurs of the conference was a Jamaican, Dr. Kenneth Rattray. According to Dr. Rattray, Jamaica exercised considerable influence at the conference, to the point where, apart from advancing ideas, "we found ourselves courted from all sides," East/West and North/South.[20] Jamaica thus played a role at the conference in building bridges between states with conflicting interests and objectives. It also assumed a leadership position for the developing countries on issues such as the Common Heritage Fund. Much of this influence may be attributed to Prime Minister Manley's stature in the Non-Aligned Movement and especially his role in promoting the idea of a New International Economic Order.

Jamaica also pursued some specific regional objectives at the conference. In particular, it was one of the countries that advanced the idea of a common patrimony in regard to the Caribbean Sea and called for a Regional Economic Zone. This would involve a pooling of living and non-living resources and a system of reciprocal preferential rights for states in the zone. While the Regional Economic Zone was meant to overcome the limitations of living in a "marine desert," it was also an effort to create a regime based on regional cooperation within the larger context of the Law of the Sea Convention.

Jamaica's contribution to the Conference on the Law of the Sea was partly reflected in its securing the site of the International Seabed Authority. According to Dr. Rattray, the Jamaican "quest for the latter was not an idle one." There are tremendous benefits to be derived from having an international organization located in a small country. Apart from international prestige, the Jamaican government was especially interested in the technology that the resource-oriented Seabed Authority would attract.

Regionalism and multilateralism

The two main political parties have had diametrically opposing views, dispositions, and behaviour *vis-à-vis* Caribbean unity, whatever its form. In the process leading up to the West Indies Federation before Jamaica's independence, Norman Manley and the PNP were committed federalists, while the JLP and Alexander Bustamante were firm isolationists. The PNP lost both the 1961 federation referendum and the 1962 general elections. Jamaica thus ironically became independent under the JLP – the party that was not very enthusiastic about independence. But although the West Indian political federation had been dissolved in June 1962 there was still considerable interest among other West Indian leaders in regional economic integration, notwithstanding Jamaica's reservations.

The mid-1960s were a propitious time for regional economic integration among the English-speaking Caribbean states. Lack of development in the region, combined with the possibility of losing British preferential treatment of export products in light of that country's application to the European Economic Community, and the closing off of migration opportunities to the United Kingdom, Canada, and the United States, sent a signal for "unity in diversity."[21] In those circumstances, Guyana and Barbados announced an integration scheme in the form of a free trade agreement under the rubric of the Caribbean Free Trade Association (CARIFTA), to take effect in January 1966. An open invitation was extended to all other English-speaking Caribbean states to join, which was actually achieved in October 1967 with the adoption of the CARIFTA Agreement.

The "virulent localism" that had gripped Jamaica during the growth years of the 1950s and into the mid-1960s, and that asserted itself during the federation question, eventually gave way to economic interest. On the one hand, the foreign investment cycle that had begun in the late 1940s was bottoming out, while, on the other, Jamaica correctly calculated that it had the most to gain from a free trade zone given its relative industrial strength in the region. But even this was accompanied by what was increasingly being recognized for what it was, namely, typical Jamaican reservation. The anchor of any successful attempt at regional economic integration thus joined the CARIFTA on 26 June 1968, but with the proviso that Jamaica "conceived of regional free trade merely as an exercise in economic cooperation – not integration."[22]

Things were to change dramatically with the PNP electoral victory in 1972. If Bustamante and Shearer were equivocal about Caribbean unity, Michael Manley was deeply committed to it. His 1970 *Foreign Affairs* article in which he denounced "insularity" was a good indication of things to come.[23] With this political opening, the integrationists (ostensibly the rest of the CARIFTA countries minus Jamaica before Manley, and minus Trinidad and Tobago) seized the opportunity to transform CARIFTA. Their strategic intervention was articulated in a document published under the title *From CARIFTA to Caribbean Community*, in which they outlined plans for a common market and around which they began to mobilize political support. The scope and magnitude of this document went far beyond the erstwhile CARIFTA Agreement. To no one's surprise Jamaica appended its signature to the Treaty of Chaguaramas in July 1973 and thus formally inaugurated the Caribbean Community (CARICOM). This was in many ways the apogee of Caribbean multilateralism.

The annual Heads of Government conference and the Common Market Council of Ministers are the two chief organs through which CARICOM operates. The former is responsible for the long-term and strategic development of the integration movement and is the highest decision-making authority, while the latter is more concerned with "supervising the operations and development of the common market areas of the agreement."[24] The organization also has a number of permanent standing committees of ministers, each of which specializes in and is responsible for specific issue areas and policies. There are also a number of regional bodies with associate status. These include "the Caribbean Development Bank, the Caribbean Examinations Council, the Council of Legal Education, the University of Guyana, the University of the West Indies, the Caribbean Meteorological Organisation and the West Indian Shipping Corporation."[25] CARICOM also has a secretariat located in Georgetown, Guyana.

In broad terms, three areas of cooperation may be delineated. First, there was a commitment to intensify economic integration via a common market. One notable feature of the undertaking was a modicum of consensus in respect of the "deepening of industrialization," a proposition hitherto anathema to the Jamaicans. Secondly, there was to be increased functional cooperation in areas such as health, transportation, and education. Thirdly, the treaty provided the basis for closer coordination of the foreign policies of the independent states of the community.[26] In due course, this had a significant impact on Community states in the United Nations and other multilateral agencies.[27]

Manley's conception of regional integration was in fact extraregional. In his thinking, Caribbean integration was merely one step in the direction of a more global third world programme of self-reliance. Thus at Chaguaramas, where he replied on behalf of all visiting delegations to the Seventh Conference of Heads of Government, he stated:

We sir, as I think must by now be known, are firmly committed to regional cooperation. We are firmly committed to the process by which we may achieve economic integration. And this is not said as a matter of diplomatic courtesy, but rather reflects our own, may I say overview, of third world strategy in the world at large today.[28]

This broader conception of regionalism in fact led Manley to expand Jamaica's definition of the Caribbean to include Latin American states. His pursuit of JAVEMEX, an arrangement among Jamaica, Venezuela, and Mexico jointly to develop an enhanced alumina production capacity outside the framework of the bauxite multinationals, was, in part, due to this expanded vision of the Caribbean region. This venture not only strained relations with Trinidad and Tobago, but also shook the already weak foundations of the Caribbean Community. The intersection between Manley's conception of regional cooperation and a more general third world strategy could be understood only in terms of his strategic vision of "counter-hegemony" in the global political economy as a whole, a problem that is explored below.

The Caribbean Basin Initiatives (CBI)

During the 1980s under Prime Minister Edward Seaga, Jamaica returned to the provincialism of the 1960s.[29] There was a strategic withdrawal from the Community in favour of bilateralism *vis-à-vis* the United States. Seaga's foreign policy quickly distanced Jamaica from its recent past and in an about-turn tempered relations with the third world bloc. Instead of a policy of solidarity with the South, he seemed more intent on establishing himself as "America's man in the Caribbean." And, unlike Michael Manley, he was well disposed to the logic of the market mechanism, an open field for multinational capital, and faith in the structural adjustment policies of the International Monetary Fund. Apart from a definitive realignment with the West, however, Jamaica's policy in the United Nations did not go through any other significant changes.

Instead of non-alignment, regional integration, and self-reliance, Seaga was more instrumental in forging an American-led mini Marshall plan for the Caribbean via the Caribbean Basin Initiatives. Announced in February 1982, the plan was, *inter alia*, aimed at accommodating preferential treatment for exports going from the Caribbean Basin to the United States as well as facilitating more direct foreign investments in the other direction. In reality this essentially American–Jamaican plan was an expression of both countries' retreat from multilateralism, and concomitantly the attempt to foster a network of partisan bilateralism was ultimately aimed at disciplining "recalcitrant states" in the area. Thus Manderson-Jones is correct when he argues that:

in short, the CBI was not aimed at promoting economic regionalism through cooperation among the beneficiary countries themselves. It was merely an aggregation of bilateral relations between the United States and each beneficiary arising from a common offer to all. In this way it emphasised the traditional dependency of these countries on United States economic and political support.[30]

In addition to the CBI, Seaga was also instrumental in forming the Caribbean Democratic Union (CDU) in 1986 and the Concerned Caribbean Leaders (CCL) in 1987. Both groups have attempted to circumvent CARICOM in important decisions pertaining to the Caribbean. The CDU, which is an ultra-conservative group, is dedicated to the promotion of liberalization in the region. As with the case of Grenada, Seaga bypassed CARICOM and instead used the CDU and the CCL in dealing with the Haitian crisis that developed after the fall of Duvalier. This was underlined when in 1988, at an emergency CARICOM meeting regarding Haiti, Seaga insisted that the meeting be dubbed a meeting of the CCL.[31] These two organizations may, therefore, be seen as political arms of the CBI.

Seaga, currently the opposition leader in Jamaica, is still circumspect about Caribbean regional integration. At the July 1992 regional summit of Caribbean heads of state, he suggested that Jamaica should break away from CARICOM and "not tie [itself] into any grouping which will require [it] to seek arrangements and approval to take major decisions that are in [its] interest."[32] This goes against current thinking in the region, which has demonstrated renewed interest in regional integration. At the last summit a number of positions were adopted in principle that, if implemented, would undoubtedly strengthen integration. Among the proposals are the formation of a Caribbean Court of Appeal, an Assembly of Caribbean Parliamentarians, and a common currency for Caribbean nations. Further, after years of disagreement, the Community has finally resolved problems concerning a common external tariff, which is crucial to an effective CARICOM single market.[33] Finally, the CARICOM heads of state held a special summit in October 1992 to discuss and plan the implementation of 225 recommendations of the West Indian Commission. The Commission's mandate was to review existing economic integration arrangements in the Caribbean Community and to chart a future direction for the Community into the twenty-first century.[34] The voluminous 600-page report was tabled at the summit and was received with satisfaction by the CARICOM heads of state.

The impact of domestic social forces

The structure of a social formation configures the social basis of political power, including state power. In turn the social structure itself is conditioned by the dialectic of competing social forces on the one hand, and the form of state on the other. First, it is important to recognize that the form of state has a determining influence on the production structure and simultaneously on the social relations of production.[35] Essentially this encompasses what is produced, the relations of authority and "cooperation" at the point of production, and the principles of distribution of the social product.[36] Secondly, the form of state develops in relation to two phenomena, namely world order pressures and the configuration of domestic social forces.[37] With respect to the latter, the balance of class forces is of particular significance. This balance conditions the social basis of the state and thereby determines the structure of opportunities for and constraints on state action. As Robert W. Cox argues, "however autonomous such political action may be, it is constrained by its social basis."[38]

As will be shown presently, Jamaica's multilateral policies have varied considerably since independence depending on the party/government in power. Yet it is not sufficient to take "government" as a given and use it as the central concept or site of explanation. On the contrary, "government" is itself part of what has to be explained. In so doing it becomes necessary to subsume government as one element within the more general category of state. Of course the concept of state itself is highly contestable and thus requires some clarification.

The form of state

Notwithstanding their divergent epistemologies, liberal/plural, élitist, and various strands of Marxist theories of the state (namely, instrumentalist, structuralist, and derivationist) share one common denominator.[39] They all see the state as a site of power, an entity that is generally fixed but that is occupied by different groups and interests at different times. Their basic disagreement is over who controls state power and to what end this power is put to use. The respective claims and propositions of these schools are too well known to be repeated here.

In contrast to the schools identified above, the works of Antonio Gramsci and Robert Cox provide the basis for a more dynamic concept of state. Gramsci has both a "restricted" and an "extended" concept of the state. Stephen Gill points out:

the restricted concept of the state corresponds to the "political society" which refers to the state's formal governmental apparatus (administrative, legal and coercive). The "extended" concept sees the state as fused with both "political" and "civil" society.[40]

The restricted concept is thus concerned with the institutional materiality of the state and its authoritative allocation of values, while the extended concept focuses on the way in which power relations are diffused through various institutional and ideological practices in the body of civil society. Hence, state and civil society are not mutually exclusive; rather they are reciprocal co-implications of each other. The relationship between the two lies in the fact that a specific form of state is underpinned by a structural correlation of social forces. The latter is known as a historic bloc.

The concept of a historic bloc makes possible an alternative conceptualization of the state. The state can be seen as a historic bloc constituted by the dominant fractions of capital, which, *inter alia*, provide "intellectual leadership," along with other subordinate fractions. In this way it is possible to see the state as a matrix of class relations integrally bound up with the social structure of accumulation as well as other prevailing social forces. Thus the state is not a permanent thing/institution, but a sequence of historic blocs that take certain concrete organizational and institutional forms. Forms of state are transformed on the basis of the constant metamorphosis of social forces as well as changes in the specificity of their combinations. The intellectual leadership referred to above is provided by what Gramsci calls "organic intellectuals," that is, by the leaders of the historic bloc.[41] The task of intellectual leadership is to provide a comprehensive world-view aimed at incorporating the disparate and recalcitrant (those who resist) groups in the society so as to maintain and reproduce the social order in the image of the power bloc. This is essentially what Gramsci means by hegemony. The principal characteristic of a hegemonic order therefore is that its principle of unity and legitimacy is produced through strategies of consent rather than coercion.

It is crucial to recognize however that a hegemonic order is never fully sutured or completely closed, since this would mean that social transformation would be impossible outside of revolutionary violence. In fact it may be argued that history is propelled by the dialectic of hegemony and its attempted totalizing practices on the one hand, and the resistance and counter-hegemonic alternatives on the other. This dialectic figures prominently in the *making* of Jamaican multilateralism.

The social structure

The social structure of Jamaican society is characterized by a polarized and discordant class system and equally by a sharp division of labour based on race and colour. The relationship between race and class is symbiotic and structural rather than contingent, deriving as it does from the institutions of slavery and plantation society. In the latter, the division of labour was defined on a strict and ossified racial basis. A relatively small number of European planters and slave owners were at the apex of the social and political pyramid, while at the bottom were the mass of blacks brought from Africa as slaves to work on sugar plantations. Free whites made up an intermediary group.[42] After emancipation in 1838, large portions of the black labour force left the plantations, creating a critical labour shortage. The planters responded by importing East Indian indentured labour, as they did for the rest of the Caribbean. The East Indians joined the ex-slaves at the bottom of the social rung. Long before this, of course, the indigenous Arawak Indians were completely wiped out.

Apart from the addition later of Syrians and Lebanese (invariably called "Jews") and Chinese merchants and the emergence of a distinctive group of coloureds, the profile of the social structure has remained intact in its broad outlines.[43] The fundamental difference of course is that there has been steady upward social mobility of educated blacks. The modern form of the social structure is thus conditioned by race as a *longue durée* element.[44] In the post-war conjuncture the economy became deeply penetrated by foreign capital in the form of direct foreign investment. Expatriate capitalists, especially from North America, along with white or (socially) near-white merchants and manufacturers consolidated themselves as the dominant class in the society. Further, in respect of state power, they constitute the historic bloc that underpins the social and political hegemony that reproduces the social structure of accumulation and its attendant social relations. Beneath this group are the mulattoes (alias: browns or coloureds), Indians, and Chinese. This middle group, of which some are petit bourgeois, are mostly engaged in the professions, small businesses, management, trading, and retailing. Mulattoes and educated blacks have moved into important government positions since independence.

The rapid pace of industrial expansion and overall economic growth during the 1950s and 1960s created a differentiated working class. The upper echelon of this class is made up of bauxite and alumina workers who, by virtue of their wage level and political consciousness, constitute a labour aristocracy. They are followed by:

a mass of low-skilled and unskilled labour manning the machines in the "sweat shops" factories, serving the guests in hotels, serving as domestic helpers for middle class and bourgeois homes, performing simple clerical and casual tasks for the state and working in service industries such as gas stations, transport and so on.[45]

To this we may add agricultural workers who labour on sugar, banana, and coffee plantations and immigrant workers who travel to the United States to work in the cane fields of Florida, and to Canada to work in tobacco and farmland areas in Ontario. One of the most significant features of the working class as a whole is that it is overwhelmingly made up of black men and women.

In the case of Jamaica it has already been shown that, in macrostructural terms, the technical division of labour is integrally bound up with the social division through race. Thus, while there are strong grounds for Cox's proposition that social classes stand between production and state, it is equally necessary to add that in the case of Jamaica race is also a mediating structural factor. This is especially so since it has already been demonstrated that race is a *longue durée* element in the "historical structure," where the latter is defined as "persistent social practices, made by collective human activity and transformed by collective human activity."[46] As used here, race is a social category derived out of embedded social relations immanent in the social structure. In other words, it does not exist as a static fact or mere datum, but rather operates vigorously in the constitution and reproduction of the society. In view of the architecture of the social structure already described, it is easy to see that the masses of black Jamaicans are socially dispossessed. This takes many forms but is conspicuous in widespread unemployment, low-paying manual work in the industrial, agricultural, and government services, and a large ghetto population that has been systematically marginalized.

According to Kaufman, "the magnitude of the poverty is staggering."[47] As late as 1977, for example, "only 40.6% of urban dwellings and 6.4% of rural dwellings had piped water; 45% of rural dwellings were only one room."[48] For the same year, 84 per cent of small farmers earned less than 30 Jamaican dollars per week, while 94 per cent of the lower working class and 50 per cent of the working class earned less than 50 Jamaican dollars per week. In all of these categories the average income is either below, or borders on, the poverty line. And, while one and a half times the recommended daily protein (68 grams) was available to Jamaicans (1973/4), the poorest 70 per cent of the population had an average daily intake of only 37 grams. Kaufman also points out that at that time, "in all, one in three preschool children does not receive sufficient food energy and protein. Almost half of pregnant and lactating women are anaemic."[49]

In addition to economic marginalization there is also a combination of cultural/ideological "problematics" that further places blacks at the periphery of Jamaican society. This large mass of subaltern blacks have become critical to popular mobilization for the two dominant political parties. To put it differently, black Jamaicans and the politics of their identity are a decisive social force in the body politic.

Garvey's legacy and the politics of cultural criticism

It has already been suggested that one of the most consistent issues pursued by Jamaica at the United Nations and in other international forums has been black liberation in Africa. In a real sense the antecedents of such a policy began with the struggle of Marcus Garvey in Jamaica in the early twentieth century. Garvey's conception of black freedom burst out of the proximate conditions of Jamaican society but was not restricted to that theatre of struggle. In his judgement, the oppression of blacks was a global phenomenon and thus required a strategy that privileged race over national identity. For Garvey, the specificity of the political form of black oppression, wherever it existed, was imperialism. When the Universal Negro Improvement Association (UNIA) and its publication *The Negro World* were launched, race was the principal articulation of a counter-hegemonic global social force. Thus Horace Campbell argues that "the importance of Garvey and Garveyism can be analyzed not only in the thrust of the UNIA in its form, but also in terms of the content of *the real philosophical basis of the challenge* which was essentially taken up by a movement of poor oppressed blacks."[50] Domestically the impact of Garvey on cultural consciousness has been enormous. The fervent religiosity of black Jamaicans combined with Garveyism has produced some peculiar cultural forms. One such peculiarity is that the concept of redemption has been reformulated to mean a return to Africa: Jamaica is Babylon. Garvey is often retrieved and deployed by the masses of black Jamaicans in their struggle for equality and social justice. According to Chevannes, "myths about Garvey are therefore part of the national consciousness of the Jamaican poor, dispossessed blacks, once the object of enslavement, still the object of oppression."[51]

The Rastafari movement is the most developed and philosophically cohesive cultural expression of this phenomenon. The Rastafari built a movement of cultural resistance upon the foundation laid by Garvey, and in this sense it constitutes an extension of Garveyism. Rastas have a strong and visceral identification with Africa, their homeland, from which they have been wrenched by imperialism. According to Campbell, "the Rastaman started from the point of view that black people should never forget their African heritage, and in this they linked their future to the redemption of Africa."[52] Politically, they were unfailing in their support for national liberation movements in Africa. This was picked up by reggae musicians who popularized the liberation struggles.

The historical structure of race has had a definite impact on Jamaica's international relations, especially in international organizations. The pan-African movement of which Garvey was the symbolic leader has placed Jamaica in the forefront of black liberation since the early twentieth century. This legacy and the subsequent development of the Rastafari movement and the culture of "dread" that the latter spawned have impelled Jamaican political leaders to join the cause. At the popular level, reggae played a vital role in "alerting" the masses on the question of African liberation. Campbell puts it this way:

the combined efforts of the Rastafarians and their leaders helped to place Jamaica in the anti-imperialist camp, so that by the time the South Africans in-vaded Angola in 1975, the Rasta movement and Jamaica consistently opposed the system of apartheid. Groups like Burning Spear, Bob Marley and the Wailers presented a variant of reggae music which centralized the question.[53]

The diplomatic activity of Jamaican governments in various multilateral institutions in respect of the liberation of Africa should therefore be seen as an extension of social forces within the domestic realm. While indeed the state does have some relative autonomy in the formulation of international policy, clearly in this case government has principally been restricted to determining the form such policy should take. In this instance, race as a radicalized social category in the historical structure has propelled the issue of African liberation and thus constitutes the social basis of state behaviour. Thus, in assessing the relationship between reggae artists and politicians, it was noted that "these artists, who were spearheading the development of a popular culture, were uncompromising in their identification with Africa, such that in 1969 both the ruling party and the opposition leader made pilgrimages to Africa and Ethiopia in an effort to keep abreast of this new pace."[54]

It was suggested earlier that the JLP pushed human rights at the United Nations during the 1960s because, *inter alia*, it was universal enough for a small and newly independent nation to get to the question of African liberation. But why was such a route necessary at all?

Two reasons come to mind. First, the heightened consciousness of the black masses in Jamaica in conjunction with the continuing resonance of forms of Garveyism virtually compelled the first government after independence to address the issue. After all, blacks, apart from comprising more than 85 per cent of the population, also constituted the largest constituency in a clientelistic electoral system.[55] Secondly, the JLP government was sworn to a pro-Western policy, a rather significant factor during the height of the Cold War given Jamaica's proximity to Cuba. In addition, the government was pursuing a development policy that was heavily reliant on foreign capital, US markets, and technology, not to mention American tourists, who also featured heavily in the development path, which mimicked "Operation Bootstrap" of Puerto Rico. This model was underpinned by an alliance of expatriate capital and a local supporting cast of merchants and manufacturers who view the subaltern classes with marked derision.[56]

How then should the government address the plight of black people in Africa? Domestically, there were two antagonistic social forces, one calling for decisive action and the other afraid that such action would be anathema to economic expansion by scaring away foreign capital. Further, too radical a policy would contradict the government's pro-Western (mostly pro-American) position. It is argued here that the pursuit of a policy that promoted human rights was universal enough to accommodate a progressive African policy without incurring penalties from the local dominant classes, international capital, multinational financial institutions, or the United States. Seen this way the government's human rights policy and its African policy were two sides of the same coin.

Between 1972 and 1980 the Jamaican government broached the question of Africa frontally. In large measure this was due to a re-alignment of domestic social forces. At the broadest level the government adopted "democratic socialism" as its official ideology. The development strategy pursued was based on self-reliance, which meant a reworking of the relationship with foreign capital, an expanded role of the state in the economy, the restructuring of production relations through cooperatives, a more egalitarian distribution of the social product, nationalization or increased national control of certain key concerns, and, among other things, increased participation of the masses in the development process.[57]

A number of policies were introduced that specifically benefited the black working class and the unemployed. The legitimization of children born outside of wedlock, easier access to education at all levels, redistributive economic policies such as reflected in taxation policies, and the very ideological disposition of the government won the favour of the masses. If Garvey was Moses, Manley was Joshua.[58] The government also became popular with the academic left and Rastas. In fact, Bob Marley, the most popular reggae artist, often played at PNP political campaigns. And, significantly, reformist members of the Jamaican élite supported at least some of the government's policies.

With the overwhelming support of the black masses and a modicum of support from some sections of the élite, Manley was empowered to act on the issue of African liberation. Further, he did not feel constrained, at least during the early years of the government, by the structural power of international capital and multilateral financial institutions. His objective after all was to diversify the base of Jamaica's international economic network. In these circumstances, therefore, it is not surprising that Jamaica, and for that matter Manley himself, became "aggressive" about the liberation of Africa (that being one of the key issues that the country had pushed in multilateral institutions).

From dependent capitalist development to "democratic socialism"

By the time of independence in 1962 Jamaica was well on its way to becoming a "middle-level" developing country. Up to the Second World War the island fitted classically into the category of dependent societies whose economies are monocultural in nature, specializing in primary products while importing manufactured and capital goods. Its major exports at this time were sugar, coffee, and bananas, buttressed by a small but growing tourist industry. Things started to change dramatically in the early 1950s.

In 1951, a Ten-Year Plan that emphasized the development of a manufacturing sector was adopted. This was strengthened when a second Ten-Year Plan for the period 1957–1967 was later accepted.[59] Both plans were developed within the purview of Arthur Lewis's model, often referred to as "industrialization by invitation." According to Lewis, the limited size of domestic markets meant that industrialization could be feasible only if production was targeted for exports. Secondly, given the shortage of domestic capital, it was necessary to open the economy to foreign capital.[60] This thesis was accepted by the nationalist movement, which also became its major supporter. Contrary to traditional colonial policies, therefore, which saw colonies as suppliers of raw materials and primary products, the nationalist movement was sufficiently vibrant and mobilized to clamour for change towards a more industrial economy.

A veritable economic explosion ensued. Foreign capital, mostly of American origin, poured into the economy, especially in bauxite, alumina, tourism, and banking. Within a decade Jamaica became the largest producer of bauxite and the main supplier to the world's aluminium industry. Industrial expansion took hold in the production of furniture, metal products, chemicals, food processing, garments, and footwear.[61] Economic expansion continued throughout the 1950s and 1960s with record growth rates. Between 1950 and 1962 the Jamaican economy grew at an average annual rate of 7.5 per cent, recording the highest per capita GDP growth for all of Latin America and the Caribbean.[62] This trend continued during the 1960s with average annual growth rates of 5.1 and 6.1 per cent for the periods

1962–1968 and 1969–1973 respectively. The export base of the country thus went through a revolution. There was a general decline of agricultural exports, which were replaced by manufactured goods, alumina, and bauxite, the latter becoming the engine of growth. Thus, while sugar, bananas, and other agricultural products made up 96 per cent of the merchandise trade at the end of the Second World War, by the mid 1960s that figure had been reduced to 37 per cent.[63]

The benefits of the Jamaican miracle, however, were extremely concentrated and did not trickle down through the population. For example, between 1958 and 1968 the distribution of income worsened as the personal income earned by the poorest 40 per cent of the population declined from 7.2 to 5.4 per cent of total national income. And, in absolute terms, the annual income of the poorest 30 per cent of the population fell from 32 Jamaican dollars per capita to 25 Jamaican dollars during the same period. In the same vein unemployment rose from 13 per cent in 1962 to 24 per cent in 1972.[64] The nationalist movement that inaugurated the industrial take-off was gradually usurped by an alliance of foreign capital, merchants who were moving into manufacturing, landed interests, and the technocrats of Jamaica's version of "Operation Bootstrap." These were the forces that underpinned the development strategy and reaped its greatest rewards.

It should not be surprising therefore that Jamaica's policy in multilateral institutions took the direction and form that it did. The JLP government accepted the hegemonic views of the world order and tried to achieve as much as possible within it. In the United Nations system Jamaican policy was geared toward improving its lot in a liberal world economy instead of seeking revolutionary transformation of that order. While indeed the government did question the terms of trade and pressed for the opening of Northern markets as well as the need for a Capital Fund, these were all intended to accelerate the process of industrialization. It is for similar reasons that it joined CARIFTA and the Organization of American States. To the former, Jamaica exported the bulk of its manufactured products, while the latter was deemed to be of importance since it gave access to loans from the Inter-American Development Bank, especially its Funds for Special Operations, noted for its easy terms. Correspondingly, the country's participation in the third world bloc between 1962 and 1972 was half-hearted at best. Its taciturnity *vis-à-vis* the Non-Aligned Movement and the G77 was more of an indication that

Jamaica's destiny was rooted in the North Atlantic. As indicated earlier, much would change in the next decade.

If the industrialization by invitation version of dependent capitalist development was successful in catapulting Jamaica out of economic backwardness, it also managed to exacerbate the class division in the society. The concentration of wealth simultaneously produced a mass of unemployed or underemployed who swelled the ranks of the ghettos. And unless one was employed in the bauxite industry, which made only a meagre contribution to total employment, wages and benefits simply did not reflect the economic miracle. These objective conditions produced by rapid growth ironically became the basis for a fundamental realignment of social forces.

In these circumstances the 1972 victory of Michael Manley and the PNP was seen as a mandate for sweeping changes, and these did occur. According to Beckford and Witter, the key to this election victory was a configuration of three currents: (1) the radical youth movement and progressive intelligentsia; (2) the cultural mass movement deriving out of the Rastafari; and (3) the organization of a mass base for the PNP.[65] As such the PNP was engaged more in the politics of mobilization rather than in the more traditional politics of aggregation associated with Western democracies. Manley actually created a Ministry of Mobilization headed by the party's most astute socialist, Dr. D. K. Duncan.

Manley thus mobilized the economic refugees from Jamaica's growth miracle to rally around the concept of the structural transformation of the economy and society. Further, since the long investment cycle that had begun in the late 1940s had exhausted itself, and the world economy was heading for recession in the wake of the OPEC oil price increases, important elements of the propertied classes perceived it to be in their interest to stand by a leader whom they viewed as essentially nationalist. With this kind of coalition it became possible to launch democratic socialism. This new correlation of social forces was also propitious for a more combative foreign policy.

It was on this basis that Jamaica was catapulted into the international limelight of African liberation and the structural transformation of world order. Manley himself became one of the most eloquent champions of the New International Economic Order. Jamaica's activities in multilateral institutions thus took a radical turn from the previous JLP government. Instead of a lukewarm attitude towards the Non-Aligned Movement and regional integration in the Caribbean, the government became their most ardent advocate. This went way beyond rhetoric, as the example of the bauxite industry demonstrates.

Fighting the bauxite MNCs

Manley has stated that "there is a sense in which the bauxite story was the story of our foreign policy," and indeed there are strong grounds for viewing it thus.[66] Discontented with the total control and exploitation of Jamaica's bauxite resources by a handful of North American multinational corporations (MNCs), the PNP government decided to renegotiate the returns from the industry. The government spent two years preparing for the negotiations through the local Institute of Bauxite and had such detailed knowledge of the industry that it surprised the executives of the companies. The negotiations with the companies turned out to be "an exercise in pure farce" according to the Prime Minister. What particularly irritated the companies was the Jamaican government's insistence that the basis of royalties be switched from a fixed rate per ton of bauxite to the price of aluminium on the world market. Apart from the advantage of pegging its return to the much more value-added aluminium, the government also wanted to benefit from the inflation in the price of the product on the world market. After the companies refused to budge, the government went ahead and unilaterally instituted a 7.5 per cent levy "on each ton of bauxite mined as a percentage of the price of aluminum ingot on the world market."[67]

The government then proceeded to withdraw from the International Centre for the Settlement of Investment Disputes, thereby forestalling any action by the companies through this body. More significantly, the government helped to form the International Bauxite Association, through which it visited other bauxite-producing countries to share its negotiating strategy and mobilize support.[68] And at a regional level the government attempted to organize the industry outside of the controls of the multinationals.

During the 1970s, therefore, Jamaica utilized multilateral institutions as launching pads for structural changes in the global political economy. Unlike the JLP government in the 1960s and 1980s, the PNP challenged the very nature of the world order and, instead of seeking changes within it, the objective was to redefine the order itself. In this sense the ideas articulated and the policies pushed by the

PNP called into question the hegemony of the Northern industrialized countries. Jamaican policy during this period may therefore be termed "counter-hegemonic."

The impact of world order pressures

The foreign policy of states is affected by external factors as much as by domestic social forces. To begin with, the form of state itself is developed in conjunction with and in response to global social forces. Of these, the distribution of power among states and the distribution of "economic activity and wealth" are the most important.[69] In Peter Gourevitch's aphorism, "political development is shaped by war and trade."[70] World order may be seen as the configuration of the inter-state system and the world economy, at least since the nineteenth century.[71]

The inter-state system and world economy are constituted through specific combinations of *longue durée* structures and conjunctural forces. For example, since the Treaty of Westphalia in 1648 the nation-state has been adopted as the principal form of political organization.[72] The secularization of the state and the principle of national sovereignty that were given sanctity in this treaty were first accepted in Europe and then globalized through imperialism. They have been consolidated as historical structures, thus mapping the broad contours of the inter-state system. Similarly, the development of capitalist forms of production in Europe entailed fundamental transformations in the economic, social, and cultural bases of those societies. The political implications of these transformations have been enormous, such as the subsumption of labour by capital on a world scale. Moreover, the sustained imperialism that ensued, especially in the form of colonialism, globalized these capitalist forms of production relations.[73] The world economy thus became a global historical structure that in turn has conditioned the international economic relations of states.[74]

The conjunctural moment may be understood through the concept of regime. According to Stephen Krasner, "regimes can be defined as sets of implicit or explicit principles, norms, rules, and decision-making procedures around which actors' expectations converge in a given area of international relations."[75] While regimes are not fixed and immutable, they do tend to span relatively broad periods of history. Thus, since the Second World War, certain well-defined global regimes (such as those in security, trade, finance, and information) have dictated the terms and conditions of interaction in their respective issue areas.[76]

Perspectives on world order are never free-floating. Rather, they are ostensibly underpinned and circumscribed by their social bases. In the post-war conjuncture, the internationalization of production, finance, and the state, along with the increasing interpenetration of markets, spawned certain transnational social forces. Chief among these was the formation of a transnational historic bloc made up of the leading fractions of international capital, principally from North America, Europe, and Japan. This historic bloc became the basis of a transnational hegemony. In this context Cox explains that:

hegemony derives from the ways of doing and thinking of the dominant social strata of the dominant state or states insofar as these ways of doing and thinking have acquired the acquiescence of the dominant social strata of other states. These social practices and the ideologies that explain and legitimize them constitute the foundation of hegemonic order.[77]

The IMF and Jamaica

The "structural conflict" between the third world and "global liberalism" was especially well reflected in the struggles between the Manley government and the IMF in the late 1970s. The essential conflict between the IMF and Manley revolved around the IMF's orthodox economic liberalism and Manley's insistence on state intervention in the economy. Between 1972 and 1976 the government had introduced a number of reforms aimed at gaining more national control over the economy. This included nationalization of a number of "public utilities, those parts of the sugar economy under foreign control, some textile operations, the flour-refining industry, some financial institutions and hotels in the tourist industry."[78] According to Thomas, in addition to minimizing "economic and social dislocation," the nationalizations "were also expected to increase the state sector's influence over the pace and direction of internal capital accumulation, so that other industries could be developed and forward and backward links within the national economy forged."[79]

But already by 1974 there were indications that the Jamaican economy was on a serious downturn. This was reflected in the rapid decline of foreign exchange, increasing foreign debt, sluggish growth of the gross domestic product (which fell by 4.1 per cent in 1974), and unemployment that remained above 20 per cent. Kaufman attributes the deteriorating economic situation to "the impact of the international recession (which slowed new foreign investment and put a brake on exports), the end of expansion in bauxite/alumina and tourism, the rise of import prices, the rising cost of borrowing money, and the consequent effects of all this on local investment and production."[80] Real wages, however, were on the rise – "contracted wage increases averaged 50–60 per cent in late 1974 and through 1975."[81]

Although Jamaica had been in the IMF under Article VIII since 1963, it was not until July 1974 in the annual staff consultation report that the IMF began to express any serious concerns over economic policy. The principal issues raised pertained to "wage increases, the fiscal deficit, monetary expansion and restrictions on trade and prices."[82] According to Girvan, Bernal, and Hughes, "clearly, the government was tilting the balance between the public and private sector, and between labour and capital."[83] In reality, by March 1976 Jamaica was showing negative net foreign reserves. It was at this time and in these circumstances that Jamaica applied to the IMF for assistance.

Between then and 1980 the IMF and the Manley government entered into several agreements but at all times the relationship was strained, to say the least. In fact, according to Manley, "the IMF made its distaste for Jamaica's policies clear from the start of the discussions."[84] The IMF terms grew progressively more harsh. After Jamaica failed the December 1977 test (on a minor technicality), the IMF insisted on a new three-year Extended Fund Facility arrangement. The terms and conditions for the US$220 million (over three years) were so harsh that they "shocked" the entire Jamaican team, "including strong advocates of choosing the IMF route."[85] Stephens and Stephens point out that "the feeling was widespread among participants and observers that there was an element of revenge in the IMF team's approach for Manley's audacity to mobilize political pressure for the first agreement."[86] Manley himself notes that "it is almost as if it [the IMF] wished to punish Jamaica for daring to mobilize international support."[87] One thing is certain: the IMF used its resources to compel Jamaica to adopt a "development strategy" more conducive to global liberalism and decidedly against the path that the Jamaican government wished to follow. The differences between the government and the IMF were fundamental. Richard Bernal neatly summarizes these differences (see table 6.1).

211

Table 6.1 **Policy differences between the Manley government and the IMF**

Issue	Manley government	IMF
Type of society	Mixed	Dependent capitalist
Dominant sector	State	Capitalist
Ownership of the means of production	State/co-ops, capitalist	Capitalist
Allocation of resources	Planning market	Market
Openness	Reduce	Complete
Accumulation and distribution	State-directed capitalist/cooperatives	Laissez-faire
Investment	State/co-ops, capitalist state to invest in production, distribution, and infrastructure	Capitalist investment in production and distribution. State confined to infrastructure investment
Savings	Public and private	Emphasis on capitalist savings out of profit
Foreign capital	Aid, loans, and regulated foreign investment	Direct foreign investment
Income distribution	Increase labour's share	Increase capital's share
Economic management	Increased state intervention and planning	Laissez-faire with emphasis on monetary policy
Monetary policy	One of several instruments	Most important policy instrument
Fiscal policy	Expansionary	Contractionary
Exchange rate	Dual exchange rate	Devaluation
Exchange controls	Yes, to affect foreign exchange budgeting	Elimination of controls
Trade	Import restrictions and licensing	Removal of import restrictions and licensing
Prices	Controls and subsidies	Removal of controls and elimination of subsidies
Wages/incomes	Increase; pegged to cost of living increases	Decrease in real terms

Source: R. L. Bernal, "The IMF and Class Struggle in Jamaica, 1977–1980," *Latin American Perspectives* 2 (Summer 1984), no. 3: 68.

As table 6.1 indicates, the IMF and the Manley government differed on the most crucial aspects of economic strategy. As Manley himself saw it, the major disagreements were over the following:
- the "expansionary fiscal and monetary policies of the government";
- "the exchange rate and the profitability of tradable goods";

- excess demand in the economy, especially with respect to the level of real wages;
- the dual exchange rate that the government had introduced in 1977;
- "the general question of intervention by the government in the free market system," especially concerning import controls and the government's State Trading Corporation, and;
- "the question of whether the government favoured the public sector in terms of available credit in the banking system and in servicing the debt."[88]

It is interesting to note that the IMF policies in Jamaica during the late 1970s had considerable political ramifications for the PNP and the Manley government. The devaluation of the Jamaican dollar, the wage restraint policy, the reduction of budget expenditure in real terms, the reduction and elimination of subsidies, and the increase in indirect taxes, all of which were key components of the IMF's strategy, sharply reduced real incomes and the standard of living of workers and the unemployed. On the other hand, the freeze on taxes on profits or property along with the incentives to capital (such as price increases to ensure a 20 per cent rate of profit) served only to widen the gap between haves and have-nots in the country.

The opposition JLP seized the opportunity offered up by widespread discontent among workers and the poor severely to criticize "democratic socialism." As expected, the PNP lost the 1980 general elections and Prime Minister Seaga was the first head of state received by President Reagan in Washington. And, although the IMF continued its liberalization policies in Jamaica, the circumstances were remarkably different. To begin, the Fund's policies were ideologically consistent with those of the new government. The IMF seal of approval opened up the vast resources of private commercial bank loans that were so difficult to come by under Manley. Moreover, President Reagan was quick in establishing the US Economic Committee on Jamaica, which was aimed at channelling US investment to the island. At the personal request of Reagan, the Committee was chaired by Chase Manhattan's chairman, David Rockefeller. Foreign aid increased sharply, making Jamaica the third-highest recipient (per capita) of American aid in the world. In the meantime, the Caribbean Basin Initiatives, the Reagan/Seaga grand strategy for the region, was already on the drawing board. Clearly, if Manley and the PNP were punished by Washington and the IMF for challenging global liberalism, Seaga and the JLP were richly rewarded.

Conclusions

For a small country, Jamaica has certainly played an active and at times significant role in global multilateralism. Although there has been continuity between the JLP and PNP governments, it is clear that the two parties have brought different perspectives to the country's international relations. The JLP's conservative and pro-Western position has often resulted in following the American attitude towards multilateral institutions. This was most conspicuously revealed throughout the 1980s when the Seaga administration accepted the liberalism of the IMF and worked tirelessly to build a closer bilateral relationship with the United States.

The *modus operandi* of post-war hegemony is to be found in the regimes constructed through the Bretton Woods agreements and, in a wider context, the United Nations and its specialized agencies. Although principally formed by Western industrialized nations (led by the United States) and exclusive in nature, they have been flexible enough to accommodate the interests of a sufficiently large number of other states to give them legitimacy.

Two other powerful global social forces in the post-war period emerged in the international communist movement, especially in the Eastern bloc countries, and the anti-colonial struggles of third world states. While the Soviet Union was militarily strong enough to be an active participant in the world security regime, it did not have the capacity to assume the broader project of global "leadership." In other words, although it had the capacity for dominance, it did not have the capacity for hegemony; this in part led to its disintegration.

The third world states of Asia, Africa, and the Caribbean, having won their political independence, joined forces with the Latin American states. Together they became a major force in the international system and in multilateral institutions. While many accepted the leadership of the West, others resisted, sometimes by joining with the communist bloc. Some, such as Jamaica, have gone back and forth, depending on the configuration of domestic social forces. Either way, the impact of world order pressures on Jamaica is critical to understanding its position in the multilateral system. The new states became a major force in the states system, generating a whole new category of world order pressures. Any third world state that was willing to experiment with alternative development paths with the aim of reforming or fundamentally transforming its domestic social order was invariably drawn to this new movement. Moreover, it was felt that for domestic transformation to occur there had to be simultaneous (if not prior) changes in global regimes. Thus "developing countries have consistently endorsed principles and norms that would legitimate more authoritative as opposed to more market-oriented modes of allocation."[89] In this respect the non-aligned and the Group of 77 have been the central articulating and institutional instruments of global reform.

Their position was much more congruent with that of the PNP in Jamaica, which has consistently called into question the principles and norms of the various regimes that have dominated the post-war global political economy. Often, this meant taking a leadership position in the struggle against global liberalism and the institutions in which it is embedded. Despite their differences, the experience of both the JLP and the PNP makes it clear that Jamaica's multilateral policies have been conditioned by domestic social forces, the form of state, and world order pressures.

Notes and references

1. It measures only 146 miles in length and 51 miles in breadth (at its widest point). It is located in the Caribbean Sea – 90 miles south of Cuba and 100 miles west of Haiti, with a population of 2.5 million.
2. It is estimated that there were over 150 well-populated Arawak villages when Columbus first landed on Jamaica. By 1611, only 74 individuals were counted. See Erna Brodber, "Socio-cultural Change in Jamaica," in R. Nettleford, ed., *Jamaica in Independence: Essays on the Early Years* (Kingston: Heinemann Caribbean, 1989), 56.
3. In delivering Jamaica's first policy statement to the UN General Assembly in 1962, Mr. Hugh Shearer stated that Jamaica is a country that had "moved beyond the first stages and [is] just on the point of attaining self-sustaining growth" (see *Policy Statements of Jamaica at the United Nations, 1962–1987*, Information Division, Ministry of Foreign Affairs, Trade and Industry, December 1987).
4. For a comprehensive study of Jamaica's policy and attitude to regionalism, see R. B. Manderson-Jones, *Jamaican Foreign Policy in the Caribbean, 1962–1988* (Kingston: Caricom Publishers, 1990).
5. Hugh Shearer, quoted in *Policy Statements of Jamaica*, 5.
6. Harry Glen Matthews, "Jamaica in the United Nations 1962–1966," unpublished Ph.D. dissertation, Claremont Graduate School, 1968, 85–86.
7. For an analysis of Jamaica's voting record in the United Nations, see Jacqueline A. Braveboy-Wagner, *The Caribbean in World Affairs: The Foreign Policies of the English-Speaking States* (Boulder, Colo.: Westview Press, 1989), chap. 5.
8. Donald Mills, "Jamaica's International Relations," in Nettleford, *Jamaica*, 140.
9. Michael Manley, *Jamaica: Struggle in the Periphery* (London: Writers and Readers, 1982), 104–105.
10. Ibid., 105.
11. The Jamaican Prime Minister was awarded a gold medal by the United Nations for his contribution to the struggle against apartheid in South Africa.

12. See J. Phillips, "Renovation of the International Economic Order: Trilateralism, the IMF, and Jamaica," in H. Sklar, ed., *Trilateralism: The Trilateral Commission and Elite Planning for World Management* (Boston: South End Press, 1980), 479.
13. Mills, "Jamaica's Internal Relations," 137.
14. Hugh Shearer, quoted in *Policy Statements of Jamaica*, 3.
15. Manley, *Jamaica*, 106.
16. For an excellent collection of essays on regime theory, see Stephen D. Krasner, ed., *International Regimes* (Ithaca, N.Y.: Cornell University Press, 1983).
17. Mills, "Jamaica's Internal Relations," 146–147.
18. Ibid., 148.
19. Ibid., 147.
20. Dr. K. Rattray, personal interview, February 1992.
21. Anthony Payne, *Politics in Jamaica* (New York: St. Martins Press, 1988), 155.
22. Ibid., 158.
23. See M. Manley, "Overcoming Insularity in Jamaica," *Foreign Affairs* (October 1970).
24. Clive Y. Thomas, *The Poor and the Powerless: Economic Policy and Change in the Caribbean* (New York: Monthly Review Press, 1988), 309.
25. Ibid., 310.
26. See Ramesh Ramsaran, *The Commonwealth Caribbean in the World Economy* (London: Macmillan, 1989), 169–172.
27. According to Thomas (*The Poor*, 318), since 1973 coordination of foreign policies has centred on:
    (i) joint work in promoting the interests of small island states and in protecting them in the international community, especially from the threat of "private mercenary invasion";
    (ii) a joint call to declare the Caribbean a "zone of peace";
    (iii) regional support for the view that ideological pluralism is an irreversible fact of international relations and should not therefore constitute a barrier to strengthening CARICOM;
    (iv) regional support for Guyana and Belize in their territorial disputes with Venezuela and Guatemala respectively;
    (v) a joint statement condemning destabilization, which, it was alleged, was being directed against Manley in Jamaica and Burnham in Guyana; and
    (vi) a unified reaction of a somewhat critical nature to the limited perspective of President Reagan's Caribbean Basin Initiatives.
28. Quoted in Manderson-Jones, *Jamaican Foreign Policy*, 91.
29. For an excellent account of Jamaica's retreat from regionalism under the Seaga government, see Manderson-Jones, *Jamaican Foreign Policy*, chaps. 9–11.
30. Ibid., 145.
31. Ibid., 170.
32. *Jamaica Weekly Gleaner*, 10 July 1992.
33. Ibid.
34. *Equality*, 11 July 1992.
35. Robert W. Cox, *Production, Power, and World Order: Social Forces in the Making of History* (New York: Columbia University Press, 1987), 355.
36. See ibid., 11–15.
37. Ibid., 147–148.
38. Ibid., 355.
39. See Martin Carnoy, *The State and Political Theory* (Princeton, N.J.: Princeton University Press, 1984).
40. Stephen Gill, *American Hegemony and the Trilateral Commission* (Cambridge: Cambridge University Press, 1990), 43.
41. See Antonio Gramsci, *Selections from the Prison Notebooks*, ed. and trans. Q. Hoare and G. N. Smith (New York: International Publishers, 1987), chap. 1. See also J. V. Femia, *Gramsci's Political Thought* (New York: Oxford University Press, 1987), chap. 4.

42. George Beckford, *Persistent Poverty: Underdevelopment in Plantation Economies of the Third World* (London: Zed Books, 1972), 35.

43. See G. Beckford and M. Witter, *Small Garden ... Bitter Weed: Struggle and Change in Jamaica* (London: Zed Press, 1982), 67–71.

44. *Longue durée* is used here in the Braudelian sense. It designates the "long term" or broad expanses in time. Braudel also uses the concepts of "conjuncture" and "event" to designate the medium term and short term, respectively. See Fernand Braudel, *On History*, trans. S. Matthews (Chicago: University of Chicago Press, 1980), 25–54.

45. Beckford and Witter, *Small Garden ... Bitter Weed*, 68.

46. Ibid., 4.

47. Michael Kaufman, *Jamaica under Manley* (London: Zed Books, 1985), 19.

48. Ibid., 19.

49. Ibid., 20.

50. Horace Campbell, "Garveyism, Pan-Africanism and African Liberation in the Twentieth Century," in R. Lewis and P. Bryan, eds., *Garvey: His Work and Impact* (Trenton, N.J.: Africa World Press, 1991), 168, emphasis added.

51. Barry Chevannes, "Garvey Myths among the Jamaican People," in Lewis and Bryan, *Garvey*, 127.

52. Horace Campbell, *Rasta and Resistance: From Marcus Garvey to Walter Rodney* (Trenton, N.J.: Africa World Press, 1988), 89.

53. Ibid., 139.

54. Ibid., 135.

55. For an excellent study on the impact of clientelism in Jamaica, see Carl Stone, *Democracy and Clientelism in Jamaica* (London: Transaction Books, 1980).

56. See Walter Rodney, *Groundings with My Brothers* (Chicago: Research Associates School Times, 1990).

57. For two authoritative accounts on the attempt at fundamental transformation of the political economy of Jamaica, see Kaufman, *Jamaica*; and E. H. Stephens and J. D. Stephens, *Democratic Socialism in Jamaica: The Political Movement and Social Transformation in Dependent Capitalism* (London: Macmillan, 1986).

58. Michael Manley is popularly known as Joshua to most Jamaicans.

59. O. Davies and M. Witter, "The Development of the Jamaican Economy since Independence," in Nettleford, *Jamaica*, 88.

60. See Stephens and Stephens, *Democratic Socialism*, 21–22.

61. Carl Stone, "Power, Policy and Politics in Independent Jamaica," in Nettleford, *Jamaica*, 2.

62. Owen Jefferson, "Some Aspects of the Post-War Economic Development of Jamaica," in N. Girvan and O. Jefferson, eds., *Readings in the Political Economy of the Caribbean* (Kingston: New World Group, 1977).

63. Thomas, *The Poor*, 211.

64. Ibid.

65. Beckford and Witter, *Small Garden ... Bitter Weed*, 78–79.

66. Manley, *Jamaica*, 103.

67. Ibid., 99.

68. Stephens and Stephens, *Democratic Socialism*, 79.

69. Peter Gourevitch, "The Second Image Reversed: The International Sources of Domestic Politics," *International Organization* 32 (Autumn 1978), no. 4: 882–883.

70. Ibid., 882.

71. Cox, *Production, Power, and World Order*, 107.

72. See Adam Watson, *The Evolution of International Society* (London: Routledge, 1992), 195–196.

73. Christopher Chase-Dunn, *Global Formation: Structures of the World-Economy* (Cambridge, Mass.: Basil Blackwell, 1989), chap. 3.

74. See, for example, Immanuel Wallerstein, *The Modern World System I* (New York: Academic Press, 1974).

217

75. Stephen D. Krasner, "Structural Causes and Regime Consequences: Regimes as Intervening Variables," in Krasner, *International Regimes*, 2.
76. See Susan Strange, *States and Markets: An Introduction to International Political Economy* (London: Pinter Publishers, 1988).
77. Robert W. Cox, "Towards a Post-Hegemonic Conceptualization of World Order: Reflections on the Relevancy of Ibn Khaldun," in James Rosenau and Ernst-Otto Czempiel, eds., *Governance without Government: Order and Change in World Politics* (Cambridge: Cambridge University Press, 1992), 140.
78. Thomas, *The Poor*, 213.
79. Ibid.
80. Kaufman, *Jamaica*, 75.
81. N. Girvan, R. Bernal, and W. Hughes, "The IMF and the Third World: The Case of Jamaica, 1974–1980," *Development Dialogue* 2 (1980): 119.
82. Ibid.
83. Ibid.
84. Michael Manley, *Up the Down Escalator: Development and the International Economy – A Jamaican Case Study* (London: Andre Deutsch, 1987), 154.
85. Stephens and Stephens, *Democratic Socialism*, 200.
86. Ibid.
87. Manley, *Up the Down Escalator*, 160.
88. Ibid., 146.
89. Krasner, *International Regimes*, 5.

7

Sierra Leone and the United Nations system

Abiodun Williams

It is not unusual for studies of Sierra Leone to begin on an apologetic note.[1] Writing about a small country that is not often the subject of scholarly analysis, is seldom in international headlines, and is not a major player in the international system seems to require justification. Small may be beautiful, but in the study of international relations it is hardly a characteristic that generates immediate, regular, or widespread attention. The majority of the members of the United Nations, however, are small states such as Sierra Leone that lack significant political, diplomatic, economic, or military influence. This fact has been reinforced by the spate of new members that have joined the United Nations during recent years, and this trend is likely to continue as other newly independent states and micro-states seek UN membership in an age of increasing nationalism.

In a general sense, Sierra Leone's story is that of many weak states that have turned to the United Nations system to achieve a variety of national goals. It demonstrates the faith such countries have had in multilateral institutions, but it also reveals unfulfilled objectives. Their faith was based on the ideals of the organization, such as its commitment to decolonization around the world. It highlights the issues that have been of particular concern to African states, which as a bloc account for one-third of the United Nations' members. It reveals how a small country such as Sierra Leone acting with other members of the African bloc can increase its influence in the United Nations, but how even such a bloc has limits to its influence and effectiveness. As Sierra Leone's economy deteriorated during the 1970s and 1980s, it turned to multilateral institutions, especially the World Bank and the International Monetary Fund (IMF), for assistance, as did many other developing countries that were in the same predicament. As its economic problems continued unabated, Sierra Leone became more dependent on these organizations and the scope of their involvement in the country broadened. The prescriptions they offered carried significant political and social costs, and did not always achieve the intended results. The specific elements of Sierra Leone's relationship with the World Bank and IMF further our understanding of the nature and impact of multilateralism on vulnerable states in the international arena.

The first section of the chapter discusses Sierra Leone's goals in the United Nations and the major issues that have been of concern to it. It argues that participation in the UN system has served three goals for Sierra Leone: achieving recognition, articulating its views, and using the United Nations as an effective instrument to achieve certain ends. Of the three, recognition was the easiest goal to accomplish, and Sierra Leone has had many opportunities to articulate its views in UN organs. Its record in using multilateral institutions as instruments, however, has been mixed. This can be seen in the discussion of the three issues that have been of enduring importance to Sierra Leone, namely, decolonization, apartheid, and economic development. The second section surveys the nature of state–society relations in Sierra Leone, and it demonstrates that foreign policy is essentially an élite activity. It argues that leaders can also view a more active involvement in multilateral institutions as a way of enhancing their domestic prestige, as was the case with Albert Margai and Siaka Stevens. The third section focuses on the role of the World Bank and the IMF in Sierra Leone and some of the consequences of their activities. The final section discusses the future role of Sierra Leone in the UN system.

Gaining UN membership

A striking feature of the evolution of the United Nations has been the dramatic increase in its membership, due primarily to the dismantling of the colonial empires of the major European powers in Africa and Asia after the Second World War. More recently, the independence of the republics of the former Soviet Union has added a number of new members to the organization. When the United Nations was founded in 1945, only four independent African states were among its ranks: Egypt, Ethiopia, Liberia, and South Africa. As successive African countries gained their independence in the 1950s and 1960s there was a concomitant growth in African representation and, currently, Africa accounts for about one-third of the total membership.

On 27 April 1961, Sierra Leone gained its independence from the United Kingdom, as the winds of political liberation blew across the African continent. Like other newly independent countries, Sierra Leone immediately sought admission to the United Nations. Five months later, on 27 September 1961, the General Assembly (by acclamation) admitted Sierra Leone as the one hundredth UN member state. That year, Sierra Leone also joined the International Monetary Fund and the World Bank. For Sierra Leone, membership in the world body provided first and foremost what has been referred to as "accreditation" – "a symbolic and collective recognition by the international political community that [it] was sovereign and independent."[2] And, as has been argued by Robert Jackson and Carl Rosberg, in order to understand why Africa's weak states survive, *juridical* statehood (international recognition) is of more relevance than *empirical* statehood (the capacity to control one's territory).[3] Although many states with juridical statehood or "negative sovereignty" lack the political power and material resources to provide social and economic benefits for their citizens, the principle of sovereign equality is "a stabilizing mechanism of international society."[4] Secondly, the United Nations provided an important international forum for the articulation not only of particular national objectives but of concerns and priorities that were shared by other African states as well. Thirdly, the United Nations was viewed as a potentially effective instrument that could be used to achieve national and continental goals. In this connection, emphasis was placed on using the collective influence and numerical preponderance of the African bloc. Sierra Leone acting on its own would have limited impact on the actions of the organization, but in concert with other African states its influence could be increased. The major arena for the activities of African states has been the General Assembly, which can be considered a global forum. While the General Assembly has less authority than the Security Council, and General Assembly resolutions are not binding on member states, over the years the General Assembly has asserted greater authority in many areas, including the maintenance of international peace and security.

Promoting key issues

One of the enduring concerns of Sierra Leone in the United Nations has been the end of colonialism in Africa. The idea of self-determination gave impetus to its own struggle for independence and liberation from British colonial rule. The United Nations contributed to the spreading of the idea and gave it new legitimacy. Article 1(2) of the Charter declares that one of the major objectives of the United Nations is the development of "friendly relations among nations based on respect for the principle of equal rights and self-determination of peoples." Chapter XI of the Charter, entitled "Declaration Regarding Non-Self-Governing Territories," required colonial powers to promote self-government and to ensure the political, economic, social, and educational advancement of non-self-governing peoples. Colonial powers were also required to transmit regularly to the Secretary-General information on the economic, social, and educational conditions in the territories. Although Chapter XI was a series of compromises between the colonial powers and the countries – primarily the United States – advocating independence for the colonies,

the anti-colonialist forces chipped away at the colonial bastions by seeking to put into operation the principles of Article 73 of the Charter, to expand the coverage of the article to establish the principle of international accountability for the administration of non-self-governing territories, and to mobilize world opinion on behalf of the self-determination of dependent peoples.[5]

In 1960, led by the newly independent countries, the General Assembly adopted Resolution 1514 (XV), a Declaration on the Granting of Independence to Colonial Countries and Peoples.[6] Significantly, the Declaration departed from the earlier UN view of decolonization as an evolutionary process, and asserted that self-determination is a basic right for all peoples regardless of their stage of political, economic, social, or educational development. The following year, the General Assembly created a special committee to oversee the implementation of the Declaration. Originally composed of 17 members, it was later enlarged to become the Committee of 24, under which name it played a major role in the decolonization efforts of the United Nations.

The priority that Sierra Leone would give to decolonization was apparent from the moment it joined the United Nations. Speaking to the General Assembly on the day of its admission, the Prime Minister, Sir Milton Margai, emphasized the importance of the principle of self-determination for African countries. He went on to say that:

When, in future, both within and without the United Nations, we persistently champion the cause of a speedy and final end to ... colonial rule everywhere in the world, we wish the fact to be remembered that we do not speak out of bitterness, but out of conviction that the right of self-determination which we ourselves now enjoy is a right which all men everywhere must enjoy.[7]

The conviction that self-determination is a right that had to be exercised in the colonies and that Africans should govern themselves shaped the policies of successive Sierra Leonean governments on the issue. Sierra Leone's independence was also viewed as inextricably linked with the independence of the remaining colonies, and its own freedom would become really meaningful only when the entire African continent was liberated from colonial subjugation.[8]

As most of the British and French colonies had either gained their independence or were on the road to becoming self-governing when Sierra Leone joined the United Nations, Sierra Leone's anti-colonial energies were focused on Portugal, which was resisting the independence of its colonies (Angola, Guinea-Bissau, and Mozambique), Southern Rhodesia (now Zimbabwe), where the white settler minority was opposed to majority rule, and Namibia, which was administered by South Africa. A major component of Sierra Leone's strategy was rhetorical condemnation in the Committee of 24 and the various organs of the United Nations. Its condemnations were consistently repeated and increasingly trenchant. Speaking before the General Assembly in October 1961, Gershon Collier, the Permanent Representative, warned Portugal that "there will be no peace in Angola until the people of Angola completely shake off the last vestiges of the foreign yoke."[9] The following year, the Foreign Minister, John Karefa-Smart, criticized South Africa's policies in Namibia (South-West Africa) and told the General Assembly that the South African government "insists on flouting the authority of the United Nations by attempting to convert a mandate of the League of Nations into an imperial right to govern the indigenous people against their will."[10] With regard to Rhodesia/Zimbabwe, he deplored the "totalitarian policies and methods of the white minority who, claiming a totally false and undemocratic 'self-government', continue to trample on the rights of the African majority."[11]

While verbal criticism had its place, it could not by itself accomplish the desired goal of political freedom for countries not yet independent. Since 1962, Sierra Leone has been a member of the Committee of 24 and has supported its increasingly forceful demands. Sierra Leone also sponsored and supported resolutions calling for the self-determination and independence of the remaining colonies. In the case of Namibia, it voted for General Assembly resolutions aimed at preventing the annexation of Namibia by South Africa, and calling for the termination of South Africa's mandate on Namibia.[12] With regard to Rhodesia/Zimbabwe, Sierra Leone's first objective (and that of other African countries) was to put the situation in Zimbabwe on the General Assembly's agenda despite the opposition of Zimbabwe's colonial power, the United Kingdom.[13] As the threat of a unilateral declaration of independence (UDI) by Ian Smith's white minority government grew imminent, the central focus was to prevent UDI. Sierra Leone criticized the failure of the United Kingdom to implement the resolutions of the General Assembly on the question of Zimbabwe and urged the Security Council to keep the situation under constant review.[14] After UDI was established by the Smith regime in November 1965, Sierra Leone tried to persuade other states not to recognize the UDI and vigorously opposed Rhodesia's admission to the United Nations. It also supported the imposition of mandatory sanctions against the Smith regime. In an attempt to further the independence of Portugal's African colonies, Sierra Leone supported resolutions critical not only of Portugal, but of countries that were Portugal's allies in NATO. By 1963, the government had banned the importation of Portuguese goods to Sierra Leone and prohibited citizens of Portugal from entering the country. It also advocated financial support for groups fighting for independence from Portugal.

The condemnation of South Africa's apartheid policies has been another consistent theme in Sierra Leone's pronouncements at the United Nations and one of its central concerns. Sierra Leone's opposition to colonialism and its support of the right of self-determination fuelled its opposition to apartheid. Shortly after gaining independence, the new government banned all trade and commercial ties with South Africa, South African aircraft were denied landing rights in Freetown, white South Africans in Sierra Leone were refused re-entry visas, and all white South Africans were prohibited from entering the country.

The United Nations had been dealing with South Africa's racial policies since its inception, before the new wave of African members joined the organization. The issue was first raised in the General Assembly in 1946 in connection with South Africa's treatment of people of Indo-Pakistani origin.[15] In 1952 South Africa's apartheid policy was included as a separate question on the General Assembly's agenda. (Both issues were considered separately until they were combined under the general question of apartheid in 1962.) Because of opposition from the Western powers, however, especially France and the United Kingdom, it was not until 1960 that the Security Council first discussed the apartheid issue. The Security Council's involvement was prompted by the Sharpeville massacre in March 1960, when South African police killed nearly 70 blacks and wounded about 187 others who were peacefully protesting the pass laws. As a result of events at Sharpeville, 29 African and Asian states requested an urgent meeting of the Security Council to consider the situation, which they viewed as having grave potential for international friction, and which endangered international peace and security.[16]

Gershon Collier, Sierra Leone's first Permanent Representative to the United Nations, was outspoken in his denunciation in the General Assembly of apartheid. In his first speech in the General Assembly he condemned South Africa's "nefarious and odious practice of race discrimination" and pledged that Sierra Leone would do all it could "to hasten the day when men of color in that troubled land will be accorded the ordinary rights and decencies which are the true entitlement of every human being."[17] In 1962, Sierra Leone joined 33 African and Asian delegations in sponsoring a resolution calling for a series of measures to be taken against South Africa because of its apartheid policies. On 6 November 1962, the General Assembly for the first time adopted a resolution that recommended the imposition of sanctions against South Africa.[18] Member states were asked to break off diplomatic relations with South Africa or to refrain from establishing them; to close their ports to all vessels flying the South African flag; to enact legislation prohibiting their ships from entering South African ports; to boycott South African goods and refrain from exporting goods (including arms and ammunition) to South Africa; and to refuse landing and passage facilities to all South African aircraft. The resolution also established an 11-member special committee to monitor the racial situation in South Africa and keep the General Assembly and Security Council informed of relevant developments.

On the establishment of the Organization of African Unity (OAU) in May 1963, African states decided on a strategy to persuade the Security Council to impose sanctions against South Africa. They adopted a resolution calling for a meeting of the Security Council to discuss the explosive situation in South Africa, which they regarded as a threat to international peace and security. The OAU designated the Foreign Ministers of Sierra Leone, Liberia, Madagascar, and Tunisia as its representatives to the Security Council. The Foreign Minister of Sierra Leone, Dr. John Karefa-Smart, opened the debate on apartheid in the Security Council in the summer of 1963. He criticized the brutality of apartheid, and argued that the Security Council should impose sanctions against South Africa. He declared:

The South African Government, which is now evading the obligations it has accepted under the Charter, particularly Articles 4 and 25, cannot disregard our decisions indefinitely. The time has come for the Security Council to take positive, firm and immediate action to dispel any doubts as to the determination of the United Nations to ensure that the aims of the Charter are achieved without delay in the Republic of South Africa. The Security Council can take no other position on resolution 1761 (XVII) as I see it – than to support it fully and take up the South African Government's present challenge to the whole international community.[19]

But the resolution subsequently adopted by the Security Council did not impose the mandatory and comprehensive sanctions that the General Assembly had recommended. It did, however, recognize the situation in South Africa as "seriously disturbing international peace and security [and] called upon all states to cease forthwith the sale and shipment of arms, ammunition of all types and military vehicles to South Africa."[20]

Sierra Leone consistently supported the imposition of economic sanctions by the Security Council, although this aim was thwarted by the vetoes of the permanent members, particularly France, the United Kingdom, and the United States. In 1974 Sierra Leone supported an attempt to get South Africa expelled from the organization. After this attempt failed as a result of the opposition of the Western powers that are permanent members of the Security Council, Sierra Leone voted for the suspension of South Africa from participation in the work of the General Assembly in November 1974. Although African states have been instrumental in keeping apartheid on the international agenda, their unsuccessful attempts to get the United Nations to impose economic sanctions against South Africa and to expel it from the ranks of its membership highlight the limitations of the influence and power of smaller states in the organization. As such actions are considered substantive rather than procedural, and thus require the concurring votes of the five permanent members of the Security Council, an exercise of the veto by one of them is sufficient to prevent the passage of any resolution. As Inis Claude has pointed out, "the veto is a weighting device, an acknowledgment of the inequality of states and a means of giving effect to the principle that the most powerful and important states should have special status in international organizations."[21]

Sierra Leone's economic development and its place in the global economic system have been another part of its continuing concerns within the United Nations system. Although the East–West conflict was raging when Sierra Leone joined the United Nations, it has focused from the outset on the importance of North–South relations. It has emphasized economic interdependence as an important element of the relationship between developed and developing countries, and multilateral economic assistance as central to its development efforts. These themes were highlighted by its Permanent Representative, Gershon Collier, during Sierra Leone's first participation in the Assembly's general debate:

We live in times when no one nation can withdraw from the fate and fortunes of the others. It is in this context that the great nations can give economic help and technical skill to the underdeveloped countries of the world. And such help can be most acceptable through international channels and organizations.[22]

There were a number of reasons for this preference for multilateral aid. First, there was a fear of the fact that bilateral aid usually comes with strings attached, such as being linked to the purchase of goods and services from the donor country, often at uncompetitive prices. There were concerns that this would perpetuate the economic influence of the Western countries on Sierra Leone's economy and result in "neo-colonialism." But as Sierra Leone's experience with the World Bank and IMF (discussed below) makes clear, multilateral assistance also came with severe conditions and increased the country's dependence on those organizations. Secondly, multilateral assistance would be in keeping with the declared principle of non-alignment that was one of the tenets of its foreign policy. Thirdly, using international institutions as the channels for economic aid would make it unnecessary to enter into several bilateral arrangements with different countries, which would be time consuming and require significant diplomatic resources.

The prevailing attitude toward economic development in the developing countries in the 1960s is reflected in Sierra Leone's approach to this question. Many Western analysts expected that African countries would follow the pattern of development of the developed countries. This meant a heavy emphasis on industrialization as the key to development and modernization. Accepting fully the prevailing logic, Sierra Leone consequently made repeated requests in the early 1960s for capital investment funds and technical assistance to fuel its development plans. In order to increase the flow of capital investment and technical expertise to Africa, it supported a resolution calling for the establishment of the African Development Bank (ADB) and the Institute for Economic Development and Planning (IEDP) in 1961.[23] Although politically independent, Sierra Leone was nevertheless part of a world economy that was dominated by the major powers, which determined the rules and mechanisms of control. The liberal economic principles supported by the hegemonic powers were reflected in multilateral economic organizations. Furthermore, Sierra Leone felt that the arms race among the major powers, especially between the United States and the Soviet Union, severely restricted the amount of money that they could spend on aid to developing countries. It was receptive to the idea that disarmament would result in a peace dividend that could be devoted to multilateral assistance. In 1953, the General Assembly had adopted a resolution in which member states agreed that, when sufficient progress had been made in disarmament, they would use the savings to create a fund to aid developing countries.[24] Thus, Sierra Leone supported the creation of the Special United Nations Fund for Economic Development.

At the start of the 1980s, Africa was in the throes of a major economic crisis fuelled by a decline in income, high external debt, and declining agricultural production. Sierra Leone's economy was in a particularly serious condition as a result of the international economic situation, a decline in the value of its mineral exports, inappropriate domestic economic policies, and mismanagement. Between 1971 and 1979, economic growth was less than 1.5 per cent, and it continued to decline during much of the 1980s; the public debt increased from Le 60.4 million in 1972 to Le 299.9 million in 1981; and the debt service ratio more than doubled from 10 per cent in 1971 to 22 per cent in the early 1980s.[25]

At the thirteenth special session of the General Assembly in May 1986, the Assembly adopted the United Nations Programme of Action for African Economic Recovery and Development, 1986–1990 (UNPAAERD). Under the UNPAAERD, African governments were to undertake certain policy reforms to improve economic management and restructure their economies. They were to eliminate constraints on agricultural development, encourage greater participation of women in development, adopt effective population policies, and implement programmes to deal with desertification and drought. Developed countries were to aid these efforts by providing increased aid and assistance. The financial response of the developed countries fell short of what was anticipated. During the five-year period of the UNPAAERD, external assistance declined from US$25.9 billion in 1986 to US$22.6 billion in 1989. In real terms, official development assistance remained around US$16 billion. Meanwhile, there was a dramatic increase in Africa's external debt from US$204 billion in 1986 to US$272 billion in 1990.

The weakness of the economy, the continuing decline in real incomes, rising prices, and shortages of basic goods led to widespread discontent, strikes, and protests. It became more difficult for the government to get private credit, and the country became increasingly dependent on the IMF for financial support. As will be demonstrated later in the chapter, financial support from the IMF came with a number of conditionalities that carried political, economic, and social costs. Political leaders were not enthusiastic about implementing the IMF's reforms because they realized that such measures were potentially risky for any government that intended to remain in power.[26] Although Sierra Leone, because of its weak economic position, could not afford to challenge the policies of the IMF directly, or be too critical of the conditionalities imposed, Sierra Leone used more "friendly" forums such as the United Nations to express its dissatisfaction. Speaking to the General Assembly in 1987, the Sierra Leonean representative criticized the IMF's structural adjustment programmes in the following words:

The rigid enforcement of structural adjustment policies which always insist on import restriction and unregulated internal economic liberalization – wholesale removal of subsidies, massive devaluations, auctioning off of public enterprises – has merely accelerated the decimation of the structural foundations of the target economies, spawning grotesque social and political problems in the process.[27]

State–society relations in Sierra Leone

Civil society in the African context has been defined as "society in its relation with the state ... in so far as it is in confrontation with the state" or as "the process by which society seeks to 'break' and counteract the simultaneous 'totalization' unleashed by the state."[28] Civil society is pluralistic in nature and includes institutions such as political parties, legislatures, trade unions, as well as the entire "social space."[29] From this perspective, since Sierra Leone's independence in 1961 there has been a progressive centralization of the power of the state and a parallel weakening of the institutions of civil society. This has had important political and social consequences. During most of the post-independence period, Sierra Leone has had a one-party authoritarian government or military regime, and the formulation of foreign policy has been the preserve of the ruling élite, with all major decisions being taken by the head of state and/or the Foreign Minister. Policies regarding multilateralism are thus shaped significantly by the attitudes of the governing élite, who regard foreign policy as another means of maintaining power. Policies of multilateral institutions that threaten or undermine the political control of national leaders are ultimately resisted.

In 1961, political control in Sierra Leone was transferred to a new indigenous political élite. Although the old élite (which consisted of traditional chiefs) was still influential, effective political control was wielded by the new élite, who comprised roughly 2 per cent of Sierra Leone's population. The new élite was not a monolithic entity, and, as Martin Kilson points out, an upper stratum of the new élite could be distinguished from a lower stratum in terms of the education, occupation, and wealth of its members. The upper stratum included doctors, lawyers, senior civil servants, teachers, wealthy merchants or traders, and bankers; the lower stratum included junior civil servants, clerks, tailors, and carpenters. Those in the upper stratum "dominated the development of modern nationalist politics."[30]

Although the new élite represented a small minority of the population, a substantial proportion consisted of Creoles and, to a lesser extent, Mendes, who (with about 30 per cent of the population) were one of the two largest ethnic groups in the country.[31] The Creoles were descendants of freed slaves who had been settled in the colony of Sierra Leone in the eighteenth century. A culturally distinct group, they were Christian and valued professional achievement. As British subjects the Creoles had early access to education; they were well

230

represented in the legal, medical, and educational fields and held important positions of authority in the colonial administration. The colony of Sierra Leone (including its capital Freetown) had been administered separately from the rest of the country, which was known as the Protectorate. Unlike the Creoles, the indigenous peoples of the Protectorate, such as the Mendes, were not regarded as British subjects but were "British protected persons." When modern education was introduced in the Protectorate in the early twentieth century, the Mendes (especially the sons of chiefs) became the first beneficiaries.[32] Consequently, the Mendes had greater opportunities for economic and social advancement than did other indigenous groups.

Sierra Leone belongs to a handful of African states that adopted an open, competitive, multi-party system after independence. The governing party at independence was the Sierra Leone People's Party (SLPP), led by Sir Milton Margai. The SLPP was not a mass-based party but drew its main support from the chiefs.[33] Although Sir Milton was a conservative ruler with a high regard for traditional authority, he tolerated competition and openness in the political system.[34] During his tenure there was a relatively "balanced opposition" between the state and the institutions of civil society. In contrast to the policies of the more stridently anti-colonial and nationalist governments such as that of Kwame Nkrumah in Ghana and Sekou Touré in Guinea, the SLPP's economic development policy favoured private capital and encouraged Western investment. It continued the basic pattern of economic relationships established during the colonial period. As John Cartwright has argued, Sir Milton's "open door" economic policy was "a policy of *laissez-faire* in economic development, a willingness to accept whatever kind of investment might be offered, regardless of its effect on the overall economic position of Sierra Leone."[35] This "open door" policy also extended to multilateral institutions.

After Sir Milton's death in April 1964, he was succeeded by his brother, Sir Albert Margai, who had previously served as Minister of Finance. Charismatic, flamboyant, and combative, Albert's personality was radically different from that of his reticent and self-effacing older brother. While "Milton epitomized a 'Tory' or aristocratic tradition of belief in the value of fixed ranks in society, Albert, in both statements and actions, epitomized the drive for self-advancement of bourgeois man."[36] Albert began the politicization of the civil service and the military by installing a number of people from his ethnic group (the Mende) in key positions. In particular, Albert Margai's policy of Africanizing the officer corps of the military was designed to ensure that the army would be dominated by Mendes.[37] He used his position to increase his wealth significantly by engaging in numerous private economic schemes. In a bid to perpetuate himself in power, he also attempted to create a one-party state in Sierra Leone. This was, however, strongly resisted by the opposition party, the All People's Congress (APC), the judiciary, and the academic community.

Albert Margai sought a more active role on the international stage and adopted a more militant rhetorical posture on issues such as decolonization and apartheid within the OAU, the Commonwealth, and the United Nations.[38] Unlike Sir Milton, Sir Albert took a keen interest in pan-Africanism and embraced leaders such as Kwame Nkrumah of Ghana and Sekou Touré of Guinea, who were ardent proponents of African unity. Albert Margai's external involvement was also an attempt to strengthen his domestic position, and his tendency to project an inflated image abroad increased as his domestic popularity decreased. Ultimately, however, Albert Margai's foreign adventures could not stem the growing resentment many Sierra Leoneans felt as a result of his domestic policies.

In March 1967 there was a general election and the opposition APC, led by Siaka Stevens, won the majority of seats and was asked by the Governor-General to form a new government. Stevens was a Limba, and the APC was a coalition composed predominantly of northern ethnic groups such as the Limba, Temne, and Susa. The victory of the APC ended the exercise of governmental power by the SLPP, which was dominated by the Mendes of the south. However, before Siaka Stevens could appoint his cabinet, the army commander, Brigadier David Lansana, a Margai supporter, staged a *coup d'état*. Two days later, Lansana was toppled by his own officers, who formed a military regime, the National Reformation Council (NRC), headed by the chairman, Lieutenant-Colonel Andrew Juxon-Smith.

Following a counter-coup 13 months later, the APC eventually came into office in April 1968. During the next 17 years, Siaka Stevens centralized the power of the state, strengthened his personal rule, and became increasingly authoritarian. He consolidated his power and control over the state by ensuring that those in positions of authority were answerable to him, completed the politicization of the civil service begun by Albert Margai, limited the power and autonomy of chiefs, and established a wide network of patron–client relationships. Stevens also undermined other institutions of civil society such as the university, trade unions, business, and professional organizations. After the official establishment of a one-party state in 1978, which Stevens had vehemently opposed as leader of the opposition, competitive party politics ended and parliament became no more than a rubber-stamp for his policies.[39] As Fred Hayward observes, under Siaka Stevens the state became "increasingly repressive, predatory, and rapacious."[40] Stevens was an avaricious politician with an insatiable appetite for unrestrained power and the acquisition of wealth by dishonest means. During the Stevens years, power became an instrument for the acquisition of private wealth, and the state became the primary channel for economic accumulation by the state élite, which included Stevens, the party, the bureaucracy, the police, and the military.

This personalist rule meant that foreign policy concerns were determined by a small ruling circle. Siaka Stevens put great emphasis on foreign policy, particularly the promotion of regionalism. He supported the establishment of regional organizations as a way of furthering economic development, and considered them potential mechanisms for resolving disputes between African states. In 1973 President Stevens and President William Tolbert of Liberia signed a declaration establishing the Mano River Union.[41] It provided for the creation of a customs union, coordination of postal services, and cooperation in economic and social areas.[42] A secretariat was established in Freetown to administer the programmes of the Union. The Mano River declaration also provided for other states in the region to become members if they so desired, and Guinea joined the Union in 1980. In 1975 Stevens and the heads of state of other West African countries signed a treaty in Lagos, Nigeria, establishing the Economic Community of West African States (ECOWAS). The ECOWAS treaty provided for economic union, and a West African Clearing House was established in association with ECOWAS to promote the use of local currencies in financing trade among member states.[43]

Stevens also had less noble motives in being actively engaged internationally, and, like his predecessor Sir Albert Margai, he viewed foreign policy activities as a means of bolstering his domestic image and prestige. In 1980 Stevens hosted the annual OAU summit meeting, an expensive undertaking that exacerbated the country's financial difficulties.[44] The decision was widely criticized in Sierra Leone, and the profligate spending to host the conference contributed to protests and strikes the following year. As had happened in the case of

Sir Albert, Siaka Stevens' grandiosity actually undermined his position, but unlike Sir Albert's SLPP government, Stevens' one-party APC government could not be removed from power through the ballot box.

Management of the economy during Stevens' regime was dismal. External strains and pressures included the dramatic increase in oil prices in 1979 and the drop in the international price for diamonds (Sierra Leone's major export), as well as a decline in the price of other commodities (including coffee and cocoa). These enormous strains on the economy, however, were compounded by misguided economic policies and corruption, which was a recession-proof industry. By 1985, Stevens had become very unpopular, the state had lost much of its legitimacy, and the economic situation was critical. In 1985, facing increasing pressure for political change, the embattled Stevens, who was by then in his eighties, announced that he would retire at the end of the year. Major-General Joseph Momoh, the head of the Sierra Leone military and an appointed member of parliament, was Stevens' hand-picked successor. The APC's National Delegates Conference nominated Momoh as the sole presidential candidate in the presidential election. Not unexpectedly, Momoh, who resigned his military commission, won the election and became President in November 1985. There were high expectations that his presidency, which he pledged would create a "New Order," would indeed be a significant improvement on the Stevens era.[45]

President Momoh called for national elections in 1986 in the hope of strengthening his position. His hope was realized as several incumbents lost their seats and Momoh then had a parliament with many new members with whom he could work.[46] Momoh, however, proved incapable of fulfilling his promises to end corruption, control prices, and ameliorate the country's economic crisis. His government became increasingly unpopular owing to widespread poverty, economic austerity measures, and rampant corruption by government officials and their cronies. In March 1987 a plot to overthrow the government was uncovered, demonstrating Momoh's unpopularity and vulnerability. Eighteen people were arrested and tried for treason. They were all found guilty and six of them, including the former first vice-president, Francis Minah, were executed in October 1989. The others received sentences of life imprisonment.

Momoh's government also had to cope with a significant influx of Liberian refugees fleeing the civil war that began in their country in

December 1989. The situation was exacerbated when Charles Taylor, the leader of the National Patriotic Front of Liberia (NPFL), one of the main factions in the Liberian civil war, began transborder attacks in the south-east of Sierra Leone.[47] Taylor resented Sierra Leone's participation in the Economic Community of West African States' Monitoring Group, a peace-keeping force that had intervened in the Liberian conflict and that he viewed as an impediment to his goal of achieving complete military and political control in Liberia. Taylor accused Momoh's government of harbouring forces of the United Liberation Movement for Democracy, composed largely of troops loyal to the ex-president of Liberia, Samuel Doe, who were using Sierra Leone as a base to attack the NPFL. To make matters worse, rebel Sierra Leoneans led by Corporal Foday Sankoh formed the Revolutionary United Front (RUF) and joined the NPFL in the fight against the Sierra Leonean government. Corporal Sankoh was seeking to topple the unpopular Momoh government. The alliance between the RUF and NPFL was an opportunistic one of convenience, and the unpopularity of Momoh's government was increased by its inability to deal effectively with the border war in the south-eastern section of the country, which was resulting in tremendous financial and human costs. Beginning in 1990 there were a number of disturbances and strikes as people demanded higher wages and political change.

Following a student protest in early 1992 calling for Momoh's resignation, the government banned all demonstrations. On 30 April 1992, Momoh's government was overthrown in a military coup led by junior army officers, and Momoh fled into exile in neighbouring Guinea. A National Provisional Ruling Council (NPRC) was formed, and the Council's chairman, 27-year-old Captain Valentine Strasser, became the new head of state. Many of the members of the NPRC had been fighting against Liberian and Sierra Leonean rebels in the border war in the south-east and were angry with Momoh's government for not paying them or giving them adequate food or ammunition.[48] The new military government considers ending the rebel war one of its top priorities and a precondition for handing over power to a civilian government. Nevertheless, it has established a 15-member council to advise it on the modalities of re-introducing a multi-party democratic system. Although the economy remains in dire straits, the NPRC remains popular to date, not least because it has made concerted efforts to eradicate corruption.

The domestic impact of multilateralism: The role of the World Bank and the International Monetary Fund

During the last 30 years, multilateral institutions, especially the World Bank and International Monetary Fund, have played an important part in the formulation of Sierra Leone's national economic policies. In the early years of independence, the government instituted programmes and policies that resulted in a financial crisis by 1965. The crisis was in large part due to the activities of the Sierra Leone Produce Marketing Board (SLPMB), which began a number of unsuccessful agricultural and industrial projects. These projects depleted the capital reserves that the Board gained from export crop earnings, and resulted in an annual loss of Le 1 million. The SLPMB, which had committed its liquid assets to long-term projects in agricultural production and processing, was unable to meet its operating expenses or to pay its buying agents and farmers.[49] The government's fiscal policies also resulted in increasing debt service payments from Le 2 million in 1963/64 to Le 8.5 million in 1967. The nation's fiscal health declined from having a surplus of Le 2 million in 1963/64 to incurring a deficit of around Le 2.8 million in 1966/67.[50]

Faced with a trade deficit and balance-of-payments problems, the government turned to the IMF for assistance in 1966. The IMF's diagnosis was that budget deficits were being financed by increasing bank borrowing and the use of cash deposits, thus creating higher prices for goods and depleting external reserves. A three-year standing arrangement was reached with the IMF in October 1966 under which the government agreed on a stabilization programme to improve fiscal management and reorganize the SLPMB. The programme called for a reduction in public expenditure, tax increases to reduce the deficit, and the cancellation of development contracts that had not yet begun. The domestic impact of such proposals would have been great. National elections were, however, due in March 1967 and, as these measures were not going to be popular, Albert Margai's SLPP government did not implement most of these proposals.[51]

The NRC military government that seized power in 1967 was able to implement the unpopular demands of the IMF, as gaining public support in order to win an election was not one of its concerns. As Thomas Cox notes, "accountable to almost no civilians, the NRC did not particularly see fit to gauge the political consequences of its austerity measures with the same degree of sensitivity as might a civilian government."[52] Nevertheless, even a military government was not wholly insensitive to the political implications of IMF involvement in the economy. In his budget statement of June 1967, Colonel Juxon-Smith, the chairman of the NRC declared:

I wish to reassure my countrymen that Fund visitation is neither a sign of national failure nor an abrogation of national sovereignty. Rather it is a sign of our determination to seek and implement sound economic policies. It is an indication to interested observers that we recognize our difficulties and that with international support we are resolved to overcome them.[53]

In order to obtain credits of around Le 9 million during the next three years, the NRC took steps to reduce the budget deficit, including raising taxes and making the system of collecting taxes more efficient. In November 1967 the government devalued the leone, following the devaluation of the sterling to which the leone was pegged. The NRC reorganized the SLPMB, restricted its functions to the marketing of produce, and closed down unproductive plantations. The government's austerity measures, however, had enormous social costs, especially increasing unemployment. For example, the closing of the SLPMB plantations resulted in the loss of over 2,000 jobs.[54]

During the 1970s and 1980s Sierra Leone's economy experienced a continuing decline. The mining of minerals, in particular diamonds and iron ore, had been the mainstay of the economy and the major source of foreign exchange earnings. In the mid-1970s, the yield and value of Sierra Leone's mineral exports decreased, thereby slowing economic growth and creating a major recession in the mining sector. In the 1970/71 financial year, 2 million carats of diamonds were mined, but by the 1978/79 financial year production had declined to 834,000 carats. This problem was compounded by the fact that a substantial quantity of diamonds was being smuggled out of the country, mainly by Lebanese businessmen and their accomplices in the government.[55] In 1976 the iron mine at Marampa, which had been in operation for more than four decades, was closed because the remaining deposits of ore were low in iron content and difficult to produce. International economic developments such as the 1973–74 and the 1979 oil price increases also had a negative impact on the economy. Thus, at the start of the 1980s Sierra Leone was experiencing slow growth, balance-of-payments pressures, increasing budget deficits, rising inflation, and a collapsing exchange rate. In addition, the mining-led growth policy of several years had resulted in major distortions in the private economy, and the benefits from mining had not been extended to other sectors of the economy.[56]

The economic woes of the country prompted a pragmatic response by the government of Siaka Stevens to foreign economic assistance: it would seek financial aid from whatever source possible. The primary objective of foreign policy became to secure financial assistance, and external relations and alliances were pursued according to their capacity to further this goal. While not abandoning Western countries such as the United States, the United Kingdom, and West Germany, all of which were traditional sources of bilateral aid for Sierra Leone, Stevens courted the North African and Middle Eastern oil states in a seemingly endless quest for economic help. In 1980, in expectation of aid from Algeria, Stevens' government recognized the Polisario government in Western Sahara.[57] In 1982 it ratified the Islamic Conference Charter. It also established diplomatic relations with Iran, Saudi Arabia, and Jordan, the last of which took over responsibility for operating Sierra Leone's national airline.[58]

As Sierra Leone's economy deteriorated in the 1970s and 1980s, the influence and role of the World Bank and the IMF increased significantly. Private credit was more difficult to obtain and the terms required by commercial creditors became increasingly stringent. The Sierra Leonean government turned to the World Bank and the IMF in the hope of extricating the country from its economic morass. Since the late 1970s, IMF stabilization programmes have been undertaken, with their attendant conditionalities and policy prescriptions. In order to understand the nature of these stabilization programmes, the economic remedies they proposed, and their domestic consequences, it is necessary to consider the diagnosis of Sierra Leone's economic problems by the World Bank and the IMF. In the view of these multilateral agencies, after Sierra Leone's economy suffered a major external shock in the late 1970s, the government exacerbated the problem by mismanaging the exchange rate, specifically by: overvaluing the currency and thereby worsening the balance of payments; engaging in excessive spending, which resulted in inflation; and intervening in agricultural markets in a fashion that discouraged production and reduced exports.[59] However, as John Weeks demonstrates in his study of Sierra Leone's economy, the empirical basis for this assessment was not sound because:

- from the late 1970s onwards the government cut real expenditure, it did not raise it;

- compared with other currencies of the region, the leone was not overvalued;
- when the leone appreciated in the 1980s, the trade balance improved; and
- with regard to agricultural policy:
  - (a) the policies of the Rice Board seem to have had little negative effect on production;
  - (b) producer prices for the major export crops closely followed the trend in world prices; and
  - (c) there is no evidence that export crop output correlated with the gap between the producer price and the export price.[60]

This suggested that other factors were at play in determining the IMF's policy towards Sierra Leone. Nevertheless, based on its diagnosis of Sierra Leone's economic ailments the IMF stipulated certain remedies that were consistently integral elements of its programmes. These included: devaluing the exchange rate; reducing government expenditure; ending subsidies of commodities; and reducing the trade gap.

Devaluation of a country's exchange rate is a basic component of the IMF's model of a sound economic policy.[61] Specifically in the case of Sierra Leone, the IMF maintained that Sierra Leone's "overvalued" or "unrealistic" exchange rate was discouraging exports and increasing imports, increasing the smuggling of diamonds and gold, and discriminating against agriculture in favour of urban industry.[62] In November 1978, following a visit to the IMF and the World Bank by President Stevens, the leone was "de-linked" from sterling and became pegged to Special Drawing Rights. This action resulted in a 5 per cent devaluation of the leone and was required in order for Sierra Leone to receive balance-of-payments support from the IMF the following year.[63] Since 1978 the foreign exchange formula has been changed several times: in December 1982 a "two-tier" exchange rate system was instituted that further devalued the leone; in July 1983 the leone was again devalued when a new unitary exchange rate was established; another devaluation occurred in February 1985; and in June 1986 the leone was further devalued when floating exchange rates were established.[64] As a result of the devaluations required by the IMF, the value of the leone declined from US$1.12 in 1980 to US$0.03 by 1987![65] However, following the establishment of a "two-tier" exchange rate system in December 1982, which was intended to remedy the problems identified by the IMF, smuggling continued to increase rather than decrease, imports declined further, and there were shortages of spare parts and other goods that negatively affected local industries such as brewing, which ceased production.[66]

The IMF has also consistently recommended that the government increase the prices paid to farmers for agricultural goods in order to increase production and ultimately exports. Consequently, the government raised producer prices in March 1983 and again in July 1983, when the coffee price was raised by 138 per cent and that for cocoa by 108 per cent. However, as happened in the case of the "two-tier" exchange rate system, the agricultural price increases failed to accomplish their intended purpose. The overall amount of purchases recorded by the SLPMB declined, and coffee and cocoa purchases declined by nearly 50 per cent.[67] Another policy recommendation advocated by the IMF was that the government end subsidies for rice (the major staple of the population), petrol, and kerosene, and allow their prices to be determined by the market. This position was also supported by the World Bank, and by 1985 the ending of all subsidies was a condition for Bank adjustment loans.[68] This was a major issue of contention between the government and the IMF because it is extremely politically sensitive and its implementation inevitably results in general discontent. Furthermore, such increases have the harshest impact on the poor and more vulnerable groups in the society, and reinforce existing inequalities. Because the government resisted implementing all the recommendations of the IMF, the relations between them deteriorated in the 1980s and the three programmes established in 1981, 1983, and 1986 were all ended unilaterally by the Fund following the first tranche. In 1988 Sierra Leone was declared ineligible for IMF borrowing and for World Bank loans.[69] This decision meant not only that Sierra Leone had limited access to private sources of credit but that it could no longer utilize the resources of the major multilateral financial institutions, which had been its lenders of last resort. The prescriptions offered by the IMF and the World Bank for Sierra Leone's economic revival were based on classical liberal economic principles, which national policy makers could challenge only at their peril.

Conclusion and prospects for the future

One of the lessons of this case-study is that Sierra Leone's contribution to the United Nations system cannot be understood without placing it in the context of the activities pursued by other African states. The admission of independent African states to the United Nations in the 1960s had a quantitative effect on the organization, and in practical terms meant that resolutions in the General Assembly could not be adopted without their support. The increased African membership also had a qualitative effect because the agenda of the United Nations reflected increasingly the objectives of African states. In many ways, the three important priorities of Sierra Leone – decolonization, ending apartheid, and economic development – were also the key objectives of most African countries. The pressures for decolonization ensured that colonialism would be ended in Africa and political independence become more than a dream. In the persistent struggle against apartheid, theories of racial superiority were challenged and debunked, and issues such as apartheid were considered legitimate areas of international concern. By the 1970s, when their halcyon days in the United Nations were over, the African bloc as a part of the Group of 77 challenged the dominant liberal economic order through demands for a New International Economic Order. Their cries of protest and indignation, however, failed to accomplish a fundamental restructuring of the global economic system.

Sierra Leone's experiences with the World Bank and IMF have been torturous and acrimonious. It cannot be disputed that successive Sierra Leonean governments have mismanaged the country's economy, engaged in corrupt practices, and plundered its resources. Primary responsibility for the country's future welfare rests with Sierra Leoneans, especially those who direct affairs of state. Nevertheless, economic prescriptions by multilateral institutions that ignore the historical roots of economic problems, do not address structural inequalities, and disregard the political and social costs they entail will continue to be of limited value. The challenge of economic development will remain of central importance for the country well into the next century.

Although Sierra Leone's influence in international affairs is limited, it brings to multilateral institutions whenever possible, on its own or in concert with other nations, the perspective of the small and vulnerable state in the international system. This perspective is not only necessary but vital if there is to be a new age of multilateralism that will be more than a diplomatic shibboleth or a device to give legitimacy to the actions of dominant states in the international system.

Notes and references

1. Some examples are Trevor W. Parfitt and Stephen Riley, *The African Debt Crisis* (New York: Routledge, 1989), chap. 6; John Weeks, *Development Strategy and the Economy of Sierra Leone* (New York: St. Martin's Press, 1992).
2. C. T. Thorne, "External Political Pressures," in Vernon McKay, ed., *African Diplomacy* (New York: Praeger, 1966), 168.
3. Robert H. Jackson and Carl G. Rosberg, "Why Africa's Weak States Persist," *World Politics* 35 (1982), no. 1: 1–24.
4. See Robert H. Jackson, *Quasi-states: Sovereignty, International Relations and the Third World* (Cambridge: Cambridge University Press, 1990).
5. A. Leroy Bennett, *International Organizations: Principles and Issues*, 4th ed. (Englewood Cliffs, N.J.: Prentice Hall, 1988), 340.
6. Resolution 1514, 14 December 1960, was adopted by 90 votes to none, with 9 abstentions.
7. Speech by Sir Milton Margai on Sierra Leone's admission to the United Nations, UN General Assembly Official Records [UNGAOR], 16th session, 1018th Meeting, 27 September 1961, 147.
8. See, for example, the speech by the Permanent Representative, Gershon Collier, during the debate on Colonialism and the Implementation of the Declaration on the Granting of Independence to Colonial Countries and Peoples, in UNGAOR, 16th session, 1057th Plenary Meeting, 17 November 1961, 699–700.
9. UNGAOR, 16th session, 1039th Meeting, 18 October 1961, 478.
10. UNGAOR, 17th session, 1144th Plenary Meeting, 5 October 1962, 355.
11. Ibid.
12. On South African annexation, see UNGA Resolution 1899 (XVIII), 13 November 1963. On termination of South Africa's mandate, see UNGA Resolution 2142 (XXI), 27 October 1966, adopted by a vote of 114 to 2, with 3 abstentions. This resolution also established an Ad Hoc Committee for South-West Africa composed of 14 member states to be designated by the President of the General Assembly.
13. The Rhodesian Question, as it was referred to then, was first placed on the agenda of the Fourth (Trusteeship) Committee in 1962. Its recommendations were subsequently adopted by the General Assembly as Resolution 1754 (XVI) in February 1962.
14. See, for example, the speech by Mr. Rogers-Wright in UNGAOR, 19th session, 1303rd Plenary Meeting, 15 December 1964, 6–11.
15. For a study of the evolution of the treatment of South Africa's racial policies in the United Nations, see Abiodun Williams, "The United Nations and Apartheid, 1946–1985," unpublished Ph.D. dissertation, The Fletcher School of Law and Diplomacy, Tufts University, 1987.
16. Following the Sharpeville massacre, the Security Council adopted its first resolution on South Africa's apartheid policies. Resolution 134 was adopted on 1 April 1960 by 9 votes to none, with 2 abstentions (France and the United Kingdom).
17. UNGAOR, 16th session, 1039th Plenary Meeting, 18 October 1961, 478.
18. UNGA Resolution 1761 (XVII), 6 November 1962, adopted by 67 votes to 16, with 23 abstentions.
19. UN Security Council Official Records [UNSCOR], 18th session, 1050th Meeting, 31 July 1963, 8.
20. Resolution 181 (1963), 7 August 1963, adopted by 9 votes to none, with 2 abstentions (France and the United Kingdom).
21. Inis Claude, Jr., *Swords into Plowshares: The Problems and Progress of International Organization*, 4th ed. (New York: Random House, 1984), 153.
22. UNGAOR, 16th session, 1039th Plenary Meeting, 18 October 1961, 478.
23. See UNGA Resolution 1718 (XVI), 19 December 1961. The IEDP was established in 1963 and the ADB in 1964.

24. Resolution 724 (VIII), 7 December 1953.
25. Jeff Haynes, Trevor W. Parfitt, and Stephen Riley, "Debt in Sub-Saharan Africa: The Local Politics of Stabilisation," *African Affairs* 86 (July 1987), no. 344: 357.
26. See the speech by Mr. A. K. Koroma in UNGAOR, 41st session, 14th Meeting, 29 September 1986, 76–87.
27. UNGAOR, 42nd session, 19th Meeting, 5 October 1987, 26–38.
28. Jean-François Bayart, "Civil Society in Africa," in Patrick Chabal, ed., *Political Domination in Africa: Reflections on the Limits of Power* (Cambridge: Cambridge University Press, 1986), 111. See also Donald Rothchild and Naomi Chazan, eds., *The Precarious Balance: State and Society in Africa* (Boulder, Colo.: Westview Press, 1988).
29. Bayart, "Civil Society," 112.
30. Martin Kilson, *Political Change in a West African State: A Study of the Modernization Process in Sierra Leone* (Cambridge, Mass.: Harvard University Press, 1966), 69.
31. The other large ethnic group, the Temnes living in the north, also forms approximately 30 per cent of the population. Cited in Irving Kaplan, *Area Handbook for Sierra Leone* (Washington, D.C.: American University, 1976), 66.
32. Western missionaries and later the colonial government concentrated their efforts on the Mendes in the south of the country because they were mostly pagan, in contrast to the northern ethnic groups who were Muslims (see Kilson, *Political Change*, 77).
33. For a more extensive discussion of party politics in Sierra Leone, see Kilson, *Political Change*, part 5.
34. See John R. Cartwright, *Political Leadership in Sierra Leone* (Toronto: Toronto University Press, 1978), chap. 4.
35. Ibid., 74.
36. Ibid.
37. Jimmy D. Kandeh, "Politicization of Ethnic Identities in Sierra Leone," *African Studies Review* 35 (April 1992), no. 1: 93.
38. For a basic overview of Sir Albert Margai's approach to foreign policy, see Amadu Sesay, "Sierra Leone's Foreign Policy since Independence: Part One: The Era of the Margais, 1961–67," *Africana Research Bulletin* 9 (1979), no. 3.
39. Fred M. Hayward, "Sierra Leone: State Consolidation, Fragmentation and Decay," in Donal B. Cruise O'Brien, John Dunn, and Richard Rathbone, eds., *Contemporary West African States* (Cambridge: Cambridge University Press, 1989), 167–170.
40. Ibid., 166.
41. The Union was named after the Mano River, which forms part of the border between Sierra Leone and Liberia.
42. Kaplan, *Area Handbook*, 195.
43. For a useful study of ECOWAS, see Uka Ezenwe, *ECOWAS and the Economic Integration of West Africa* (New York: St. Martin's Press, 1983).
44. The official estimated cost of the conference was Le 100 million, but even the President admitted that it was a conservative estimate (see Colin Legum, ed., *Africa Contemporary Record: Annual Survey and Documents 1979–80*, New York: Africana Publishing Co., 1981, B637).
45. Stephen Riley and Trevor W. Parfitt, "Party or Masquerade? The All People's Congress of Sierra Leone," *Journal of Commonwealth and Comparative Politics* 25 (July 1987), no. 2: 175.
46. Fred M. Hayward and Jimmy D. Kandeh, "Perspectives on Twenty-Five Years of Elections in Sierra Leone," in Fred. M. Hayward, ed., *Elections in Independent Africa* (Boulder, Colo.: Westview Press, 1987), 25–59.
47. For a study of the origins of the Liberian civil war and role of ECOWAS, see Abiodun Williams, "Regional Peacemaking: ECOWAS and the Liberian Civil War," in David D. Newsom, ed., *The Diplomatic Record 1990–1991* (Boulder, Colo.: Westview Press, 1992), 213–231.

48. *New York Times*, 1 May 1992, A10.
49. Kaplan, *Area Handbook*, 213.
50. Colin Legum and John Drysdale, eds., *Africa Contemporary Record: Annual Survey and Documents 1968–69* (London: Africa Research Ltd., 1969), 592.
51. Ibid.
52. Thomas Cox, *Civil–Military Relations in Sierra Leone* (Cambridge, Mass.: Harvard University Press, 1976), 180.
53. Quoted in George O. Roberts, *The Anguish of Third World Independence: The Sierra Leone Experience* (Lanham, Md.: University Press of America, 1982), 58.
54. David Fashole Luke, *Labor and Parastatal Politics in Sierra Leone* (Lanham, Md.: University Press of America, 1984), 78.
55. Haynes, Parfitt, and Riley, "Debt in Sub-Saharan Africa," 357.
56. Weeks, *Development Strategy*, 33.
57. Legum, *Africa Contemporary Record 1979–80*, B636.
58. Colin Legum, ed., *Africa Contemporary Record: Annual Survey and Documents, 1983–84* (New York: Africana Publishing Co., 1985), B578.
59. Weeks, *Development Strategy*, 107.
60. Ibid., 125–126.
61. Cheryl Payer, *The Debt Trap: The IMF and the Third World* (New York: Monthly Review Press, 1974), 33.
62. Weeks, *Development Strategy*, 108.
63. Colin Legum, *Africa Contemporary Record: Annual Survey and Documents 1978–79* (New York: Africana Publishing Co., 1980), B777.
64. Haynes, Parfitt, and Riley, "Debt in Sub-Saharan Africa," 360–361.
65. Weeks, *Development Strategy*, 114.
66. Haynes, Parfitt, and Riley, "Debt in Sub-Saharan Africa," 361.
67. Ibid., 362–363.
68. Weeks, *Development Strategy*, 36.
69. Ibid., chap. 3.

Conclusion

States, societies, and the United Nations in a multilateral context

W. Andy Knight and Keith Krause

The case-studies in this book have been informed by the general sociological orientation discussed in the Introduction, and have focused on the changing relationship between particular state/society complexes and the institutions of the UN system. In doing so each makes a significant contribution to the corpus of case-studies on the UN system. Combined, these cases also throw considerable new comparative light on national (state/society) orientations toward multilateral participation in world politics, and force us to reflect on some of the broader theoretical and analytic issues that emerged from them.[1] This Conclusion examines some of these issues and draws on the collective body of studies to inform our conceptualization of what we call the state/society perspective, particularly as it pertains to multilateralism and multilateral institutions like the United Nations system.

State/society perspective: Broadening the lens

The central task of each study was to explain the pattern of involvement of its state/society in the UN system, in light of certain questions that went beyond an examination of government-to-government relationships. These included the way in which a state situated itself within the multilateral UN system; the influence of a diverse range of internal, transnational (and/or global) social, ideological, or political forces on the sorts of policies that state representatives pursued within the multilateral system; and the impact of multilateral activity on political and socio-economic structures within the state/society complex.

In addressing some of these questions, many of the case-studies departed significantly from previous work on the UN system. Instead of treating foreign policy-making in the state-centric manner of the realist scholarship that has dominated the international relations literature since the Second World War, or treating it in the pluralist fashion of liberal institutionalist scholars, the authors in this volume utilized an eclectic range of explanatory tools that, taken together, not only offer a stiff challenge to the traditional foreign policy and international relations approaches but also point towards the outline of a state/society perspective on the UN system that draws on Robert Cox's historicist theoretical approach to the somewhat neglected issue of multilateralism.[2] This approach is built on a number of arguments that have emerged out of recent scholarship in sociology and international relations, arguments that not only challenge, but overturn, the traditional realist and liberal institutionalist intellectual conventions that have contributed to the definition of international relations since 1945.

The first argument challenges the value of a commitment to parsimonious explanation as an essential element of (or the correct path to) theory-building. Explanations that view state policies as framed by an unproblematically invoked "national interest" (as defined by foreign policy élites) have not proven to be theoretically productive (except perhaps at a very high level of abstraction), and they are certainly not an accurate reflection of reality.[3] Likewise, viewing the UN system simply as a forum for exclusively intergovernmental relations does not seem to help us understand the specific roles and perspectives brought to it by member states, the way in which new issues have risen on the international agenda, and the trajectory of change in these institutions. Finally, such orientations do not capture well the "meaningful" or "purposive" element of social action, and veil their own political implications or commitments in the shroud of "objective social science." Our attempt to confront these theoretical challenges seeks instead to establish a broad sociological framework for the study of multilateralism that embraces a range of potentially important explanatory factors and that tries to assess the changes in the global political, economic, and social power relationships we have witnessed since 1945.

At a second level, empirical observations of changing international relations practice have highlighted the debates surrounding the nature, number, and variety of relevant actors involved in contemporary international relations; the range of stakes and priority of items on the international or global agenda; the diversity and complexity of the goals of various actors in the international system; the nature of the interactions; and the character and relevance of international organizations, institutions, and regimes.[4] Whereas traditional analysis has regarded inter-state interactions as the primary focus of international relations, our study looks at the roots and interstices of the state system, to subnational, transnational, and global social relations and processes, in order to find explanations of the sources of policy and change in global politics. The impact of state–society relations on the foreign policy-making process of states is increasingly being acknowledged, and for this reason the interaction of states with their civil societies has been explored in the country case-studies of this book, with the state/society complex being the preferred unit of analysis.

Third, the interdependent nature of issues and actors in the contemporary international system implies the need to examine the problems of international relations from the more holistic perspective of "world order," rather than in the fragmentary manner of the past. The fact that we can no longer easily separate domestic from foreign issues has several implications for the traditional understanding of sovereignty, for example. For that reason alone, this factor ought to be given more attention in the mainstream international relations literature.[5] The sociological approach adopted in this study is one that can be applied at both state and global levels, and is designed to flesh out not only how forms of state/society articulate aims within the UN system but also how various components of that system have an impact upon states and societies.

All of this argues for a broadened and contextualized concept of multilateralism. An expansive view of multilateralism would treat it as the organizing principle for world order, conceptualized as the "political, economic, social, ideological, and cultural structures that define the behaviour and power relationships among human groups."[6] As noted in the Introduction, multilateral institutions embody and (to a degree) perpetuate the relationships of power and understandings of world order that govern international relations at a specific juncture. But these institutions can also be conceived as a locus or arena in which competing ideologies and values clash, including those pertaining to the meaning, nature, and scope of multilateralism. Thus the study of the multilateral institutions of the UN system is an important part of understanding the changing nature of multilateralism and the extent to which multilateral institutions are adapting (or not) to accommodate new challenges, new demands, and the forces of change in contemporary world politics. It is in this light that the authors have examined the relationship between their particular state/society complex and the multilateral institutions of the UN system.

The evidence provided by the case-studies in this volume makes clear that traditional approaches to the study of international relations and international organization fail to capture, and in many cases occlude, the many ways in which states approach their participation in the world of multilateral relations. The state–society perspective attempts to overcome some of these shortcomings by examining the broader set of relations that involve the interactive struggles between the society and the state in the making of foreign policy with respect to the United Nations. As was noted in the Introduction, this approach allows for the introduction of a range of forces, not generally included in traditional international relations analyses, that we thought could significantly influence different states' multilateral policy towards the United Nations. Five sets of factors have been highlighted by the various cases in this volume: historical influences; the relationship between state power and domestic political, social, or economic cleavages; the role of individuals; political cultural and ideological influences; and transnational and global forces. The insights and issues raised by each of them can be briefly outlined and synthesized.

Historical influences

Most of the chapters in this study demonstrate how historical influences can leave a deep imprint on a state/society complex and its general approach to multilateral activity or participation in international institutions. Recent German historical experience, for example, has had a central role in shaping the self-image that evolved in the international behaviour of both the West and East German states. The stigmatization of the German states and societies as a result of the atrocities of Hitler was the reason for their "enemy state" status in the United Nations, and it ensured that neither of the two German states became members of the international organization for almost a quarter of a century after its founding. At the same time, the high profile of Germans in UN specialized agencies (such as the FAO, ILO, WHO, UNESCO, and UNIDO) during the time of quasi-isolation or moral ostracism was in large part an attempt to demonstrate to the international community that the militaristic and imperialistic elements of traditional German nationalism had been overcome. Since 1973, this has also led German representatives at the United Nations to be very conscious of how their activities are perceived by other national delegations. Also not surprisingly, Germany's pursuit of regional multilateralism in the European Union has been viewed with suspicion in many quarters, where questions have been raised about whether or not Germany's regional activity represents a renewed national quest for dominant regional power status. Similarly, Germany's historical legacy has acted as a constraint on its quest for a permanent seat on the UN Security Council (in both formal and informal ways), although its representatives have made no secret of this goal.

Sweden's historical commitment to neutrality explains its active involvement in the UN specialized agencies, on one hand, and its reluctance to become involved in collective security initiatives of the Security Council, on the other. Its long history of support for multilateralism and international governance, which goes back to its involvement with the League of Nations, has also resulted in a disproportionately high Swedish profile in efforts to maintain international peace and security; a legacy that is influenced by a domestic legalist and judicial inheritance that stresses neutrality, objectivity, and impartiality in attempts to resolve conflicts. Similarly, Romania and Chile both possess a "legalist" public service tradition (in the Chilean case, traceable to Hispanic and French Napoleonic influences) that guides their foreign policy with respect to the UN system (and earlier the League of Nations) and helps explain the persistent technocratic element in the foreign policy establishment. Obviously, however, the rise and domination of the Ceauçescu dictatorship in Romania and Chile's recent history of autocratic rule and human rights violations hindered their respective activities within the UN system, illustrating how domestic political developments can taint a UN member state's activity in the multilateral process.

The tightrope diplomacy that Romanian delegations at the United Nations became noted for may have also had its roots in the early history of that nation-state. Surrounded by three empires, Romania appears to have developed a particular orientation towards maintaining its independent field of action and, although it was forced into the orbit of the Soviet Union, it was able to preserve, rather skilfully, some relative autonomy at the international level. This historical legacy best explains Romania's penchant for a more non-aligned stance in its multilateral diplomacy.

Finally, the colonial historical experience of countries like India, Jamaica, and Sierra Leone has helped shape the kinds of policies adopted in the United Nations and other multilateral forums. It certainly explains the emphasis that Sierra Leone has placed on self-determination and its advocacy of financial support for liberation movements, as well as India's vociferous condemnation in the General Assembly of colonial practices (such as the French suppression of the Algerian liberation movement) and its strong leadership in the decolonization movement. The discriminatory features of the colonial legacy were one factor that led Indian delegates to emphasize the need for equality among all states. Correspondingly, Jamaica's history of being marginalized and exploited – qualities characteristic of a colonized and structurally dependent society – explains its criticism of the unequal North–South economic relations and its agitation for equity, fairness, and redistributive justice for similarly disadvantaged states in the international system.

This historical experience explains why Jamaica and India both supported (at least at certain points) the demand for a New International Economic Order (NIEO) and the Group of 77 in its more general quest for economic fairness. Jamaican and Indian leadership in the Non-Aligned Movement was a by-product of their colonial legacy, and fuelled its anti-colonial and anti-Western rhetoric. The failed attempts by Jamaica and other Caribbean states to bring Latin American states into some form of regional economic union with the Caribbean also testify, however, to the importance of their divergent historical experiences. In some respects, this fragmented state-formation process may be one of the primary reasons for the inability of the South to develop a coordinated counter-hegemonic strategy that could challenge the dominance of the status quo powers. As Abiodun Williams points out in chapter 7 on Sierra Leone, the failure of the NIEO demonstrates the limitations of the influence of weak states (even when they combine forces) and the extent to which Western industrialized states still dominate the multilateral process.

State power and societal cleavages

The "state/society" perspective recognizes that "the state" still plays a prominent role in defining the state/society perspective on multilateralism, provides a sense of identity for its inhabitants, and continues to be the dominant actor within the UN system. But several case-studies in this volume illustrate the inadequacy of an exclusive conception that does not raise as a basic question the relationship between state power and social forces, and the impact this could have on the orientation of the state towards the UN system. Debates over *which* character and form the state assumes under what conditions are vast (and cannot be resolved here), but several studies in this volume point out that the activities of a particular state within multilateral institutions depend heavily on the "form" of the state and on the relationship of various state and societal elements with its decision-making apparatus.[7] The potential impact of three particular state–society relationships (this is by no means an exhaustive list) is highlighted by the case-studies in this volume.[8]

The first is the way in which a "strong" state (and its apparatuses of control) can exert its own power over society by virtue of its relative strength *vis-à-vis* civil society. This is true of states such as Romania, Chile, and Sierra Leone, where the heavy hand of the state apparatus was felt (at certain periods) in the evolution of policies regarding the UN system. In such cases, state power, symbolized by the influence of the military or the presence of authoritarian rule, gained the upper hand in state/societal struggles over the development of perspectives on multilateralism. As Roberto Duran notes in the Chilean case, Chile's position on multilateralism shifted (once the Pinochet regime came to power) from being highly supportive of multilateral institutions to an anti-multilateralism that manifested itself in hostility to the United Nations, and later (between 1978 and 1983) to a form of pragmatic multilateralism that limited its multilateral activity to engagement in so-called depoliticized bodies of the UN system. In order to avoid criticisms of its human rights record, the Pinochet regime opted for selective bilateralism over active multilateral participation. In Sierra Leone, the state's approach to multilateralism became a vehicle for the advancement of particular interests, at least under Albert Margai and Siaka Stevens.

In other cases this process is more subtle. In Jamaica and Sweden, an enlarged role in regional or global multilateralism was used to obtain a greater measure of legitimacy for certain governments or to advance the interests of particular leaders (such as Michael Manley or Olof Palme). In Germany, participation in the UN system has been used as an instrument to legitimize its entire political system, validate a global presence, and demonstrate that its society had changed after the Second World War.

251

The second variation is one in which profound domestic political or social cleavages play a role in allowing various groups within society to exert greater influence on multilateral policy, depending on the way in which domestic political arrangements have been constructed. This is arguably the case in Jamaica, where labour unions have at different times had a greater influence on the state and where racial cleavages complicate and undermine Jamaica's rhetoric of anti-apartheid in multilateral institutions. It is also the case in Sierra Leone, where the Creoles and Mendes enjoyed greater access to political and socio-economic power. In both instances, the influence of such groups goes beyond the normal interplay of "interest group politics" because the weak, fractured, or divided nature of the state/society complex allows the state to be partially captured by particular interests. This also has had a demonstrable impact on the multilateral policies pursued by the state in the UN system.

Third, the Swedish and Romanian cases illustrate (in benign and pathological variants) the possibility of the fusion of state interests with society. The authors of the Swedish case reject the idea of a state/society cleavage as an adequate description of Swedish domestic social and political relations, because in Sweden organized interests have been more or less institutionalized into the state machinery. Accommodation of interest groups and other social forces within Sweden helped to form the basis for that country's position towards multilateralism generally and the activities of UN bodies in particular. As a consequence, participation in the UN system often took the "moral high road," avoiding entanglement in issues over which the social consensus was weak or in which a divisive debate could have resulted (such as the Persian Gulf War). In the Romanian case, during the Ceauçescu period the state ruthlessly controlled civil society, effectively confining organized interests within its coercive embrace, and suppressing or driving underground other societal interests. Thus participation in the multilateral system became a vehicle used to enhance the domestic status of the ruling élite, and the primary goal of the government's involvement in UN and multilateral activity was to legitimize its international status.

The evidence allows us to conclude not only that there are varieties of "forms" of state, but that different forms of state are likely to pursue different multilateral policies. In addition, the particular form of state may determine the input that groups within civil society can have in the formulations of multilateral policy. Conversely, the form of state may also be in part determined by the amount of pressure that societal forces can bring to bear on the state. In any case, within a state/society approach, the state cannot be viewed as an unproblematic expression of the "national interest" (as in the realist account), a neutral arbiter of societal interests (as in the liberal institutionalist account), or a tool of a particular class or élite (which would fit a Marxist account). It is rather a locus of potential power, one that could reflect a pluralistic balance of political and social forces, but that also could be captured by specific groups, forces, or even individuals in a society. Therefore, we suggest that, in order to understand more fully a state's international behaviour, including the self-image it projects on the world stage, one must expose the form and nature of the state/society complex itself.

The role of individuals

Popular historical accounts populate the stage of world politics with individuals who shape and determine historical developments. Yet in much of the traditional international relations literature, the role of individuals tends to be occluded in the interests of broader structural explanations of outcomes. While the state/society perspective focuses most clearly on social and political forces that influence and shape the behaviour of individuals, and on structural constraints to their agency, it nevertheless jettisons structuralist determinism precisely because that notion tends to reduce individual action to merely a function of the social order. As Anthony Giddens points out, actors in (for example) a Marxist structuralist conceptualization are treated as little more than structural "dopes."[9] The reality is that, although social and political forces can act as structural constraints on agency, they can also be enabling devices for individual action. Structure–agency interaction is therefore dynamic, and agency and structure can causally condition each other over time.[10] The state/society perspective thus recognizes individual actors' capacity for strategic and tactical action, and allows some scope for individual action, within the context of the state/society complex, in the pursuit of multilateral policy.

The cases in this volume highlight the prominent role of specific individuals in shaping or constraining the evolutionary path of multilateralism in particular states. The negative cases are those of Sierra Leone and Romania, where individuals such as Siaka Stevens and Nicolae Ceauçescu appear at the apex of authoritarian political processes that they bend to their will. The chapter by Mircea Malitza, a former Romanian ambassador to the United Nations, gives one an insider's view of the extent to which the cult of personality was pushed to absurd levels by Ceauçescu. From 1965 until his violent death, Ceauçescu progressively eliminated anyone who could rival his influence in Romania's foreign policy, steadily reduced the significance of the Foreign Ministry in foreign policy through staff purges (among other things), and ultimately initiated most multilateral or bilateral contact by himself.

On the more positive side is the case of Sweden. This country's international reputation has been enhanced considerably by the high-profile work of such notables as Östen Undén, Dag Hammarskjöld, Gunnar Jarring, Judge Emil Sandström, Olof Palme, Gunnar Myrdal, Hans Blix, and Inga Thorsson (among others) in the United Nations and other multilateral organs. Of course, the presence of so many individuals raises the question of the social context informing their actions, and part of the reason for this plethora of individual contributions to the multilateral system may be rooted in shared beliefs within Swedish domestic political culture. These beliefs manifest themselves in, for example, the general assumption that international public opinion exists and can be influenced and persuaded. The engagement of individual Swedes in various multilateral activities hence could influence international public opinion along positions in keeping with Sweden's domestic and international interests.

Nehru and Gandhi provide perhaps stronger examples of how the "personalist factor" can make an indelible impression upon the multilateral policy of a state. Their respective accents on self-determination and pacific approaches to conflict resolution left a legacy that has continued to serve as a reference point for India's multilateral role. Nehru, the Prime Minister of India from 1947 to 1964, more or less dominated Indian foreign policy. He not only acted as his country's Foreign Minister but also, because of his charismatic personality, was able to give India a high profile within the international community. His example (along with that of Michael Manley in Jamaica) suggests that weaker states can make up for their lack of material clout if credible individuals are identified with specific foreign policy orientations. By projecting abroad, through the UN system, India's own struggle for self-determination, Nehru successfully created a niche for India on the international stage. Gandhi's legacy of non-violent civil disobedience against the United Kingdom during India's independence struggle helps to explain India's preoccupation with issues of colonialism and apartheid. Hari Mohan Mathur reminds us that

India led the way, through trade, travel, sports, and cultural exchange boycotts, in the international pressure to bring about change in South Africa. The dismantling of apartheid in South Africa, symbolized by the 1994 all-race elections, is a reminder of the importance of agency in affecting international and domestic outcomes, and perhaps also demonstrates the socio-political dimensions of power and influence in world politics, which are often recognized (if not utilized) within traditional approaches.[11]

One caveat is worth noting here, however. The psychological and ephemeral character of the personalist dimension makes it difficult to attribute with any certainty specific outcomes of multilateral processes to individual action. The goal in elaborating a state/society approach is not to overstate such influences, but to make room for them to be addressed in theoretically informed case-studies of the UN system. A realist account leaves little room for individual influences, except in the tradition of "great statesmen" who creatively uncover and defend the national interest. The liberal institutionalist approach, with its emphasis on pluralistic state/society relations, likewise restricts the domain of agency to the creative manipulation of the process of interest aggregation (i.e. coalition-building). By contrast, a state/society approach understands the influence of individuals on *contemporary* developments in terms of the political and socio-economic relations within a state/society complex that accords them a position of power (whether this be legitimate or illegitimate), and their *historical legacy* as mediated through their influence on the persistent structures of thought and patterns of behaviour that mould policy directions within and towards the UN system.

Political cultural and ideological influences

Perhaps the most difficult and intangible set of influences can be grouped under the rubric of political culture and ideology. Here the links between such influences and the state's orientation towards the UN system are difficult to trace, in part because cultural and ideological factors do not, in any direct sense, determine state policies. They do, however, form the backdrop or mental horizon against which specific policy debates are conducted, and can act as limiting or constraining factors.

For example, in the Indian case a strong "self-image" as a peace-loving nation has been influenced by Buddhist and Ashoka teachings, as well as by Gandhian and Panchsheel principles.[12] This

255

cultural and ideological heritage informs the Indian government's rhetorical policy towards disarmament, even if specific policy acts may be inconsistent with this. In Sweden, the legalistic heritage, the "*lagom* code," and the corporatist ideological espousal of a "third way" between capitalism and socialism informed Swedish policy on disarmament, neutrality, and economic development. In Germany, the political culture that emerged out of the ashes of the Second World War is central to explaining the reluctance of Germany to assume certain multilateral roles (such as peace-keeping) and the nature of the domestic political debate around them. In Jamaica, Garveyism, the reggae music of internationally recognized groups like Bob Marley and the Wailers, and the Rastafarian movement of cultural and ideological resistance all form part of the backdrop to Jamaica's policy at the United Nations on African liberation struggles. The heightened consciousness of the majority of Jamaican blacks concerning the race issue and pan-Africanism helped to catapult these items onto the state's foreign policy agenda, and helps explain why various Jamaican governments have been preoccupied with opposing apartheid and supporting liberation struggles throughout Africa, even though this progressive agenda has clashed on occasion with the agenda of the dominant economic élite within Jamaican society.

Political cultural and ideological influences are excluded by a realist account and obscured by a liberal institutionalist one, as they are not articulated in a univocal fashion that can be easily incorporated as one input into policy-making. But, as John Ruggie points out, the operation of different "logics" within domestic political discourse can affect the preferences of states for the form and scope of multilateral cooperation.[13] These factors are difficult to incorporate within any approach that emphasizes the rational calculation of state interests, because a state's "value preferences" (i.e. the emphasis it may place on particular issues) are taken as a given or considered irrelevant in calculations of interests. But a state/society approach can open a space in which such factors, and their impact on a state's orientation towards the UN system, can be analysed, explained, and understood.

External factors

For structural realists, exogenous influences on a state's orientation towards the UN system would be a product of state-to-state relationships, mediated through alliances, regional organizations, or bilateral processes. Certainly, throughout the Cold War the direct influence of external actors on Germany and Romania was evident, as were the efforts of states such as India and Jamaica to insulate themselves from such influences via participation in the Non-Aligned Movement and Sweden's adoption of a policy of neutrality. But the state/society perspective alerts one to additional sorts of external influences that may originate from the multilateral process itself, or that may not be mediated through state institutions. While the primary focus in this volume has been on the position that the various forces within the state/society complex take with respect to the UN system and multi-lateralism, the authors have recognized that the UN system and the multilateral process can have an impact on the state/society config-uration. Special attention in some of the case-studies has been paid to the impact of multilateral institutions and structures on domestic politics, most prominently the impact of the structural adjustment policies of the IMF on Jamaica, Sierra Leone, and India. Acknowl-edgement of this reversed influence on states and their societies chal-lenges the notion that international organizations derive their sus-tenance exclusively from states, and that the relationship between multilateral institutions and states is unidirectional.

In some cases, the impact of participation in the multilateral system is manifest directly in the "options" a state has or pursues at the in-ternational level, via the creation of a space for relatively indepen-dent activity and policy-making. As Malitza argues, Romania's inser-tion into the United Nations helped it to move towards normalization with the West during the Cold War, to develop its bilateral contacts, and to eke out a measure of autonomy from the USSR. Romania took a distinctly different position from the Soviets during the Cuban missile crisis and on the issue of denuclearization of the Balkans in 1963. It refused to break ties with Israel in 1967 (even though most Soviet satellites did so) and it established relations with Bonn in 1967 despite protest from the Warsaw Pact states. It also refused to take part in the invasion of Czechoslovakia, and went so far as to re-pudiate the Brezhnev doctrine during a General Assembly session. In doing so, Romanian delegates were deliberately opening up space in which Romania's autonomy could be preserved. This was in part ac-complished through the forging of links with neutral and non-aligned states at the United Nations, and through repeated references in bilateral and multilateral forums to fundamental world order princi-ples that supported its position (sovereignty, non-interference in do-mestic affairs). What this suggests is that the insertion into multilateral bodies may offer a certain degree of immunity for countries like Romania that find themselves under the forceful influence of a great power.

In other cases, insertion into multilateral organizations has an indirect impact on state policy by shifting the balance of political, social, and economic forces within a state. For example, an international body like the IMF or the World Bank can influence a state and the "form" it takes by intervening in its economic policy and planning, as is suggested by all the developing world cases. In Jamaica, IMF regulations and structural adjustment recommendations were used to impose certain conditions on that country's government as well as on its society; in Sierra Leone, the policies enforced by multilateral institutions had a disruptive and profound effect on the configuration of domestic politics. On the more positive side, as manifest in the cases of India and Romania, government policy and processes have been affected by major UN conferences on such themes as the environment, the law of the sea, human rights, and science and technology. Mathur notes that in India several government departments were created to mirror some of these multilateral concerns. This pattern has been repeated in several countries, in some cases with UN standards or norms being adopted by national legislatures, and it could be argued that, in almost all the studies, debates at the multilateral level played a role in setting parts of the agenda of national governments and that ultimately this process can feed back into influencing a state's foreign policy positions within the UN system.

The state/society perspective's sociological orientation also highlights the fact that the interaction between international society and domestic societies is not always mediated through the state. For instance, the domestic political changes that occurred after the collapse of the East European regimes ushered in an era of political pluralization that led to a very different kind of representation within the UN system. Several domestic non-governmental organizations (NGOs), including charitable, voluntary, environmental, youth, and professional organizations, have entered into political associations within the international network of NGOs with links to the UN system. In Romania, for example, information and knowledge passed on from the international network of non-governmental organizations to local community groups within Romania have been used to intensify the agitation for changes in political structures and processes in that country. This mirrors the previous experience of East European movements such as Solidarity or Charter 77. This kind of phenomenon was perhaps accelerated by the presence of several UN institutions in Romania and by the fact that the Romanian government hosted several international meetings and seminars on the United Nations in the 1960s and 1970s. Likewise in the Swedish case, an internationally attentive Swedish élite that has been plugged into the UN specialized agency network for some time has been successful in transposing issues of global significance into local debates. The Romanian and Chilean cases also illustrate the impact of diffuse human rights norms on the diplomatic *modus operandi* adopted by state representatives in New York or Geneva, and the legitimization process used by societal groups as a result of various UN human rights instruments and resolutions. In Chile, for example, relatively weak social groups took sustenance from their multilateral involvements and were empowered to challenge the ruling élite to embrace a more democratic posture. In Romania, the specific incident of Secretary-General Trygve Lie's visit in 1964 and the subsequent release of political prisoners suggest that even authoritarian regimes can be affected to some degree by public criticism from UN bodies or officials of their human rights violations.

In the (somewhat unique) German case, the redefinition of Germany's position in world politics and the impact of this on its "collective national identity" that occurred after the fall of the Berlin wall were facilitated by external multilateral arrangements. Unification itself was both a multilateral as well as a domestic process, and Germany's embrace of multilateralism as the legitimizing tool for unification (via the "two plus four" process) proved to be a more useful way to address its problems in the international environment than a nationalist strategy would have been. The German government was able to utilize multilateralism as a tool for promoting unification and other national interests while at the same time employing it as an "effective antidote against the temptations of neo-nationalism" in that country.

Together these examples raise the issue of the extent to which domestic politics have been "internationalized," in the sense that the evolution of domestic political, social, and economic arrangements can no longer be understood without reference to developments at the global or regional level. Certainly when one shifts focus away from the major Western industrial states towards small and medium-sized states (in the developing world and elsewhere), the influence appears clear. The attempted transformation of Jamaican or Indian society, or Sweden's evolving neutrality, do not make sense without some reference to multilateral economic and political institutions.

Finally, under the rubric of external forces, one must note the impact in almost all the cases in this volume of the "regionalization" of international relations. As was suggested in the German case-study, multilateral activity can be regional, transregional, or global. The multilateral activity of each state under examination was placed within the context of competing visions of the appropriate forums, and almost every state examined has at various times supported each form of multilateralism. The studies reveal, however, that the pull of regionalism is manifest in different ways in various cases. In the Jamaican case, Caribbean regionalism is a means to assert a more prominent Jamaican role and to encourage self-reliance among people of the region. For Sierra Leone, regional multilateral activity in the Economic Community of West African States is viewed primarily as a means of promoting economic growth. In the Indian case, the fragmentation of the Non-Aligned Movement enhances the attractiveness of regionalism via the South Asian Association for Regional Cooperation. Chile finds itself drawn into the orbit of South American free trade arrangements (such as MERCOSUR) and broader North and South American regional activities. In Europe, the progression towards European Union (EU) has had a profound impact on Swedish and German domestic policy and could significantly shape the future direction of both states' foreign policy with respect to the UN system (and it may have a similar impact on Romania). As Ulrika Mörth and Bengt Sundelius suggest in chapter 3, it is possible that in the future the United Nations may no longer be at the centre of the Swedish engagement in multilateralism, as the global organization is perceived to be less relevant and less efficient than regional multilateral bodies in Europe.

This raises the general question: to what extent will regional and transregional forms of multilateralism eclipse global multilateralism in the future? This question is more than speculative, in light of the increasingly competitive activity of institutions such as the EU, CSCE, OECD, OAS, OAU, CARICOM, and ASEAN. Several contributors to this volume have noted how a particular regional focus seems to be replacing a traditional UN focus in the declaratory and substantive foreign policy positions of some countries. But, to make sense of the future trajectory of these competing multilateralisms, one must look not only at concrete manifestations of state interests (in such issues as regional economic integration) but at the underlying notions of community and society that they implicate. Membership in the European Union is, for Sweden, in part an existential issue. Ultimately, what is at stake theoretically is the issue of whether or not it will be meaningful to speak of a singular "international society," existing within a particular world order, and manifested concretely through participation in global multilateral activities.

Conclusion

The so-called "crisis of multilateralism" of the 1980s was not merely a political crisis but an intellectual and scholarly one, as the tools and concepts used to study the UN system proved ill suited to understanding the changing nature of political life in the late twentieth century. Since the end of the Cold War, however, opportunities for creative scholarship have paralleled those for creative diplomacy, and the study of the UN system is enjoying something of a renaissance. In this light, the cases in this volume contribute positively to this renaissance, and they shed some light on little-examined corners of the multilateral experience.

Broad claims for theoretical and conceptual innovation should always be viewed sceptically, and will be eschewed here. Nevertheless, the cases in this volume taken together demonstrate the utility of more flexible, encompassing, and "sociological" approaches to the study of multilateralism and the UN system. These have been described here under the umbrella of a "state/society perspective," signalling that the basic unit of analysis is not the state but the complex of social relationships that coalesce within and across states and are projected into the international dimension. However, once this move is made, the character of the state itself needs to be examined, and it can no longer be considered as an immutable entity, or one whose character is irrelevant to international relations. Particular forms of state are shaped in part by specific institutional elements (formal governmental apparatus) and in part by broader political and ideological practices that permeate civil society at a specific historical juncture. In this regard, a state's transformation will depend in some respects on the constellation of social forces within the society over which it presides. Several of our cases offer clear signals that the renegotiation of the relationship between the state and civil society is under way, and they emphasize that this process could result in different approaches to foreign policy-making and multilateralism.[14]

Although the factors analysed by traditional international relations approaches do not necessarily disappear within a state/society perspective, this analysis, as demonstrated by the foregoing chapters, extends considerably beyond the traditional government-to-government relationships between the state and central institutions of the UN system. Without exception, each study provides empirical evidence and specific examples of the changing relationships between states and social forces; the influence of these forces in shaping states' perspectives on multilateralism; the linkage of domestic and foreign policy issues at the level of the multilateral agenda; and the impact of subnational, transnational, and global forces on the state's position with respect to regional and global multilateral institutions. These cases also suggest that the relationship between the state/society complex and multilateral institutions is not unidirectional (from the state to multilateral institutions), and that forces within a state can gain strength from ideas in circulation, or institutions operating, outside of the state itself. The studies in this volume support the notion that the position a state takes towards participation in multilateralism is conditioned in part by world order pressures (such as the internationalization of production and finance or the prevalence of certain dominant ideologies and practices) and in part by the way in which the state has been inserted into multilateral processes and institutions.

According to Robert Cox, multilateralism can be examined from two distinct but related standpoints: "as the institutionalization and regulation of established orders," and "as the locus of interaction for the transformation of existing order."[15] The UN system embodies the post-1945 established order, but, as material circumstances change or prevailing meanings and purposes are challenged by new ideas and practices of multilateralism, the United Nations will be expected to adapt or face irrelevance. Changing state/society perspectives on the United Nations system revive the debate of "reform versus transformation" of this global multilateral institution, and this issue receives greater impetus as one realizes that several authors in this study have questioned whether or not the United Nations will remain the central focus of their country's multilateral engagement.

The case-studies in this volume hint at the magnitude and importance of some of the rapid transformations in world politics, although they do not offer a single set of conclusions on the future direction and character of global and/or regional multilateralism. What these cases demonstrate, however, is that few of the changes in the focus of multilateral activity, or the pressures on the UN system, can be explained with reference only to intergovernmental or state-to-state relationships. The fact that there exist different visions of multilateralism should alert one to the realization that its future trajectory is not necessarily the same as its past, and that this is a theoretically important issue for international relations.[16] Theoretical and methodological approaches developed during (and suited to) a static or more stable environment are poor guides to the current evolution of the UN system and global multilateralism. Ultimately, the phenomenon of multilateralism is best understood through a variety of approaches, which come closer to capturing the diverse forces at work in the various institutions of the UN system and their differing impact on states and peoples around the world.

Acknowledgements

We have benefited from comments by various participants in the original conference, and from those provided by Jennifer Milliken.

Notes and references

1. One other major contribution of several of the cases in this book is the inclusion of non-English and non-North American sources, many of which are not easily accessible to North American and English-speaking scholars.
2. For a discussion of the neglect of multilateralism in international relations theory, see James Caporaso, "International Relations Theory and Multilateralism: The Search for Foundations," *International Organization* 46 (Summer 1992), no. 3: 630; on Robert Cox's approach see "Multilateralism and World Order," *Review of International Studies* 18 (April 1992), no. 2: 161–180.
3. This, of course, touches on a large debate in the philosophy of social science that we cannot replay here. For significant turns in the debate in international relations, see Robert Keohane, ed., *Neorealism and its Critics* (New York: Columbia University Press, 1986), especially the contributions by Kenneth Waltz, Richard Ashley, and Robert Cox; Mark Hoffman, "Restructuring, Reconstruction, Reinscription, Rearticulation: Four Voices in Critical International Theory," *Millennium* 20 (1991), no. 2: 169–185; Mark Hoffman, "Critical Theory and the Inter-Paradigm Debate," *Millennium* 46 (Summer 1987), no. 2: 231–249; Alexander Wendt, "Anarchy Is What States Make of It," *International Organization* 45 (Spring 1991), no. 2: 391–426; Robert Keohane, "International Institutions: Two Approaches," *International Studies Quarterly* 32 (December 1988), no. 4: 379–396.
4. This debate is conventionally understood to have opened with the work of Robert Keohane and Joseph Nye, eds., *Transnational Relations and World Politics* (Cambridge, Mass.: Harvard University Press, 1971).
5. As one author notes, much of the recent dialogue and debate concerning the nature of the state, the reconceptualization of state sovereignty, and the relationship between the domestic and the international is taking place "well outside the scope of international relations" (Justin Rosenberg, "A Non-Realist Theory of Sovereignty?: Giddens' The Nations-State and Violence," *Millennium: Journal of International Studies* 19, 1990, no. 2: 258).
6. Robert Cox, "Programme on Multilateralism and the United Nations System," unpublished paper, United Nations University (April 1991), 2.
7. This juxtaposition of domestic structures with international behaviour finds a parallel in the "democracies and war" debate. See Michael Doyle, "Liberalism and World Politics,"

American Political Science Review 80 (December 1986), no. 4: 1151–1169; Carol Ember, Melvin Ember, and Bruce Russett, "Peace Between Participatory Polities: A Cross-Cultural Test of the 'Democracies Rarely Fight Each Other' Hypothesis," *World Politics* 44 (July 1992), 573–599.

8. See, for a theoretically sophisticated series of case-studies, Peter Evans, Dietrich Rueschemeyer, and Theda Skocpol, eds., *Bringing the State Back In* (Cambridge: Cambridge University Press, 1985). See also James Caporaso, *The Elusive State* (Newbury Park, Calif.: Sage Publications, 1989).

9. See Anthony Giddens, *Central Problems in Social Theory* (London: Macmillan, 1979), 52.

10. Walter Carlsnaes, "The Agency–Structure Problem in Foreign Policy Analysis," *International Studies Quarterly* 32 (1992), 245–270; David Dessler, "What's at Stake in the Agent–Structure Debate," *International Organization* 43 (Summer 1989), 441–473; Alexander Wendt, "The Agent–Structure Problem in International Relations Theory," *International Organization* 41 (Summer 1987), no. 3: 335–370.

11. Many realist formulations of the components of power emphasize "soft" or socio-political aspects such as leadership or morale. Hans Morgenthau's listing of the "elements of national power," for example, includes such factors as national character, national morale, and the quality of diplomacy (Hans Morgenthau, *Politics among Nations*, 3rd ed., New York: Alfred A. Knopf, 1964).

12. For more on this, see R. P. Arnand, *Cultural Factors in International Relations* (Columbia, Mo.: South Asia Books, 1981).

13. He offers the example of the relative immunity of Japanese trade policy to considerations of institutional efficiency (John Gerard Ruggie, "Multilateralism: The Anatomy of an Institution," *International Organization* 46, Summer 1992, no. 3: 591–592).

14. See, on this point, James Rosenau, *Turbulence in World Politics* (Princeton, N.J.: Princeton University Press, 1990); Mark Zacher, "The Decaying Pillars of the Westphalian Temple: Implications for International Order and Governance," in James Rosenau and Ernst-Otto Czempiel, eds., *Governance without Government: Order and Change in World Politics* (Cambridge: Cambridge University Press, 1992), 58–101.

15. Robert Cox, "Multilateralism and World Order," 163.

16. See J. Martin Rochester, *Waiting for the Millennium: The United Nations and the Future of World Order* (South Carolina: University of South Carolina Press, 1993).

Contributors

Wilfried von Bredow is a professor of political science at Philipps-University, Marburg. He is predominantly interested in international relations with special regard to the East–West conflict and its heritage. Among his recent publications are: *Krise und Protest. Ursprünge und Elemente der Friedensbewegungen in Westeuropa*; *Der KSZE-Prozeß. Von der Zähmung zur Auflösung des Ost–West-Konflikts*; (with Thomas Jäger) *Neue deutsche Außenpolitik. Nationale Interessen in internationalen Beziehungen*.

Roberto Duran is a professor of international relations at the Institute of Political Science, Catholic University of Chile, and professor of Chilean foreign policy at the Chilean Diplomatic Academy (Santiago). He has held visiting professorships at Würzburg (1984), Heidelberg (1987), London (1989), and Georgetown (1993). He has published widely on Chilean foreign affairs in Argentina, Brazil, Chile, and Germany. His research interests include Chilean and Latin American multilateralism, Latin American security, and Chilean diplomacy in the nineteenth and twentieth centuries.

W. Andy Knight is an assistant professor of political science at Bishop's University, Quebec. He has written numerous chapters on United Nations reform, and is the editor of *An Agenda for United Nations Reform: Reconstructing Human and Global Security* (forthcoming). His current research work examines financial and structural problems in the United Nations, regional and universal approaches to global governance, and Japan's emerging prominence within multilateral institutions.

Keith Krause received his D. Phil. in international relations from Oxford in 1987, where he studied as a Rhodes Scholar, and is an associate professor of political science at York University, Toronto. He is the author of *Arms and the State: Patterns of Military Production and Trade* and the co-editor of a forthcoming volume, *Critical Security Studies*. His current research includes chapters on multilateralism and the United Nations, new concepts of security, and militarization and conflict in the Middle East. He has also served as the deputy director and acting director of the Centre for International and Strategic Studies at York University.

Mircea Malitza is a professor of mathematics at the University of Bucharest and of international relations at the Black Sea University. His extensive diplomatic experience includes service as vice-minister for United Nations affairs from 1962 to 1970, ambassador to the United Nations (Geneva), 1980–1982, and ambassador to the United States (1982–1985). His research has concentrated on Romanian diplomacy and foreign policy, and on mathematical models for international relations and multilateral negotiations. He has written several books including: (in Romanian) *Pages of the History of Romanian Diplomacy*; *Diplomacy, Schools and Institutions*; *The UN Charter*; *The Theory and Practice of Negotiations*; *Mechanisms for the Peaceful Settlement of Disputes*; (in English) *Mathematical Approaches to International Relations*; and *Romanian Diplomacy, An Historical Outlook*.

Hari Mohan Mathur (Ph.D.) is a development administration specialist and an anthropologist with wide practical and academic experience. A senior government official in India, he has also been Vice-Chancellor of the University of Rajasthan. As a staff member, adviser, and consultant to various United Nations agencies, Dr. Mathur has worked in many countries in Asia, the Pacific, and Africa. His current research interests include participatory development, human resources development, sustainable development, indigenous peoples, development-generated resettlement, NGOs, and the UN system. He has written extensively on development issues, and his books include *Sociocultural Factors in Human Resources Development*; *Anthropology and Development in Traditional Societies*; *Administering Development in the Third World*; and *Development Projects, Displaced Peoples: Resettlement Experience in Asia* (forthcoming).

Ulrika Mörth is a fellow in European politics at the Swedish Council for Research in the Social Sciences and Humanities, Stockholm. She has written extensively on Swedish foreign policy, focusing on the United Nations, high-technology trade and development, and the Korean War.

Randolph B. Persaud is a doctoral candidate in political science at York University, Toronto, a researcher at the Centre for International and Strategic Studies, and affiliated with the Centre for Research on Latin America and the Caribbean. His research interests focus on the foreign policy of small states and on international political economy.

Bengt Sundelius is a senior fellow in European international relations at the Swedish Council for Research in the Social Sciences and Humanities, posted at the University of Stockholm. He has published widely on problems of international interdependence, foreign policy analysis, and security studies, with a focus on the Nordic nations. He has served as vice-president of the International Studies Association and as founding chairperson of the Nordic International Studies Association and is currently editor of *Cooperation and Conflict: Nordic Journal of International Studies*.

Abiodun Williams is an assistant professor of international relations at the School of Foreign Service, Georgetown University, Sierra Leone, where he teaches courses in international organization, the theory and practice of international relations, and power and justice in the international system. He has taught at the University of Rochester and at Tufts University. His research focuses on international organization, multilateral negotiations, and conflict resolution. He is the editor of *Many Voices: Multilateral Negotiations in the World Arena*.

267